SHAKESPEARE'S COMEDIES

LONGMAN CRITICAL READERS

General Editors:

RAMAN SELDEN, late Emeritus Professor of English, Lancaster University and late Professor of English, Sunderland Polytechnic;

STAN SMITH, Professor of English, University of Dundee

Published titles:

K.M. NEWTON, *George Eliot*

MARY EAGLETON, *Feminist Literary Criticism*

GARY WALLER, *Shakespeare's Comedies*

JOHN DRAKAKIS, *Shakespearean Tragedy*

RICHARD WILSON AND RICHARD DUTTON, *New Historicism and Renaissance Drama*

PETER BROOKER, *Modernism/Postmodernism*

PETER WIDDOWSON, *D.H. Lawrence*

RACHEL BOWLBY, *Virginia Woolf*

FRANCIS MULHERN, *Contemporary Marxist Literary Criticism*

ANNABEL PATTERSON, *John Milton*

CYNTHIA CHASE, *Romanticism*

MICHAEL O'NEILL, *Shelley*

STEPHANNE TRIGG, *Medieval English Poetry*

ANTONY EASTHOPE, *Contempory Film Theory*

SHAKESPEARE'S COMEDIES

Edited and Introduced by

GARY WALLER

LONGMAN

LONDON AND NEW YORK

Longman Group UK Limited,
Longman House, Burnt Mill, Harlow,
Essex CM20 2JE, England
and Associated Companies throughout the world.

Published in the United States of America
by Longman Inc., New York

First published 1991
Second impression 1993

British Library Cataloguing in Publication Data
Shakespeare's comedies. – (Longman critical readers).
   1. Drama in English. Shakespeare, William, 1564–1616
I. Waller, Gary F.
822.33

   ISBN 0-582-05926-7
   ISBN 0-582-05927-5 pbk

Library of Congress Cataloging-in-Publication Data
Shakespeare's comedies / edited by Gary Waller.
     p. cm. – (Longman critical readers)
   Includes bibliographical references and index.
   ISBN 0-582-05926-7. – ISBN 0-582-05927-5 (pbk.)
   1. Shakespeare, William, 1564–1616 – Comedies. 2. Comedy.
I. Waller, Gary F. (Gary Fredric), 1945–   II. Series.
PR2981.S496 1991
822.3'3–dc20   90-20546
                                       CIP

Set in 9/11½pt Palatino

Produced by Longman Singapore Publishers (Pte) Ltd.
Printed in Singapore

Contents

General Editors' Preface

The outlines of contemporary critical theory are now often taught as a standard feature of a degree in literary studies. The development of particular theories has seen a thorough transformation of literary criticism. For example, Marxist and Foucauldian theories have revolutionized Shakespeare studies and 'deconstruction' has led to a complete reassessment of Romantic poetry. Feminist criticism has left scarcely any period of literature unaffected by its searching critiques. Teachers of literary studies can no longer fall back on a standardized, received, methodology.

Lecturers and teachers are now urgently looking for guidance in a rapidly changing critical environment. They need help in understanding the latest revisions in literary theory, and especially in grasping the practical effects of the new theories in the form of theoretically sensitized new readings. A number of volumes in the series anthologize important essays on particular theories. However, in order to grasp the full implications and possible uses of particular theories it is essential to see them put to work. This series provides substantial volumes of new readings, presented in an accessible form and with a significant amount of editorial guidance.

Each volume includes a substantial introduction which explores the theoretical issues and conflicts embodied in the essays selected and locates areas of disagreement between positions. The pluralism of theories has to be put on the agenda of literary studies. We can no longer pretend that we all tacitly accept the same practices in literary studies. Neither is a *laissez-faire* attitude any longer tenable. Gerald Graff argues that literature departments need to go beyond the mere toleration of theoretical differences: it is not enough merely to agree to differ; they need actually to 'stage' the differences openly. The volumes in this series all attempt to dramatize the differences, not necessarily with a view to resolving them but in order to foreground the choices presented by different theories or to argue for a particular route through the impasses the differences present.

The theory 'revolution' has had real effects. It has loosened the grip of traditional empiricist and romantic assumptions about language and literature. It is not always clear what is being proposed as the new agenda for literary studies, and indeed the very notion of 'literature' is questioned by the post-structuralist strain in theory. However, the uncertainties and obscurities of contemporary theories appear much less worrying when we see what the best critics have been able to do with them in practice. This series aims to disseminate the best of recent criticism, and to show that it is possible to re-read the canonical texts of literature in new and challenging ways.

RAMAN SELDEN AND STAN SMITH

Acknowledgements

One of the most interesting trends in the current retheorization of literary
and cultural criticism is that the critic should not hide behind a pretence
of objectivity, but rather acknowledge his or her own commitments and
place them within current ideological struggles. Some of mine will
become explicit in my introductory essay. But in addition, I wish to
acknowledge that in sorting out some of my sense of how we articulate
'our' Shakespeare, I have more than the usual personal debts, in
particular to a quarter century of students, at Cambridge, Auckland,
Dalhousie, Wilfrid Laurier and Carnegie Mellon, who have proved to me
not that the play's the thing so much as the commitments and discoveries
which the play opens up in us. I single out, among so many, Andrew
Brown and Michael Wheeler for nurture and nature, Andrea Clough for
magic, Margaret McLaren for courtesy, Shawkat Hussain for otherness,
Craig Dionne for politics, Havard Albright for media events, and Michelle
Osherow for poetry. Some of the ideas here were tried out in TVOntario's
Telecollege Shakespeare in 1982, and in the workshop on critical
anthologies organized by Herb Weill, Jr, at the Shakespeare Association of
America meeting in Philadelphia in April, 1990, to the members of which
many thanks, especially Ed Pechter and Len Findlay. And thanks to my
own Shakespeare teachers – the late J.C. Reid, Peter Dane, Lionel Knights
– and to those colleagues and friends with whom I have spent happy
hours watching, marvelling, listening and arguing, especially Jim Black,
Curt Breight, Beekman Cottrell, Jonathan Dollimore, Susan Rudy Dorscht,
Richard Dutton, Bernard Hopkins, Peggy Knapp, Mary Ellen Lamb, Ken
Larsen, Kathleen McCormick, Naomi Miller, Marianne Novy, Bill
Sessions, Alan Sinfield, Bob White and Elizabeth Wilson. Like Sir
Rowland de Boys, I have three sons: Michael, whose acting in *Twelfth
Night* and *As You Like It* made me revalue some of the cornier parts of
those plays; Andrew who, as the (original) younger son, hopes to find his
Rosalind, though with a camera, not poetry; and Philip, who like Sir
Rowland's other son, arrived in the final scene and who, as part of a
whole new family romance, is already a figure of Falstaffian proportions.

I am also grateful to the general editors of the series, especially to Ray
Selden, whose perceptions on both critical stance and communicability
were most helpful. Editors, teachers, students, friends, family, colleagues,
readers of this book: I feel privileged to be part, not so much (as we used
to say) a member of a timeless community so much as one contributor to
a history of the (perhaps) never-ending rewriting of the Shakespearean
text.

This book is dedicated to the students in my Shakespeare classes, who
over the years have helped turn me from a bardolator to a bardliberator,

and who have encouraged both tears and smiles and even the beginnings of a little wisdom. Also to three remarkable Shakespeare teachers – Lionel Knights, Jim Black and Peter Dane. And for Kate and Michael, Andrew and Philip, who have laughed and suffered and laughed again through a lot of it.

The publishers are grateful to the following for permission to reproduce copyright material:

Associated University Presses for extracts from Coppélia Kahn, 'The Cuckoo's Note: Male Friendship and Cuckoldry in *The Merchant of Venice*' from *Shakespeare's Rough Magic* (eds.) P. Erikson & C. Kahn; the author, Carolyn Asp for her article 'Subjectivity, Desire and Female Friendship in *All's Well That Ends Well*' originally printed in *Literature and Psychology* 32 (1986) edited by Richard Feldstein; the author, Mrs Helen Golding (née Cunliffe) for her article 'The Story of the Night told Over: D. W. Winnicott's Theory of Play and *A Midsummer Night's Dream*' which first appeared in *Ideas and Production* 8 (1988) 'Drama in Theory and Performance' Edward E. Esche (editor); International Universities Press, Inc. for extracts from Norman N. Holland, 'Hermia's Dream' in *The Annual of Psychoanalysis*, Vol. VII (1979); Johns Hopkins University Press for extracts from W. Thomas MacCary 'The Comedy of Errors: A Different Kind of Comedy' in *New Literary History*, Vol. XI, No. 3, Spring 1978, pp. 525–536; Manchester University Press for Jonathan Dollimore, 'Transgression and Surveillance in *Measure for Measure*' in *Political Shakespeare* (eds.) Jonathan Dollimore & Alan Sinfield (Manchester University Press, 1986); Northwestern University Press and the author, Frank Whigham for his 'Ideology and Class Conduct in *The Merchant of Venice*' in *Renaissance Drama*, 1979, pp. 93–115; The University of California Press for Peter B. Erickson, 'Sexual Politics and the Social Structure in *As You Like It*' in *Patriarchal Structure in Shakespearean Drama*, pp. 22–37, copyright © 1985 The Regents of the University of California; University of Massachusetts for Karen Newman, 'Renaissance Family Politics and Shakespeare's *The Taming of the Shrew*' in *English Literary Renaissance* Vol. 16 (1986) pp. 86–100; The University of Texas Press and the author, Louis A. Montrose for extracts from his 'Sport by Sport O'erthrown: *Love's Labour's Lost* and the politics of play' in *Texas Studies in Literature and Language* v.18:4, 1977, pp. 528–552; the author, Terence Hawkes for extracts from his article 'Comedy Orality and Duplicity: A Midsummer Night's Dream and Twelfth Night' which first appeared in *Shakespearean Comedy*, Vols. 5 & 6 of *New York Literary Forum*, New York, 1980; Yale University Press for abridged article Carol Thomas Neely, 'Broken Nuptials in Shakespeare's Comedies: Much Ado About Nothing' in *Broken Nuptials in Shakespeare's Plays* (Yale University Press, 1985).

List of Abbreviations

In the notes and the list of further reading, the following abbreviations have been used:

All's Well that Ends Well   *AWell*
As You Like It   *AYL*
The Comedy of Errors   *Err*
King Lear   *KL*
Love's Labour's Lost   *LLL*
Measure for Measure   *Meas*
The Merchant of Venice   *Mer*
The Merry Wives of Windsor   *MWW*
A Midsummer Night's Dream   *MSND*
Much Ado about Nothing   *MAdo*
Pericles   *Per*
The Taming of the Shrew   *Shr*
Twelfth Night   *TN*
Two Gentlemen of Verona   *2Gent*
The Winter's Tale   *WT*
Shakespeare Quarterly   *SQ*

Introduction: 'Much Joy, Some Terror: Reading Shakespeare's Comedies Today'

The essays in this book are not meant to give authoritative accounts of what Shakespeare's comedies mean, or even, rather more usefully, what readers' experiences of the plays might be, but rather to open questions, in recognizably contemporary terms, for students, readers, teachers and spectators alike about these intriguing plays. The 'true beginning of our end' as Quince puts it (*MSND* V, i, 111) is to encourage different ways to produce 'our' Shakespeare. As Terry Eagleton joco-seriously observes, 'it is difficult to read Shakespeare without feeling that he was almost certainly familiar with the writings of Hegel, Marx, Nietzsche, Freud, Wittgenstein and Derrida'. Perhaps, he goes on, 'this is merely to say that though in many ways we appear to have left Shakespeare and his age behind, there are other ways in which we have yet to catch up with him'.[1] The essays have been selected to suggest ways of doing so, to place Shakespeare's comedies within the exciting developments in current literary theory, and to invite readers to share in that excitement.

The functions and effects of comedy

Comedies – depending on how we define comedy, and whether we include the late so-called romances (*Pericles, Cymbeline, The Winter's Tale, The Tempest* and (perhaps) *Henry VIII* and *Two Noble Kinsmen*) – make up a large proportion of the Shakespearean canon. *The Comedy of Errors* (?1592–94) may have been the first play Shakespeare wrote (though it is probable that he wrote the three parts of *Henry VI* and possibly *Richard III* earlier) and his contributions to *Two Noble Kinsmen* (1613) probably the last. Both, using the term broadly, are comedies, and in between he wrote – depending on how restrictive the definition is – between eleven and seventeen plays regarded as comedies. This collection of essays is restricted to eleven plays, mainly written in the first fifteen or so years of his career, the latest of which is *Measure for Measure* (1604). It excludes *Troilus and Cressida* (1601) – which is sometimes linked to *All's Well that*

Ends Well and *Measure for Measure* as a 'problem play', but which many critics see as a tragedy. Early in the first decade of the seventeenth century, Shakespeare was writing comedies (if they can be so termed) that called much of his earlier work in the comic mode into question, and with these complex plays, categorization is certainly difficult. I have also excluded the late romances – a category not recognized by early editors, but one that has become overwhelmingly accepted this century. Inevitably, however, reference will be made to these later plays, since they figure prominently in contemporary arguments about the comedies. The essays are arranged in order of the probable dates for the plays. While there are no separate essays on *Two Gentlemen of Verona* or *The Merry Wives of Windsor*, these plays are commented upon in passing, and references to recent criticism on them may be found in the Further Reading section.

What is comedy? Readers of Umberto Eco's novel *The Name of the Rose* will recall the battle to preserve or destroy Aristotle's lost treatise on comedy. It is as well that no such work has survived (or perhaps even existed) since, as happened in the case of tragedy, we might have to struggle with an overlong tradition of formulaic definition supposedly based on Aristotle's authority. Better to ask, as Joseph Westlund does, what does comedy *do* for us?[2] We find multiple and contradictory answers to that question. It makes us probe deeply into the ways we are constructed psychologically and culturally, and to consider the power of humour, fantasy and, in particular, memory in our lives.

At the start of Alain Resnais' film *Mon Oncle d'Amérique*, a psychobiologist voice-over – reflecting the behaviourist theories of Henri Laborit, who appears later in the film – explains how, at times of crisis, humans will often fall back on deeply ingrained responses produced by a mixture of biological and cultural determinations. This ability to 'remember' experiences, whether individual, encultured, even biological, demonstrates how we no longer react instinctively to crises to which our more primitive humanoid ancestors would have had simpler responses. Our larger brains, with their complex layers of memory, are therefore the source of both what *The Winter's Tale* calls our 'joy' and 'terror' (IV.i.1), which terms may be usefully respectively applied to comedy and tragedy. As a starting point (almost immediately to be qualified), I suggest that tragedy 'represents' the 'terror' in human experience. 'Represents' is necessarily metaphorical, heavily charged with ideological baggage, as would be any of its alternatives, like 'embodies', 'imitates', 'deals with', 'shows us', the wordy 'invites us to participate in/think about', or the banal 'is about'. Likewise, 'terror' is a necessarily slippery term. It can be conceived individually, socially, historically, even cosmically – and Shakespeare's tragedies have been represented in different ages and societies in different terms. Comedy 'represents' (the same alternatives apply) the 'joy'. Both 'terror' and 'joy' are primitive emotions that throughout our lives become overlaid with multiple layers of experience. But these memories are not simply subjective: even the most basic areas of our experiences – the 'joy' of love, family life, political liberation, self-assertion, discovery, reconciliation, the 'terror' of weaning, differentiation, entrapment, loss, death – are articulated through historically specific, culturally inherited forms and material practices. We draw on both our most primitive and our most deeply encultured memories when we respond to and reproduce Shakespeare's comedies in our own histories. Stephen Orgel describes Shakespeare's plays as 'collaborative fantasies'. Such collaboration involves not just the author but also readers, critics and audiences. Indeed, in his essay, Terence Hawkes argues that comedy is 'an art of the audience: the audience's participation finally constitutes the comedy' (p. 171).[3]

Thus the functions and effects of comedy – a better way of putting it than 'what comedy *is*' – may vary both from person to person and from one historical period or social formation to another. Comedy cannot be defined ahistorically. There is no 'essence' of comedy. Nor should it be thought of simply as light or trivial or less demanding than tragedy – as, say, merely pleasant entertainment designed to make us laugh, or help us escape the tensions of our lives, however important these characteristics may be in different experiences of comedy. Some of the greatest comedies may produce as much tears as laughter, a phenomenon that is explained by the typical happy endings providing us with what some psychoanalysts term a 'safe haven' for the release of pent-up anxieties. The 'joy', in short, may be inextricably connected to, and even dependent upon, the 'terror'.[4]

The history of the comedies' reception

One of the commonplaces of contemporary criticism is that meanings are constructed by the interaction of text and reader: they are not found solely 'in' the text. No reading of a text is, therefore, ever objective or disinterested; all readings are what Malcolm Evans calls 'readings-for' – readings supporting particular viewpoints – or 'strong' readings. Thus a reader or critic needs, in Louis Montrose's phrase, to 'foreground his [and her] instrumental role in the productions of meaning'. 'Instrumental' and 'production' are key terms here. They imply that a reading can never be merely subjective, since it is always produced within what Tony Bennett terms a 'reading formation': all readers bring a culturally produced repertoire of assumptions and expectations to their reading experiences; these interact – either clashing with or matching – the repertoire of the text. Both text and reader are, in turn, produced (to use a theatrical metaphor) by both the specifically literary ideology and the more general ideology of his or her society. Thus when we read Shakespeare's plays, we bring particular ideological repertoires – our expectations, preferences, beliefs, hopes, anxieties, our class, racial, or gendered, or culturally specific assumptions – into dialogue with the particular repertoire of the text – *its* demands, pressures, its formal structure, conventions, the history of its productions, its current critical reception. Such interaction is inherent in all reading experiences; we could call it a 'dialogue' between text and reader, but we should perhaps talk of 'polylogue' since it involves many voices. This interaction is particularly evident with drama – what we call a 'play' is a script, words (and the eloquent silences that surround words) that can be used to produce different effects in different ways. A play is not a text *requiring* us to read it in a certain way, as if it were directions on how to assemble a bookcase. Our experiences may be different each time – they may be gripping or boring, intellectual or emotional, fearful, joyful, puzzling.[5]

In reading, watching, and thinking about a Shakespeare play there are, therefore, no fixed, original, let alone any obligatory meanings. Some readings may seem to us more natural than others, but if we survey the history of the criticism of the comedies, what seemed 'natural' in one historical period or society may seem puzzling or less interesting in others. There is not a *true* or *original* interpretation of Shakespeare that different readings or productions have somehow covered over, but rather a continuing process of struggle and difference within the history of ideologies. All societies attempt to regulate the arts, directly and indirectly, and the more powerful a text's potential to challenge what is perceived to be the established beliefs and assumptions of a society, the more directly control may be exercised. There are, therefore, historically or culturally *dominant* meanings, readings that we (or our teachers or powerful critics) prefer. The production of dominant readings is part of the mechanism by which 'Shakespeare' (in this sense a complex cultural construct not simply a historical person with definite, or more or less likely, birth and death dates) has become part of our culture.[6]

If we ask what the dominant views of Shakespeare's comedies today are, as compared with sixty, or even thirty, years ago, we can point roughly to three phases of criticism. Before the 1950s, they were predominantly regarded as, in Dover Wilson's phrase, 'happy' plays, delightful entertainment, escapist crowd-pleasers, golden effusions of romantic celebration and sentimentality.[7] In so far as the comedies were treated seriously, they were read in terms of general, universal (and frequently binary) 'themes', such as appearance and reality, courtship and marriage, idealism and cynicism, innocence and experience, order and disorder. While such 'themes' were often seen to 'reflect' aspects of the (usually intellectual rather than material) history of Shakespeare's time, they often had very little connection with either the material practices from which the plays grew or those within which they might be read. The comedies were also widely seen – however inadequately they measured up alongside the tragedies – as revelations of 'character'. Derived in part from the nineteenth-century fascination with biography (but in fact having deeper philosophical roots in the history of Western ideologies), character criticism tended to moralize and (especially after the impact of Freud was assimilated by Shakespeare studies) psychologize Shakespeare's characters, treating them as if they were real people not dramatic representations, speculating about their motives and behaviour, off stage as well as on. While much recent criticism is interested in both character and theme, this is inclined to be in more sophisticated contexts. Norman Holland's essay on *Twelfth Night* offers some illuminating comments on developments in this mode of criticism – and incorporates some attempt to revive it with the help of ego psychology.

The second phase of criticism, which dates from the 1950s and is especially associated with the influence (still strong today) of Northrop Frye and C.L. Barber, tended to see comedy as a socially produced form – or as Frye put it, 'mode' – of literature. By such a reading comedy was the expression or enactment of a society's most profound myths and rituals. An analysis of what he saw as timeless, mythic patterns in the plays, Frye's views in *A Natural Perspective* (1965), which elaborates more schematic insights in his monumental theory of literature, *Anatomy of Criticism* (1957), focused on a recurring pattern: a movement from disorder into a 'green world', often represented by the forest or countryside, and the final establishment of a renewed society, frequently represented by marriage. Frye saw such patterns not merely as socially produced but as 'universal' or, borrowing a term from Jung, 'archetypal'. Thus critics writing under Frye's influence will often see the plays as repeating the same 'archetypal' situations. Even what is probably the least interesting of Shakespeare's comedies, *Two Gentlemen of Verona*, which at times reads like a first draft of *Twelfth Night*, can be read in this way and so anticipating many of the motifs, characters and situations of later plays – tempests, strong heroines, adolescent love, a debate on friendship versus love, male bonding, a heroine disguised as a man, music, witty servants, a romantic setting and a more or less happy ending. It echoes the same recurring 'mythic' pattern of initiation, self-discovery, and reconciliation. Barber, in *Shakespeare's Festive Comedy* (1959), similarly related comedy to pre-modern community festive rituals, and saw a pattern of tension, release, clarification and celebration, 'the release from family ties on a tide of communal, seasonal, family feeling'.[8] More recently, the influence of the Russian formalist critic Bakhtin – commented upon in Terence Hawkes's essay (pp. 169–74) – has redirected such an approach, drawing attention to the irreverent, playful, subversive and grotesque elements in the plays, and in relating them to the rituals and myths of 'popular' rather than to those of 'high' culture or of 'archetypal' experiences. According to this more recent view, comedy provided those members of Shakespeare's audiences who were not nobility with a potentially subversive play-space, that (like a fantasy or day-dream) was fenced off from the restrictions of everyday reality, and which encouraged the contemplation of social alternatives, the revisioning, if only in wish-fulfilment, of apparently inescapable class or gender assignments.

One recent overview of the comedies that incorporates the attention paid to the formal structures of comedy by Barber or Frye and also considers the complex experiences produced by comedies in their readers and spectators is W. Thomas MacCary's *Friends and Lovers: the Phenomenology of Desire in Shakespearean Comedy* (1985). In common with a number of recent critics, MacCary finds the quest for personal identity in both homoerotic and heterosexual relationships as both the structural principle and the major human impact of the comedies. He uses a psychoanalytic theory of narcissism to point to the kinds of pleasure we receive from them, and links their techniques with the ancient Greek comic writers Aristophanes and Menander. He suggests that Shakespeare's comedies are not merely designed to evoke laughter, but to produce complex emotional and intellectual effects centred on an acceptance, even a celebration, of our at-one-ness with ourselves and our societies. Such harmony is frequently represented by the marriages and family reconciliations that usually occur or are promised at the plays' ends.

Shakespeare our contemporary

Third – and most recently – the comedies, along with both 'canonical' texts and those outside the canon, have been increasingly read within the major retheorizing of the discipline of English studies that has occurred since the late 1970s. Feminism and psychoanalytic criticism have raised fundamental questions about the comedies' concerns with gender and family structures, and (as has just been noted) their functions in relation to both individual and collective fantasies. The rethinking of historical approaches to literature – by feminism, the so-called New Historicism, and the more politically focused Cultural Materialism – has revitalized the consideration of the plays in their own time and in the history of their subsequent reception. Feminism, Psychoanalysis, New Historicism and Cultural Materialism represent the most powerful kinds of criticism of the comedies today, and consequently dominate (often in combination) the essays chosen.

The assumption that underlies most criticism before the late 1960s and 1970s, including Frye's, was that meanings – or what are still widely termed a play's *themes* – were not only inherently 'in' the text, but that they were accessible to close, empirical attention to the text itself. In Britain, the influence of F.R. Leavis, I.A. Richards and others enshrined 'practical criticism' as the dominant mode of reading, while Cleanth Brooks, John Crowe Ransom and Allen Tate shaped American New Criticism in a similar fashion. The fundamental reading strategy of both – the means by which a play's supposed 'themes' were elucidated – was 'close reading', by means of which texts were supposed somehow to yield up their hidden meanings. Rather than acknowledging the constructed nature of meaning, such an approach tended to be objectivist, assuming that meanings were independent of the historical or cultural context of the reader or critic. In an obvious sense close reading underlies all approaches to literature: it is important to pay careful attention to one's interactions with the text, and to the questions and issues one finds oneself posing to explain those interactions. But the assumption that meanings are 'in' the text has, in recent years, been increasingly seen as naive empiricism, ignoring what the reader brings to the text and what pressures were on the text when it was written. But a close reading technique of a particularly intense kind has been revived in deconstruction, where the literary text is subjected to a rigorous – indeed, some would say perverse – close reading. The term 'deconstruction' has recently been applied loosely to any reading that refuses to take a text's surface or preferred meaning for granted, but in its heyday – between, say, 1975 and 1985 – a deconstructive reading focused primarily on the duplicity of rhetoric and, in particular, the power of metaphorical language to cover over a pretended objective and full meaning seemingly contained 'in' the text. It was thus a technique of 'close' reading that looked particularly rigorously at the details of texts. A recent collection, *Shakespeare and Deconstruction*, provides useful examples of its application to Shakespeare, but some of the most interesting essays criticize the formalistic residue of deconstruction and call for accommodation with historical analysis, even while they 'acknowledge its use and potential and employ its strategies'.[9]

One of the most important works of Shakespeare criticism this century – not least because it deeply influenced many leading theatre directors, productions, especially Brook's *A Midsummer Night's Dream*, which was such a startling departure from the traditional view of the play as 'light entertainment' – has been *Shakespeare our Contemporary*, by Jan Kott, the Polish director and critic, published in 1964. Kott unabashedly insisted that we should search for the meaning of the plays here and now, especially in the politics of our post-holocaust, nuclear age. His approach represents an important strand of current criticism that insists that we ask not only 'what does that mean?', but rather 'what does that say to us now? How can we make that work for us, here in our place and time?' When we read or listen to Katherine's final speech in *The Taming of the Shrew*, how do we, as late-twentieth-century women or men, sensitive to issues of gender, read it? As an affirmation of traditional patriarchal marriage, when men, however careful and subtle, are believed to be dominant? Or as a satire on male chauvinism – especially given the framework of the play provided by the Induction, where in the play is presented as an entertainment for Christopher Sly, a tinker who is indulging his repertoire of drunken sexist remarks. It was noticeable that Jonathan Miller left out the Sly scenes from his BBC television production as, indeed, many directors do. In her essay on the play, however, Karen Newman gives them great prominence. Both are asking the question I am suggesting we all, as critics, readers and spectators, implicitly or explicitly, ask: what *can* and what do I *want* to do with this play? Over the course of its history, the dominant reading of the *Shrew* is undoubtedly closer to Miller's, but that does not make his the *true* meaning. After all, among the dominant beliefs in the past four hundred years have been that racial superiority is a God-given fact, that women are intellectually and sexually inferior to men, and that war is a glorious expression of the best instincts of a culture. There is no inherent reason why the dominant view is the correct or inevitable one, and Shakespeare's plays are certainly not immune from this process.

If the specific ways that we speak of Shakespeare's comedies are not given by the text itself, but are produced by the interaction of the text and its readers, within their specific cultures and histories – something that was also true for Shakespeare, in his theatre and in his mind as the plays took shape – so today, as we read, watch, act in, direct or write about Shakespeare we too are part of that history. We are producing *our* Shakespeare. Therefore it is crucial that we make our Shakespeare as powerful and interesting an intervention as we can, not only in the history of Shakespearean criticism, but also in the broader cultural life of our own time. The essays collected here, which were all written between the mid-1970s and early 1990s, are designed to help readers of the plays do that. While they by no means exhaust what constitutes 'our' Shakespeare, they are sufficiently representative to show both the distinctiveness of current criticism and significant continuities with earlier work. A convenient landmark to use is the mid-1960s, when so many crucial trends in the current cultural conjunction were taking shape. The writings of Barthes, Macherey and Althusser were about to be noticed in certain Anglo-American critical circles as part of a major rethinking of the literary theory and practices of our time. Outside academe, the Royal Shakespeare Company was founded in 1960, a major milestone in the history of Shakespearean production, and in 1964, Shakespeareans all over the world celebrated the 400th anniversary of the Bard's birth. And specific to Shakespeare's comedies, in 1965 Frye's *A Natural Perspective* – a work in the background of or referred to by a number of the essays collected here – was published.

Even if current critical approaches see the comedies quite differently, the overall tendency is to treat them more seriously than earlier modes of criticism. Without their entertaining dimensions being necessarily ignored, they are more likely to be read as being concerned with no less 'serious' issues than the tragedies or histories – gender assignment, racial or social exclusion, class, determinism and freedom (what is often today termed 'agency'), or identity. *A Midsummer Night's Dream*, for instance, may still be read in a sentimental or romantic way, as the story of young lovers struggling, eventually successfully, to affirm their loves, or as a delightful combination of court and woods, mixing together for our entertainment haughty aristocrats, mischievous fairies, energetic lower-class buffoons, songs, dances and culminating marriages, all celebrating the relaxed carnival spirit of the festivity referred to in the play's title. But contemporary critics are equally likely to point to an undercurrent of threat and anxiety that links the play much more closely to the disturbing and arbitrary experiences ('terror') that is usually regarded as the stuff of tragedy – fears that the celebratory might not triumph, or that the dream might turn to nightmare. Jan Kott's essay in *Shakespeare Our Contemporary* (1964) opened the way for discussions of many aspects of the play's sinister side, and has influenced many similar readings of the other comedies. Do we see the fairies as benign or malevolent? Is Puck mischievous or irresponsible, even sinister? Do the fairies represent the arbitrary in our lives? How close to violence and tragedy do the mistaken identities in the woods get? Do the suggestions of conquest and rape in the opening scene undercut the young lovers' romanticism? Are such suggestions continued in Demetrius' treatment of Helena in the forest? How close does the play come to tragedy? Likewise with *Twelfth Night*: recent criticism has stressed the play's melancholy underside, and its reminders that only in fantasy may unpredictability and loss be beneficent. Viola acknowledges that 'Time, thou must untangle this, not I', but only in the wish-fulfilment world of romance does time always oblige. Time, as the tragedies show, is also the destroyer of hopes. That realization is not far from the surface of most of the comedies, and *Twelfth Night*, with its potential for contradictory readings – epitomized in the mixture of celebratory and moody songs at the end – shows it strikingly.

But how 'serious' are such disturbances? Most of the comedies are structured around family tensions – daughters against fathers, in particular – that are frequently heightened and complicated in the middle scenes, and (usually) settled at the end. The complications provide a little 'terror' for the audience that things might not turn out happily, so that when they do, we are all the more pleased. But in some, most particularly in *Love's Labour's Lost* and *Measure for Measure* (by which time he is breaking the boundaries of comedy) Shakespeare works a radical variation. In *Love's Labour's Lost*, he puts the threat to the promised happy ending in the last scene so that, as one of the characters puts it, the play 'doth not end like an old tale', contrary to what we have been led to expect. In *Measure for Measure* contradictions in tone, characterization, plot and ending call most assumptions about comedy radically into question.

According to the dominant, celebratory reading, apart from such exceptions (though it is one mark of current criticism that every play can be read as an exception) Shakespearean comedy is a dramatization of common wish-fulfilment fantasies: unless we are feeling particularly cynical, neurotic, or masochistic, we want our love affairs to be fulfilling, our families to experience harmony and (perhaps contradictorily, a question many of the comedies pose) young men and women to overcome their anxieties (or their parents' doubts or opposition) and find their own kinds of happiness – especially if that happiness is acceptable to the dominant powers of society. Comedy, according to this view, offers us a fantasy in which all or some of these goals are achieved. The plays produce sufficient challenges to this fantasy to keep us in suspense without destroying it.

Considering the comedies as 'serious', however, might lead us to construct an alternative theory of comedy as a 'collective fantasy' to this one of indulgent, individual wish-fulfilment. The traditional reading of the comedies as reinforcing harmony and reconciliation sees them predominantly focused on love – which is conventionally treated as an ideal, an absolute, perhaps the ultimate harmony of our existence, and which the ending of the plays generally celebrate. But an alternative view is possible. As we all know – and we know this more powerfully if, as at times the comedies themselves encourage us to do, we think of 'desire' rather than 'love' – how unsettling, transgressive and painful it often is. Over and over again, the comedies show the precariousness of the institutions by which desire is socialized. Significantly, we never see what happens after the lovers are married. Our own experiences of sexuality show how easily seemingly reassuring stabilities – commitments, family ties, friendships, marriages, even our sense of being coherent selves – can be threatened, shattered, illusory. *A Midsummer Night's Dream*, for instance, ends with three marriages: but one is politically compelled; the others occur after many misapprehensions, revealing that the shifting anarchy of desire may take, like Puck, infinite shapes.

It was Frye – the major exponent of the mythical reading of the comic structure culminating in an harmonious ending – who acknowledged that a reader's perception of the 'naturalness' of the harmony traditionally accorded to the end of the comedies rested on assumptions of the 'naturalness' of the workings of a divine providence which, he argued, was 'assumed to favour happy endings'. Today, in a world in which what Freud termed the 'oceanic feeling' of traditional religion has seemed to further recede, it may seem easier to resist the seductiveness of the final harmony either as artificial or as the imposition of authoritarian power, and to find characters in the comedies who themselves feel alienated by such coercive harmony such as Jaques in *As You Like It*, Malvolio (and maybe Feste) in *Twelfth Night*, Shylock in *The Merchant of Venice*. How much weight we give such oppositional figures will vary according to the political or other agendas we bring to it.[10] Eagleton has described the late romances – in which many of the characteristics of the comedies are (some would say triumphantly) extended – as powerful and repressive mystifications of a patriarchal social order which, like many of the comedies, seem to assert the inevitability of hierarchy, class privilege, gender inequality, and political quietism. But such a view of the plays involves taking the traditional reading as if it were somehow 'there' in the texts. If we approach Shakespeare's plays as places where ideology is produced, not simply communicated, then the comedies afford opportunities for very different, oppositional, even radical readings. Michael Bristol's *Carnival and Theater* (1985) draws attention to the oppositional elements within the plays: festivity, carnival, grotesquery, misrule and licence, he argues, are not mere foolishness but signs of a resistant counter-culture. It is such transgressive or perverse elements that threaten or actively undermine the harmony, and encourage an audience to indulge itself in fantasies of defiance and liberation, pointing, as Ryan suggests, 'towards the possibilities of more desirable ways of organizing human life and relationships': if we can be seduced by the collective fantasy of the ending of *As You Like It*, say, he argues, then outside the theatre 'quite different social productions can be scripted and mounted on the stage of history'.[11] Ryan's reading opens intriguing possibilities for reading the comedies as, say, envisaging a collective utopia of class or gendered (or, if we think forward to *The Tempest*) racial justice or harmony. A systematic reading of the comedies and of comic experience as disturbing, transgressive and rebellious (*and* utopian) still waits to be done, but there are many signs in current criticism and productions that such a combination is emerging as a major part of 'our' Shakespeare.

However, while such considerations suggest that contemporary views of the comedies are likely to be very different from those a generation or so ago; nonetheless the comedies continue to intrigue critics and spectators alike. This appeal may still be seen as based, at least in part, on the ways the comedies draw out our most primitive experiences, whether we describe those as built into our basic biogrammar or (as some psychoanalytic critics argue) our fundamental psychological patterns, or as culturally determined, or as a mixture of all these. Indeed, if either (or a mixture of) bio-psychological and cultural layering makes up what Freud called our unconscious, then Shakespeare's comedies are among those works of literature that draw most deeply on what that often contentious term stands for. That is, in part, why we call them 'great' – not because they are somehow 'universal', above the material or psychological details of our personal and collective histories, but because they are deeply embedded in those histories and have consequently been read in intriguingly different ways.

Feminist readings of the comedies

Perhaps the most powerful 'contemporary' readings of the comedies are those influenced by feminism. If we go back a century or so, we find books with titles like *The Girlhoods of Shakespeare's Heroines*, in which the sweetness, virtue, or nobility of the supposedly ideal girlhoods of the comic heroines were praised in terms that today appear to be heavy-handed, sentimental and condescending. But our own century's critics have sometimes been as culpable. In the tradition of character analysis, H.B. Charlton, in *Shakespearean Comedy* (1938), saw the comic heroines as the centre of the plays' 'charm', as embodiments of elegance, wit, creativity, inspiring us 'to shape the world towards happiness', which makes them sound a little like bishops' wives or society hostesses.[12] Fifty years later, as an offshoot of one of the most important critical and political movements of our time, feminist readings of Shakespeare have developed a tradition of less patronizing, more serious and complex readings of gender in the comedies, focusing – though not exclusively – on the heroines, while a variety of critics, not all explicitly feminist, have seen the comedies as sites of contention about gender issues. The emphasis in much recent criticism on problems of sexual identity, gender roles and family relations has produced some outstanding criticism, and any serious criticism of the comedies today must grapple with issues raised by feminist theory and critical practice.

Three feminist approaches to the comedies may be broadly distinguished. First, Shakespeare has been seen as a protofeminist, reflecting, in his portrayal of strong, attractive heroines, the emergence of viable subject positions for women within the discursive practices of early modern England. Juliet Dusinberre's *Shakespeare and the Nature of Women* (1975) is an example. Second, sceptical of this reassuringly liberal view of Shakespeare, some critics have pointed to what they see as the comedies' inevitably patriarchal assumptions which still overwhelmingly marginalized women. Marianne Novy's *Love's Argument: Gender Relations in Shakespeare* (1984) and Marilyn Williamson's *The Patriarchy of Shakespeare's Comedies* (1986) are examples. Carol Thomas Neely's *Broken*

Nuptials in Shakespeare (1985), the chapter on *Much Ado* which is exerpted in this collection (pp. 138–54), points to the ways in which the plays' culminating marriages are frequently disrupted or undercut: 'broken nuptials' often counterpoint the achieved marriages, underlining the women's reluctance to marry or the need for some reformation of the men before the harmonious end can be achieved. In her essay on *The Merchant of Venice*, Coppélia Kahn terms marriage in the comedies 'the ideal accommodation of eros with society' (p. 128). Yet Neely's argument asks us to contrast the strong, clever heroines with their seemingly unambiguous capitulation to orthodox patriarchal marriage at the end of *Much Ado about Nothing* – or – as Erickson's and Asp's essays show, *As You Like It* and *All's Well that Ends Well* (see pp. 156–67 and pp. 175–92). Third, there are those critics who relate the contradictions in the comedies to both residual patriarchal assignments of gender and emergent feminist practices, finding them held in contention in the plays as they were in Shakespeare's age, which was itself characterized by change and controversy over gender roles and authority within the family. An approach that stresses the contradictory signals on gender in the comedies, in their own time, and in (to adapt a phrase of Jonathan Dollimore's) other, 'later' struggles, has strong affinities with Cultural Materialism, a critical approach which is discussed below (pp. 20–2).

Twelfth Night is a particularly interesting play for focusing on both the importance and variety of feminist (or, more broadly, gender-aware) criticism. A central focus of the play is cross-dressing, which points to, as it does in *As You Like It*, a blurring of sexual difference at the heart of the play. Viola is not merely a woman disguised as a man but one who is desired as both man and woman. Critics disagree on the significance of this insistent and sustained motif. For Stephen Greenblatt, the play simply affirms the dominance of models of male individuation in Shakespeare's time. For Jean Howard, the play makes gender identity indeterminate, though finally it does act to recuperate and so contain challenges to the dominant pattern of gender assignments. She describes the play as a 'fairly oppressive fable . . . of the valorization of the "good woman" as the one who has interiorized – whatever her clothing – her essential difference from, and subordinate relations to, the male'. By this view, the play asks us to applaud Viola's resumption of a 'properly feminine subjectivity'. For Catherine Belsey, by contrast, the very dramatization of the blurring of sexual identity opens up the possibility of undoing traditional roles. To extend her argument in a cultural materialist direction, viable alternative conceptions of gender roles are being put into discourse, making them available for adoption by the play's spectators. It was by such means that radical alternatives were made available outside the theatre, not least to the increasing number of women spectators, thus laying the ground for gradually changing gender roles and assignments.[13]

The endings of both *As You Like It* and *The Merchant of Venice* can be read in a similar manner, as the essays by Erickson and Newman suggest (see pp. 156–67 and 41–55). Indeed, cross-dressing in the comedies – in particular, the fact that on the stage in Shakespeare's time women's parts were played by boys, which afforded the dramatists the occasion for both amusing and disconcerting references – has become a major focus of recent feminist criticism. Such work often draws on the influential analysis of the spectator of film by Laura Mulvey and Teresa de Lauretis to stress ways by which women are traditionally represented as objects of the male gaze, the seemingly unchallenged pleasure of which is disconcerted when the object is a man playing a woman – who is, in *As You Like It* and *Twelfth Night*, also playing a man. Cross-dressing calls assigned gender roles into question, and allows the theatre to become a place where alternative, transgressive, or utopian gender identities might be put into play.[14] While gender issues are central to the comedies, their author and many critics are males. What insights (or ignorances) was Shakespeare articulating about his own or patriarchy's fear of or curiosity about women? And what differences does gender make to reading? These are current feminist and 'male feminist' issues. Such work as that by Mulvey and Gaylyn Studlar on, respectively, the sadistic gaze and the masochistic desire for engulfment as basic experiences of film are influencing current gender criticism on the comedies.[15]

Psychoanalytical approaches to the comedies

From Freud onwards, our century has seen a marked preoccupation with the psychological dynamics of the family – with, for example, the separation and individuation of child from the mother, a child's discovery of boundary conditions, the development of object relations, delusions of omnipotence and fears of abandonment, and the search for a lost, pre-oedipal, polymorphous sexual fulfilment. To many critics, the conflicts of Shakespeare's comedies seem uncannily close to such concerns. MacCary argues Shakespeare gives comedy the 'force of psychoanalysis: we come to see ourselves in its characters just as we come to know ourselves in analysis'.[16]

An important figure inspiring such work over the past thirty years was C.L. Barber, whose final book on Shakespeare, *The Whole Story* (1988), was completed by Richard Wheeler and published posthumously. Unashamedly speaking of how the plays served Shakespeare's own 'human needs' and so can be made to reveal his 'personality', Norman Holland likewise sees 'Shakespeare' as a text to be analysed both culturally and personally. Such an approach runs counter to the common post-structuralist insistence on the humanist illusion of the coherent subject which, it seems, Holland's approach demands.[17] Both Holland and Golding offer some comments on this controversy in their essays (see pp. 73–92 and 92–105). Less contentiously, what the psychoanalytic tradition – not only Freud, but such major figures as Melanie Klein or, as the essay by Golding shows, D.W. Winnicott – has provided is a powerful vocabulary to talk of the stages and crises of individual and familial growth, and one more congenial to discussions of drama and poetry than the positivism of much cognitive psychology or the scientism of some behavioural psychology.

For instance, in 'The Family Romance', Freud noted that 'the liberation of an individual, as he grows up, from the authority of his parents is one of the most necessary though one of the most painful' events of life. He describes a number of characteristic fantasies of changing one's family circumstances – to have richer or more powerful parents, or not have to share one's parents' love with siblings, for instance. Other symptoms include a boy's hostility towards his father coupled with an intense desire to bring his mother – the subject, says Freud, 'of the most intense sexual curiosity' – into 'situations of secret infidelity' with him. Other connected fantasies may involve incestuous feelings for siblings, desires to return to fancied (or perhaps real) conditions of early childhood when the child was unindividuated from the mother, and the child's 'most intense and momentous' general wish, simply 'to be big like his parents'. In children, such day-dreams emerge as wish-fulfilments with, Freud says, aims that are simultaneously erotic and more generally ambitious – not only to emulate (or seduce) the parents but to be free of their control. In adults, the symptoms of the family romance emerge in desires to discover or recapture a lost state of autonomy, which may be projected, negatively or positively, upon a series of love-objects – lovers, spouses, or children, even (as one of my students pointed out) pets – who thereby become incorporated into the neurotic patterns that were laid down early in the adult's own family history.[18] Many psychoanalytic critics see the comedies – and, even more intensely, the later romances – as evoking these stages and crises of individual and familial growth. Despite – as many feminists rightly point out – predicating the psychological narrative upon the development of a male subject, and despite, too, the temptation to dehistoricize its categories, psychoanalytic criticism provides suggestive ways by which we can describe the struggle for differentiation between child and parent, especially between sons and mothers, or (and this is particularly relevant to these plays) daughters and fathers. Without such struggles, the plays seem to assume, there can be no viable identity, no later close and meaningful relations with others, no fulfilling sexual identity.

Shakespeare's male characters, in particular, seem engaged in continuous struggles to form a secure gendered identity, and to find (or reject) a place for women in that identity. We can point too to the separated twin brothers who find each other in *The Comedy of Errors*, or the breaking from parental dependence and adolescent friendship to adult love in *As You Like It*. Claudio's treatment of Hero, or Bertram's of Helena can be usefully seen in this light. Later, in *A Winter's Tale*, the focus is on the self-destructive insecurities that arise from separation from the mother here (as elsewhere) represented by lost innocence of youth. It may be that (to return to Resnais' metaphor) we 'remember' such separations only in the unconscious – although for some people they may become very, and painfully, conscious. But either way, a relatively constant characteristic of the Western male identity has been an attempt to revert to a core of imaginary oneness simultaneously into which to escape and to become free from, even destroy. These contradictory feelings are projected, often violently, upon adult lovers, wives and children. In many of the comedies, Shakespeare's interest in this contradiction of Western masculine identity focuses on a male figure whose separation was incomplete or problematic – as it seems to be for most of us – and for whom anxiety arises when he is called upon as an adult to be a friend, a husband, a father. In *As You Like It*, the struggles for differentiation and maturity are relatively lightly treated, but are still linked to the dynamics of the family. In *All's Well that Ends Well*, the concentration is on the very different patterns of maturation which a man and a woman undergo, and is a major concern of the play.

Where many critics see the family as a symbol of stability in Shakespeare's plays, it can also be seen as yet another site of instability, a place of contest between generations, where often one parent (usually the mother) is missing, and where its harmonies are tentative, patched together, and founded on utopian wish rather than reassuring coherence. Even the late romances, which seem to valorize reunited families, do so through great strains and, as in *The Winter's Tale*, without restoring all that was lost. Even in what is probably the first comedy Shakespeare wrote, *The Comedy of Errors* (?1592–94), the focus is not – as in the later comedies – so much on courtship and marriage as on another, more threatening narrative. We are reminded from the outset of shipwrecks, the confusion (not wholeness) of identity, loss and futility: indeed, a violent undercurrent goes through the whole play, not the least of which is the death sentence that hangs over Egeus, who can find compassion and financial rescue from neither his captors nor the citizens of Ephesus – until the seemingly miraculous ending when his newly discovered son ransoms him. The play sets up what becomes a typical pattern of wish-fulfilment balanced by reminders that reality is more complex than our fantasies wish: hovering behind our most sought-after desires is the fear that they are unrealizable. Such anxieties are embodied in the end of the play, which invites us to join in a family reconciliation, but suggests that the other marriages of the play are far from settled.

Many such readings of the comedies by critics working within the psychoanalytic tradition draw primarily on a tradition, derived from Freud, of ego psychology which is closely related to clinical practice. In recent years, however, Lacanian theory has become a major force in psychoanalytic criticism. Rejecting the stable self of ego psychology, Lacanians focus on the misidentifications (*méconnaissances*) by which the individual subject constructs a fiction of self-coherence. Barbara Freedman's *Staging the Gaze: Psychoanalysis, Postmodernism and Shakespearean Comedy* (1990) is an attempt in the Lacanian mode to show how Shakespeare's comedies enact a fundamental scepticism towards individual identity, showing up the 'misrecognitions of language, gender and ideology by means of which the ego is sustained'.[19]

Historical approaches to the comedies

Feminist and psychoanalytical readings of these plays are clearly interactive – both there 'in' the text and also the product of 'contemporary' repertoires. The next critical category is characterized by attempts to avoid the 'contemporary' emphasis in order to emphasize Shakespeare in *his* history as opposed to ours – in other words to focus on the production of the Shakespearean text as opposed to its reception. Whether it is, in fact, possible to treat the two separately is one of the central issues of both 'contemporary' and 'historical' criticism. An 'historical' approach does not mean one that merely takes note that, fairly obviously, Shakespeare's plays were written four hundred years ago in language that is sometimes archaic, or that its characters and settings are rarely those we would expect to see in our everyday lives. Historical criticism uses such matters to establish the plays' alleged meanings. In its extreme form, it is directly opposite to an approach that stresses the contemporary relevance of the plays and appropriates the plays to current concerns (see *Shakespeare our Contemporary*, above). Complicating this distinction is a kind of criticism that claims to be 'historical', but finds the plays' meanings in 'universals', truths or insights that are supposedly always true, and in a sense located outside history. Much traditional thematic criticism that discusses the plays in terms of such ahistorical abstractions as appearance and reality, the maturing of true love, or the discovery of an underlying personal identity – as if these were unaffected by historical factors of race, class, or gender – is criticism of this type. Any claim to such universality is difficult to maintain since it endows the observer with an ability to step outside of history. One powerful version of this approach, essentially nostalgic, sees the plays as a reminder of a world supposedly lost for us disorganized and unheeding moderns, a world of cultural order and social harmony that is, contradictorily, at once timeless and yet rooted in a nostalgic version of Shakespeare's age.[20]

More properly historical are those approaches which relate the issues of the play primarily, and perhaps exclusively, to the intellectual or material conditions of production in Shakespeare's own time. An older historicism tried to explain the meanings of the plays through the construction of a 'background' to the plays that is, supposedly, objective and which gives a modern reader access to the play's 'true' meaning. While historical research on the comedies can be invaluable – for instance, in establishing the clash of class values between Falstaff and the Windsor bourgeoisie in *The Merry Wives of Windsor*, explaining the various philosophies of love represented in *As You Like It*, or helping us understand the expectations of parental control over a girl's choice of a husband in *A Midsummer Night's Dream* – these matters do not, in themselves, give us authoritative meanings for the play. There is, curiously, often an intriguing nostalgia built into the 'old' historical approach, as if we were afraid not just of our time but of the future. The alternative, after all, to conceiving of history as somehow completed and needing only to be read once and for all, an assumption which lies behind the old historicism, is to recognize the unfinished nature of history and that the past we reconstruct will help us shape – and is shaped by our conception of – the future we must live.

This realization that history is, by definition, constructed by men and women from within history itself, not from some outside, objective viewpoint, underlies the next two, newer, historical approaches. While there are important overlappings between the two – and some of the best criticism of the present time, such as the work of Louis Montrose represented in this collection by his essay on *Love's Labour's Lost* (pp. 56–72), combines aspects of both – there are sufficient differences to justify distinguishing them from each other.

New Historicist and Cultural Materialist approaches to the comedies

New Historicism has been one of the most exciting and influential movements in American and British scholarship in recent years, most notably in the Renaissance. It focuses on the Shakespearean text as part of a network of cultural forces, linking 'literary' texts with 'historical' material and material practices considered as textual: diaries, legal records, fashion, anecdotes, and patterns of political or religious authority. Plays are considered, along with these other cultural texts, as articulations of the society's dominant cultural forces. In the New Historicist view, culture, in all its rich detail, is bound together, almost like a conspiracy within which individual texts and individual subjects alike are both imprisoned and legitimated. A New Historicist essay will characteristically start with an historical anecdote – what Jean Howard terms an 'illustrative example' – often involving state violence or repression, from a field seemingly marginal to the literary text under discussion, which will demonstrate the connections and interweavings of the lines of power across disparate cultural practices in the society. A striking instance is the story recounted by Newman at the start of her essay on *The Taming of the Shrew* (pp. 42–4). Similarly, in a recent essay on Renaissance individualism, Greenblatt – often seen as the originator of the movement – uses Jacques Duval's medical account of hermaphroditism to demonstrate the 'shared code, a set of interlocking tropes and similitudes that function . . . as the conditions of representation'. Shakespeare's comedies, like one of Duval's medical cases, Greenblatt argues, are concerned with 'a love that cannot at first declare itself, and that encounters, when it finally does so, life-threatening obstacles; a dizzying confusion of identity centered on cross-dressing; an intense experience of desire . . . that seeks to satisfy itself in a sanctified union; the intervention of authority to block this union but eventually to resolve all problems'.[21]

Interestingly, despite an accumulation of impressive historical detail, there often emerges in New Historicist studies – ironically, rather like the nostalgic approach of 'old' historicism noted above – a curiously ahistorical tendency to extract from texts a world view that is no less monolithic than that of 'old' historicist views of 'order' or 'hierarchy', one concerned with the locations and forms by which power flows through all societies, both the consciously felt power of laws and institutions and the more subtly, though no less materially felt power that is articulated through family, religion and even such apparently harmless forms of entertainment as drama. Power as such – almost independent of historical details – is seen as the predominant plot of history. For New Historicism, entrapment within the currents of power occurs not because of material factors within particular social formations – not because, for instance, we are members of a particular class or gendered group, but because we are trapped by the very nature of power. For instance, Leonard Tennenhouse's *Power on Display* (1986) reads the plays in terms of an inescapable hierarchical view of power which leaves little room for direct, oppositional agency. Shakespeare, he asserts, knew 'what it was politic to say', and in his plays, no less than Jonson's court masques, 'stagecraft' collaborates with statecraft to produce 'spectacles of power'. Further, the world New Historicism depicts, as Norbrook puts it, is one 'of dominant males in which there seems no room' for specifically female agency. Feminist and other critics have sometimes claimed that New Historicism seems to avoid analysis of class and gender interests; not only, as Carol Neely points out, does it overemphasize the power of the dominant, but it often seems to be predominantly white, middle class, and male in its focus and commitments.[22] Its treatment of popular culture in the plays – the ludic, grotesque or antisocial elements that are so prominent in the comedies – is particularly revealing. The work of Tennenhouse on Elizabethan spectacle or Stephen Mullany's *The Place of the Stage* (1988), on Elizabethan underclass culture, sees the dominant power controlling potentially subversive practices. Within the comedies, the Dromios, Mechanicals, Dogberry, Feste, Lucio and Mistress Quickly are among the many characters read within the New Historicist paradigm of willing or coerced complicity with the hegemonic powers.

If New Historicism has directed our attention to the ways the Shakespearean text is produced within and constrained by the dominant structures of power in early modern England, Cultural Materialism focuses more on the potential growing points and contradictions, both referred to within the text or which, as it were, lurk on its margins. Behind New Historicism lies the genealogical history of Michel Foucault and social anthropology's emphasis on the 'thick' description of the enmeshed details of a culture. By contrast, behind Cultural Materialism are the influences of Marxist theorists like Althusser, Macherey and Williams. The material and ideological contradictions and potential sites of opposition and resistance are its primary focus. Those dramatic characters and scenes that New Historicists tend to see as complicity with or recuperated by the hegemonic court power, become in a Cultural Materialist reading the signs of emergent social subversion or potential or widespread (if repressed) opposition. Cultural Materialism investigates resistances to power rather than its apparent dominance, focusing on marginal groups like women, witches, the sexually or economically disenfranchised, on conflict among class factions and racial minorities – in short on the marginal but insistent forces that challenge and may eventually break down a monolithic construction of power. The characteristic agenda of Cultural Materialism is the quaternity of gender, race, class and agency, issues that arise from distinctively contemporary struggles, but which still acknowledge the historical differences between our society and that of Shakespeare. Consequently, where 'power' is a key word for a New Historicist, 'ideology' is the central focus for Cultural Materialism.

Unlike the New Historicists, who tend to avoid an explicit political stance, Cultural Materialist critics make clear that their readings of Shakespeare are politically strong ones – designed to make distinctive interventions in contemporary political debates. Graham Holderness's *The Shakespeare Myth* (1988) analyses the institutionalization of Shakespeare within contemporary political and social struggles. Such committed criticism has clear affinities with that of Terry Eagleton and Catherine Belsey, whose essay on the comedies in John Drakakis's *Alternative*

Shakespeares (1985) is a stimulating combination of feminist and ideological analysis.

These two forms of historical criticism, which in the 1980s have made Renaissance studies, and Shakespeare studies in particular, so exciting, have certain concerns in common and yet in many ways are very distinct. For the New Historicist, Shakespeare's texts operate within a network of shared forces, articulating (often against their will) the totalitarian and all-embracing nature of Jacobean monarchy and aristocratic power. Thus, in Jonathan Dollimore's essay in this collection (pp. 195–209), the Duke in *Measure for Measure* is widely read in relation to the power of the Jacobean conception of monarchy. *The Merchant of Venice* becomes a study of how the dominant Christian and mercantile power – represented by Antonio, Portia and Bassanio – successfully trick and marginalize the alien Shylock. For the Cultural Materialist, on the other hand, it is precisely the marginalized and disruptive on which we should focus – especially on these aspects that the dominant reading of the play wants to see defeated. Thus, as Dollimore's essay indicates, a number of recent Cultural Materialist readings see Lucio's irreverence or a possible refusal by Isabella to the Duke's proposal at the end of *Measure for Measure* as challenging the dominant assumptions of control and order the authorities of the play assert. In Terence Hawke's analysis of *Twelfth Night*, Malvolio becomes not so much a dupe as a victimized, even potentially tragic, figure whose determination to revenge his mistreatment creates a disruption to aristocratic control of the final harmony. His self-righteousness links him with the Puritans who, in Shakespeare's time, were not only hostile to the conspicuous consumption of the aristocracy on whose patronage the theatre depended, but also represented an important emergent social group. Cultural Materialism thus, potentially at least, allies with feminism in focusing on the subversive potential of women and other marginalized groups in the early modern period, and showing how the drama can be read as a site of social struggle – both in its time and in our own.

These are major and inescapable ways of rethinking how we do historical criticism. They have made the questions we tend to ask nowadays as literary and cultural historians radically different from those of even ten years ago. We can no longer speak of 'text' or 'author', or 'historical background' as if they were unproblematic, objectifiable entities, or as if we ourselves (or other readers) were uninvolved in their construction. Indeed, we have learnt that often the most important things in texts are what they don't mention – either because, as it were, they can't or they won't. So we focus, paradoxically, on things that in the older paradigm we might have rejected as not being, as we used to say, 'in' the text. How do we do this? In two ways, I suggest. In the first we read for evidence of the pressure of history on the production of the text, history as it were *in* the text. If necessary, we focus on the text's 'silences', that is on ideas or cultural practices not addressed directly by the text, perhaps where the unspoken, although certainly at the time speakable, has been repressed, censored, or marginalized, but nonetheless exerts pressure upon the text's production. In the second we read the text into history, or as Jonathan Dollimore puts it, we address history directly, making explicit what in the text's production had no voice – for Dollimore, in Shakespeare's *Measure for Measure*, a counter-discourse of deviancy, the development of which, he argues, in a cryptic but telling phrase, is 'another and later story' (p. 208). This second mode points to, adapting a term of Macherey's, the 'absences' of texts. Some 'absences' are related to what Williams terms 'the pre-emergent' places where oppositional practices are in fact struggling to be heard. And then there is reading for absences in a radically historicized way – where the reader's commitments and interests in the present open up a particular perspective on the text.[23]

Shakespeare in performance: theatre, film and television

Finally, it is important to comment briefly on the seemingly elementary fact – ignored for much of this century by mainstream academic criticism of Shakespeare's comedies – that they were written for performance. Today, the play-in-performance is a major critical focus. I write as someone who (like millions of other theatre-goers) has sat through performances of Shakespeare's plays in delight at the antics of Beatrice and Benedick in *Much Ado about Nothing*, or – with *King Lear*, or *The Winter's Tale* in my case – with tears streaming down my face. My own deepest experiences of Shakespeare's plays have been in the theatre and in the classroom, both places stressing performance. Yet when I was at Cambridge in the 1960s the dominant view of Shakespeare – derived from critics like F.R. Leavis – was that production was a decidedly lesser manifestation of Shakespeare's art. His plays were seen as dramatic poems. The words were primary; meanings were in the text. We picked out imagery, themes and ironies. If we had read Frye or Barber we related the themes to principles of structural recurrence. We were not encouraged to speak of the theatrical aspects of the plays – despite the fact that John Barton, still a Cambridge don, was at the Arts Theatre and soon to be a dominant force at Stratford, along with Leavis's sometime pupil, Trevor Nunn.

Today things are very different. As W.B. Worthen points out, a 'relocation of meaning from within the text to the ways a text can be made to perform has fundamentally altered both the practice and the consequences of criticism'. Critics have increasingly commented on theatrical productions, especially those of the Royal Shakespeare Company.[24] The company's title is of course an indication of the assimilation of Shakespeare into our dominant ideology – as if Shakespeare had been appointed Purveyor of Entertainment and Leisuretime Comfort to Her Majesty, along with the worthy makers of marmalade, beauty soap or toilet tissue. While the best and most provocative productions of the last thirty years have not always come from the RSC – especially lately, as it has struggled under the pressure of underfinancing and Thatcherism – its impact, not just in the theatre but also on criticism of the plays, has nevertheless been immense.

What the multiplicity of productions of the plays – on stage, film and television – has done for ordinary theatre-goers, readers and students alike in the past thirty or so years is to remind us that Shakespeare's plays are not primarily literature, but theatrical scripts: that their meanings are not unchanging across the ages, but arise from the many possibilities that can be opened up among script, actor, director and audience. We may not like or agree with productions we see, but they at least make us aware that the plays can be acted in different ways – with very different impacts on audiences. Productions may be exercises in nostalgia, or highly iconoclastic; they may involve elaborate settings, or be acted on a bare stage. The 'same' play can be menacing, jolly, or ambiguous. When Jonathan Miller set his 1974 production of *Measure for Measure* in Freud's Vienna, it added a whole new dimension to its insights; when the same director set his BBC television production of *The Taming of the Shrew* in the world of Jacobean Puritanism and concluded with the singing of a psalm, it told us something very different from Michael Bogdanov's contemporary production in leather and chains, or the rollicking male chauvinism of Zefferelli's film version with Richard Burton chasing Elizabeth Taylor through a barnyard, complete with door-breakings, and accidental tumblings into piles of goose feathers – knock-about farce in a literal sense.

In much current criticism, there is widespread recognition that our involvement with the plays as theatre should be a crucial dimension of our study of them. In *Shakespeare and the Energies of Drama* (1972), Michael Goldman declared that the critic should 'seek a meaning for each play in the human significance of our response as audience, in the life it awakens us to, the awareness it builds upon'. In the theatre, he argued, 'there is a unique focus on the body. The play may rise in Shakespeare's imagination and come home to our own, but it takes place between two sets of bodies, ours and the actors.'[25] Philip McGuire's *Speechless Dialect* (1983) draws attention to what is occurring on stage while characters are present but silent – Hippolita's near-silence at the start of *A Midsummer Night's Dream*, for instance. Such criticism marks a significant break with the criticism dominant before the 1960s. Today most Shakespeareans would recognize as incomplete any criticism that ignores the performative dimensions. Nonetheless, performative criticism raises difficult questions. Some critics assume that productions simply articulate pre-existent meanings: it exists, as both Worthen and James Kavanagh have argued, in a 'lapsed' relation to an authoritative text. Acting, like reading or criticism, however, is a mode of *producing*, not merely *reproducing*, meanings; it is no less the product of a particular repertoire of assumptions that are ultimately ideological. By this second, more radical view, the Shakespearean script makes 'meaning only as it is loosed into the world as production . . . within changing signifying systems'. What Derrida terms the 'infinite deferral of the signified' is enacted in each performance.[26]

Current performative criticism divides, often acrimoniously, between these two views of the authority of the theatrical script. However, one of the ironies of our present situation is that, having been dragged (in some cases reluctantly and in contradictory ways) into the theatre, Shakespeare critics now must face the possibility, as Ronald Bryden is reported to have apprehensively stated, that Shakespeare will be further 'liberated from us' (who, we might ask, is the 'us'?). By that he meant that Shakespeare's plays are not only theatre, but that they have been, for sixty years, film and now, television. In 1975, in his inaugural lecture as Professor of Drama at Cambridge, Raymond Williams argued that 'drama is no longer . . . coextensive with theatre', noting that 'most dramatic performances are now in film and television studios'. He suggested further that no society has ever been so self-conscious about 'acting', and that drama 'in quite new ways' is built into the rhythms of our everyday life, especially through the omnipresence of television.[27] Williams's argument makes us realize that when we ask 'What is *our* Shakespeare?' today, we are necessarily asking to what extent do film and television versions of the plays determine our rewritings of Shakespeare? What changes can we see in the ways we respond to, teach, or write criticism about the plays? To what extent, when film and television provide the dominant conventions of viewing entertainment, do we imagine Shakespeare according to their conventions? Such questions are especially important when we consider the culturally peripheral nature of traditional theatre for a large number even of those people who study Shakespeare, let alone those for whom Shakespeare remains a set of uncomfortable memories of a school set text, boringly taught and seemingly irrelevant to their lives. That television, even more than film, has taken on a 'bardic function' – i.e., providing a common centre, articulating the myths of our society – provides a pressing reason for taking it seriously. At the very least, we must surely consider that 'millions of people each year . . . experience Shakespeare on the screen', and it will thus 'become increasingly impossible for teachers and critics to ignore these productions'.[28]

Enjoying the comedies (seriously)

The shift in critical and stage readings of the comedies in recent years may be marked by a 1983 Canadian production of *Measure for Measure*, in which instead of the reassuringly happy ending of the Duke and Isabella presiding over a scene of forgiveness and reconciliation, a tableau of threat and violence defined the ending of the play – Isabella listened in horror to the Duke's proposition, and tried to slap his face (as she had done with Angelo and Claudio) only to find the provost violently restrain her. She found herself isolated, surrounded by a beaten group of conformists and victims of state power, assigned to distinctively subordinate gender and class roles, and without recourse to any sense of agency.[29] In reviewing contemporary approaches, productions and criticism alike, to the comedies, what has happened – in Dover Wilson's term – to Shakespeare's 'happy' comedies? Surely, we are 'meant' to reject Malvolio and Shylock? To laugh at the mistakes of identity in *The Comedy of Errors*, not see them as a potential threat to our own sense of identity? Aren't we 'meant' to enjoy happy endings? Partly, the answer to such protests lies in the fact that in reading critical essays, or considering our own sustained reading of a play, we are accounting for the impact of the plays after the fact: when we read them, or watch them in the theatre, we are less self-conscious than when we afterwards analyse the cognitive strategies with which we have responded, or the ideological contradictions we've found ourselves in. Thus we may be moved deeply by the celebrations at the end of *As You Like It* or Helena's return in *All's Well that Ends Well*, and later feel uneasy about the ways we have been manipulated into accepting an archaic patriarchal situation (and the feelings that go with it). Or by hearing or reading Portia's 'The quality of mercy is not strained' speech in *The Merchant of Venice*, and afterwards considering how we acquiesced in Portia's charm and cunning, even perhaps how 'instinctively' we were led to identify with the young and the beautiful, and the rich and powerful, and to reject (or find ourselves embarrassed by) an outsider like Shylock. Such tensions within our responses are not improper; they make up a great deal of the impact of the comedies, and the more self-conscious about how we are caught between contradictory beliefs and responses, the more we will enjoy them. To focus on the subversive or oppositional readings that may be opened up by a play, to acknowledge contradiction as an effect as important as, or even more important than, harmony – these are responses by no means incompatible with enjoyment, laughter, or lightheartedness. Laughter itself can, after all, help to dismantle monolithic power structures, whether political, academic, or psychological, probably more easily than it can be used to prop them up.

Notes

1. TERRY EAGLETON, *William Shakespeare* (Oxford: Basil Blackwell), pp. ix–x.

2. JOSEPH WESTLUND, *Shakespeare's Reparative Comedies: A Psychoanalytic View of the Middle Plays* (Chicago: University of Chicago Press, 1984), pp. 14–15.

3. STEPHEN ORGEL, 'Prospero's Wife', in *Rewriting the Renaissance: the Discourses of Sexual Difference in Early Modern Europe*, ed. Margaret Ferguson, Maureen Quilligan and Nancy J. Vickers (Chicago: University of Chicago Press, 1986), p. 57.

4. M.N. EAGLE, *Recent Developments in Psychoanalysis* (New York: McGraw-Hill, 1984), p. 97.

5. MALCOLM EVANS, *Signifying Nothing: Truth's True Contents in Shakespeare's Text* (Brighton: Harvester Press, 1986), p. 256; LOUIS A. MONTROSE, Introductory Essay to Harry Berger Jr, *Revisionary Play: Studies in the Spenserian Dynamics* (Berkeley: University of California Press, 1988), p. 8; TONY BENNETT, 'Texts in History: The Determinations of Readings', *Journal of the Midwest Modern Language Association* 18.1 (Fall, 1985), 1–16.

6. See KATHLEEN MCCORMICK and GARY WALLER, *Reading Texts* (Lexington, MA: D.C. Heath, 1987), pp. 23–7, from which some of this paragraph is adapted.

7. JOHN DOVER WILSON, *Shakespeare's Happy Comedies* (Cambridge: Cambridge University Press, 1938).

8. C.L. BARBER and RICHARD P. WHEELER, *The Whole Journey: Shakespeare's Power of Development* (Berkeley: University of California Press, 1986), p. 5.

9. See GARY WALLER, 'Decentering the Bard: The Dissemination of the Shakespearean Text', in *Shakespeare and Deconstruction*, ed. G. Douglas Atkins and David M. Bergeron (New York: Peter Lang), pp. 27–9; G. DOUGLAS ATKINS, 'Introduction', *Shakespeare and Deconstruction*, pp. 2, 3, 6.

10. NORTHROP FRYE, *The Myth of Deliverance* (Toronto: University of Toronto Press, 1983), p. 6; SIGMUND FREUD, *Civilization and its Discontents*, trans. James Strachey (New York: Norton, 1961), p. 12.

11. EAGLETON, *William Shakespeare*, pp. 96, 99; KIERNAN RYAN, *Shakespeare* (Brighton: Harvester Press, 1989), pp. 11, 40.

12. H.B. CHARLTON, *Shakespearean Comedy* (London: Methuen, 1938), p. 283.

13. STEPHEN GREENBLATT, *Shakespearean Negotiations* (Berkeley: University of California Press, 1989), p. 93; JEAN HOWARD, 'Crossdressing, the Theatre, and Gender Struggle in Early Modern England', *SQ* 40 (1989), 432; CATHERINE BELSEY, 'Disrupting Sexual Difference: Meaning and Gender in the Comedies', in *Alternative Shakespeares*, ed. John Drakakis (London: Methuen, 1985), pp. 166–90.

14. LAURA MULVEY, 'Visual pleasure and narrative Cinema', *Screen* 16.3 (1975), 6–18; TERESA DE LAURETIS, *Alice Doesn't: Feminism, Semiotics, Cinema* (Bloomington: Indiana University Press, 1984).

15. G. STUDLAR, *In the Realm of Pleasure* (Urbana: University of Illinois Press, 1988).

16. W. THOMAS MACCARY, *Friends and Lovers: The Phenomenology of Desire in Shakespearean Comedy* (New York: Columbia University Press, 1985), p. 21.

17. NORMAN N. HOLLAND, 'Introduction', *Shakespeare's Personality*, ed. Norman N. Holland, Sidney Homan and Bernard J. Paris (Berkeley: University of California Press, 1990), pp. 1, 5.

18. SIGMUND FREUD, 'Family Romances', *The Standard Edition of the Works of Sigmund Freud*, ed. and trans. James Strachey, 9 (London: International Universities Press, 1952), pp. 237–41.

19. BARBARA FREEDMAN, 'Misrecognizing Shakespeare', in *Shakespeare's Personality*, p. 257.

20. Theatre, film and television productions may declare themselves as either 'historical' or 'contemporary': by their use of sets and costume we may be asked to contemplate the difference between the world of the play and our own time, or to see the similarities. The widely available BBC/Time-Life television versions are all 'costume' productions: set in a TV version of the Renaissance, sometimes shot in actual castles and manor houses, with period costumes, and 'authentic' details in fashion, furniture, jewellery, transportation, market or crowd scenes. An exhibition of the costumes designed for the productions has been a major attraction in Stratford-upon-Avon, and from my experience as a teacher, many students unfortunately think the consistently 'olde-worlde' atmosphere of the productions give them an authentic feel. On the other hand, many stage productions deliberately choose a contemporary setting to bring home the modern impact of the plays, and it is important to note that *AYL* in leather and chains, or *AWell* set in the 1920s is no more nor less authentic than a production in Renaissance dress. What matters is the effectiveness of the production. Of course, in one important sense, all productions, whether we term them 'historical' or 'contemporary', are contemporary in that they are being mounted in the present. We need to investigate why a director chooses to do one thing rather than the other. To choose a Renaissance setting for *TN* rather than an eighteenth century or modern one is to say something about what impact the play may have, or about the cultural functions of Shakespeare. The famous 1960 Peter Brook production of *MSND*, which stressed the play's menacing atmosphere by a brightly lit, white gymnasium-like stage and fairies who looked like circus performers, appalled some who were used to experiencing the play as a reassuring exercise in charm and nostalgia.

21. JEAN HOWARD, 'Recent Studies in Elizabethan and Jacobean Drama', *Studies in English Literature* 27 (1987), 339; GREENBLATT, *Shakespearian Negotiations*, p. 86.

22. LEONARD TENNENHOUSE, *Power on display: The Politics of Shakespeare's Genres* (London: Methuen, 1986), pp. 2, 15; DAVID NORBROOK, 'Life and Death of Renaissance Man', *Raritan* 8.4 (1989), 103; CAROL THOMAS NEELY, 'Constructing the Subject: Feminist Practice and the new Renaissance Discourses', *English Literary Renaissance* 18 (1988), 5–18.

23. For class, gender, race and agency, see GARY WALLER, 'Knowing the Subject: Critiquing the Self, Critiquing the Culture', *ADE Bulletin*, 95 (Spring, 1990), 14–18, and for the silence/absence distinction, see 'The Countess of Pembroke and Gendered Reading', in *Renaissance Englishwomen in Print: Counterbalancing the Canon*, ed. Betty Travitsky and Anne B. Haselkorn (Amherst: University of Massachusetts Press, 1990), pp. 340–1.

24. W.B. WORTHEN, 'Deeper Meanings and Theatrical Technique', *SQ*, 40 (1989), 441.

25. MICHAEL GOLDMAN, *Shakespeare and the Energies of Drama* (Princeton: Princeton University Press, 1972), p. 4.

26. WORTHEN, 'Deeper Meanings', pp. 446, 448; JAMES KAVANAGH, 'Shakespeare in Ideology', in Drakakis, p. 147. See also WALLER, 'Decentering the Bard', pp. 27–9, and McCormick and Waller, chapter 7.

27. RAYMOND WILLIAMS, *Drama in a Dramatised Society* (Cambridge: Cambridge University Press, 1975), p. 3.

28. JOHN FISKE and JOHN HARTLEY, *Reading Televison* (London: Methuen, 1978), p. 86; JACK J. JORGENS, *Shakespeare on Film* (Bloomington: Indiana University Press, 1977), p. 3. For the remarks by Bryden, see 'Messina at the SAA Meeting', *Shakespeare on Film Newsletter* 4.2 (April, 1980), 1.

29. 'Shakespeare and Foucault', *Bulletin of the New York Shakespeare Society*, 3 (1983), 4.

1 The Comedy of Errors (?1592–94)

W. THOMAS MACCARY 'The Comedy of Errors: A Different Kind of Comedy'*

MacCary's essay on The Comedy of Errors – which later became part of his fuller study, Friends and Lovers: the Phenomenology of Desire in Shakespearean Comedy (1985) – moves beyond an older formalist emphasis on structure and 'theme' to root the experience of Shakespearean comedy in a psychoanalytic model of the family. He finds the quest for personal identity in both homoerotic and heterosexual relationships as both the structural principle and the major human impact of the comedies. Using a theory of narcissism to point to the pleasure of comedy, he links Shakespeare to the ancient Greek comic writers, Aristophanes and Menander. He suggests that Shakespeare's comedies are not merely designed to evoke laughter, but to produce complex emotional and intellectual effects centered on a celebration of our at-one-ness with ourselves and our societies.

MacCary's argument thus blends an analysis of structure and sources with a discussion of underlying psychoanalytical patterns. In this essay he focuses on The Comedy of Errors' central motif of not just one, but two, sets of identical twins who, after being separated from infancy, find each other. MacCary argues that this motif has not only farcical potential, but profound psychological possibilities. But this play strikes an unusual note. The later comedies typically focus on the possibilities and limitations of courtship and marriage: in The Comedy of Errors it is the family that is the main focus. The typical Shakespeare comedy involves a young man's pursuit of a young woman – a transference, if we adopt the largely male-centred psychoanalytical perspective, of the search for the mother we gave up when we struggled to differentiate ourselves. But The Comedy of Errors involves something even more primitive – the pursuit, at the level of the unconscious memory of a complete and idealized self, the 'reunion with or creation of a person like the person the protagonist would like to

---

* Reprinted from New Literary History, Vol. XI, No. 3, Spring 1978, pp. 525–536.

become', his or her 'ideal ego'. However illusory such a quest, on this level the goal of the play is to make us feel satisfied, helping us, even in the relatively self-conscious fantasy of viewing or reading, 'to recapture, in our adult, intellectualized state, the sensual bliss of warmth and satiety' that – at least in our unconscious – we had in our very earliest childhood. The reunited family at the play's end, unlike the marriages that typically end the comedies, therefore uncannily anticipate those of Shakespeare's late romances. Qualifying such an interpretation, of course, one needs to stress the disturbing notes the play sounds – the threat of Egeus's death sentence, the lost brothers, marital tensions, confusion and loss of identity. The psychological seriousness of this, probably Shakespeare's earliest comedy, is remarkable for its anticipation of later, more complex plays. (For a broader discussion of psychoanalytical approaches to the comedies, see Introduction, pp. 14–17.)

We say that the human being has originally two sexual objects: himself and the woman who tends him, and thereby we postulate a primary narcissism in everyone, which may in the long run manifest itself as dominating his object-choice.

(SIGMUND FREUD, *On Narcissism: An Introduction*)

Our comic tradition, since Menander, has been essentially romantic: boy meets girl, boy loses girl, boy wins girl and lives happily with her ever after. Much else, of course, happens in comedy from the fourth century B.C. to the present, but this 'nubile' pattern of action focuses our attention. Even in plays where the couple are of little interest as characters, their union nevertheless symbolizes the beginning of a new life, and comedy, if it differs at all from tragedy and satire, must at least make us that promise. There are some plays in the tradition which do not end in marriage, leaving many people dissatisfied: their expectations seem to have been shaped as much by dramatic conventions as by deeper needs and desires. Shakespeare's *The Comedy of Errors* is one of these plays and has been criticised for its lack of definitive marriage plans: there is brief allusion to future arrangements between Luciana and Antipholus of Syracuse, but the marriage of Adriana to Antipholus of Ephesus is left unreconstructed. In fact, this is a comedy of a different kind. Its entire argument prepares us not for the union of man and wife – its view of marriage is especially pessimistic – but for the reunion of twins with each other and with their parents, the sort of reestablishment of the nuclear family which is so important in Shakespeare's last plays. To appreciate the *Comedy* we need to master certain basic problems: the history of the development of the romantic pattern in comedy; the psychological significance of this pattern: its alternatives and their significance.[1]

Northrop Frye speaks of the 'comic Oedipus situation' in New Comedy: 'Its main theme is the successful effort of the young man to outwit an opponent and possess the girl of his choice. The opponent is usually the father (*senex*), and the psychological descent of the heroine from the mother is also sometimes hinted at. The father frequently wants the same girl, and is cheated out of her by the son, the mother thus becoming the son's ally. The girl is usually a slave or courtesan, and the plot turns on a *cognitio* or discovery of birth which makes her marriageable.[2] If the pursuit of a young woman who reminds the young man of his mother is oedipal, then the pursuit of a young man who reminds the young man of himself is pre-oedipal and narcissistic. I do not mean to propose a new cycle of forms here;[3] I do think the appreciation of certain correspondences between stages in literary history, stages in human development, and different conceptions of happiness can make our reading of a difficult text more complete. Aristophanes does not use doubles in his plays, but he does consistently develop patterns of action which lead toward the comic close that is implicit in the use of doubles by other authors, i.e., self-fulfilment and self-expression. His male characters enjoy sexual intercourse with women, but they do not pursue women as the embodiment of complete contentment. Rather, they enjoy a wide range of sensual experiences that are specifically sexual (i.e., genital) or capable of producing sexual gratification (i.e., oral or anal): masturbation, homosexual intercourse, defecation and urination in a variety of postures, flatulence, expectoration, scoptophilia, eating and drinking, kissing and fellatio. They also like to talk about all these activities. In short, Aristophanic heroes sound like psychoanalytic textbooks on perversion and, more precisely, they sound like Freud's description of the polymorphously perverse child, the pre-oedipal child, the child before he has learned to channel all his libidinal energy into the pursuit of a woman who will take the place of his mother.

If we were to formulate a kind of comedy which would fulfil the demands associated with the pre-oedipal period, it would have many of the aspects which critics find annoying in *The Comedy of Errors*. The family would be more important than anyone outside the family, and the mother would be the most important member of the family. Security and happiness would be sought not in sexual intercourse with a person of the opposite sex but in reunion with or creation of a person like the person the protagonist would like to become, i.e., his alter ego, or, more correctly, his ideal ego. There would be an ambivalent attitude toward women in the play, because the young child (male) depends upon the mother for sustenance but fears being reincorporated by the mother. Such fears of the overwhelming mother might be expressed in terms of locked doors and bondage, but the positive, nurturing mother would occasion concern with feasting and drinking. There might even be ambivalent situations, such as banquets arranged by threatening women, and ambivalent symbols, such as gold rings or chains, which suggest both attraction and restriction.

How much do we want to know about the pre-oedipal period? Can we really believe that certain conceptions of happiness develop in certain stages and all later experience is related back to these? To what extent is our appreciation of comedy based on our ability to identify with its protagonists? If we answer this last question affirmatively, then we must at least consider the implications of the other two. Most of us do not have twin brothers from whom we were separated at birth, so the pattern of action in *The Comedy of Errors* cannot encourage us to identify with Antipholus of Syracuse – clearly the protagonist, as I hope to show below – on the level of superficial actuality. There must be a common denominator, and thus the action of the play must remind us, by way of structural similarity or symbolic form, of something in our own experience. If a play has universal appeal, the experience recalled is more likely to be one of childhood than not, since the earliest experiences are not only the most commonly shared, but also the most formative: what we do and have done to us as children shapes all later experience. A good comedy 'ends happily', which means it follows a pattern of action which convinces us that we can be happy. Happiness is different things at different periods in our lives, and if the argument on development is accepted, the greatest happiness is the satisfaction of our earliest desires. By this I do not mean that comedy should feed us and keep us warm, but rather that it should cause us to recapture, in our adult, intellectualized state, the sensual bliss of warmth and satiety.

I do not think that many critics today would label *The Comedy of Errors* a farce and dismiss it as deserving no more serious analysis. The patterns of farce, like all the patterns of action in drama, are appealing for some good reason. Clearly the comic pattern involving mistaken identity appeals to us because it leads us from confusion about identity – our own, of course, as well as the protagonist's – to security. The most effective version of that pattern would be that which presents to us our own fears and then assuages them, so it must speak to us in language and action which can arouse memory traces of our own actual experience of a search for identity. While it is true that this search goes on throughout the 'normal' man's life, it is most intense in the early years. When Antipholus of Syracuse likens himself to a drop of water in danger of being lost in the ocean, he speaks to us in terms which are frighteningly real. The plight of the protagonist is felt almost physically, his yearning for his double accepted as natural and inevitable. Water itself is the most frequent dream symbol for birth, and with the mention of the mother and brother, we are set firmly in the child's world. The brother, in our own experience, is not a brother, but another self, the ideal ego which the mother first creates for us and we strive to assimilate. We are reminded of the Narcissus myth, since water can reflect as well as absorb, and Antipholus of Syracuse seeks himself in his mirror image. The water here, as ocean, is the overwhelming aspect of the mother, the mother from whom the child cannot differentiate himself. She projects to us the image of what we shall become; but it is a fragile image, and if we lose it we risk reintegration with her, reabsorption, a reversal of the process of individuation which we suffer from the sixth to the eighteenth month. Only later, when we have developed a sense of alterity, can we distinguish ourselves from the mother, and her image of us from ourselves.

Plautus, of course, does not frame his comedy of twins with a family romance the way Shakespeare does. He provides a complete view of the relation between man and wife and clearly indicates the preparation for this relation in the male child's attitude toward the mother. In Plautus we have only one set of doubles, the twins themselves, but Shakespeare gives us two more sets: the twin slaves Dromio and the sisters Adriana and Luciana. We see these women almost entirely through the eyes of Antipholus of Syracuse, our focus of attention in the play. From his first speech onwards it is from his point of view we see the action, and the occasional scene involving his brother serves only as background to his quest: he is the active one, the seeker. We meet the two sisters before he does, in their debate on jealousy, and then when he encounters them, our original impressions are confirmed. They are the dark woman (Adriana, *atro*) and the fair maid (Luciana, *luce*) we meet with so frequently in literature,[4] comprising the split image of the mother, the one threatening and restrictive, the other yielding and benevolent. The whole atmosphere of the play, with its exotic setting and dreamlike action, prepares us for the epiphany of the good mother in Luciana, the bad mother in Adriana. Antipholus of Syracuse, who seems to have found no time for, or shown no interest in, women previously, is entranced and wonders that Adriana can speak to him so familiarly:

To me she speaks. She moves me for her theme.
What, was I married to her in my dream?
Or sleep I now, and think I hear all this?
What error drives our eyes and ears amiss?

(II, ii, 183–6)

The extraordinary aspect of his reaction, though quite natural in the context of the play's system of transferences, is that he should take for his dream the strange woman's reality: in other circumstances we might expect him to say that she is dreaming and has never really met him, but he says instead that perhaps he had a dream of her as his wife which was real. She is, then, strange in claiming intimacy with him, but not entirely unknown: she is a dream image, and he goes on to question his present state of consciousness and sanity:

Am I in earth, in Heaven, or in Hell?
Sleeping or waking? Mad or well advised?
Known unto these, and to myself disguised!

(II, ii, 214–16)

If these women were completely alien to him, had he no prior experience of them in any form, then he could have dismissed them and their claims upon him. As it is, he doubts not their sanity but his own and wonders whether he dreams or wakes as they persist in their entreaties, suggesting he has dreamed of them before, and not without some agitation.

The exact words of Adriana's address which creates this bewilderment are, of course, very like his own opening remarks. She seems to know his mind exactly, and this makes her even more familiar to him though strange in fact. She takes his comparison of himself to a drop of water and turns it into a definition of married love. The impact of the repetition is due to the reversal of the protagonist's expectations. He came seeking his mirror image, like Narcissus, his ideal ego, his mother's image of himself, and finds instead a woman who claims to be part of himself; and she threatens him with that absorption and lack of identity which he had so feared: she is the overwhelming mother who refuses to shape his identity but keeps him as part of herself. In this speech he was the drop of water; in her speech the drop of water is let fall as an analogy, but he becomes again that drop of water and flees from the woman who would quite literally engulf him.

He flees, of course, to the arms of the benign Luciana, she who had warned her sister to restrain her jealousy and possessiveness, to allow her husband some freedom lest she lose him altogether. This unthreatening, undemanding woman attracts Antipholus of Syracuse, and he makes love to her in terms which recall the two drop of water speeches (III, ii, 53–64). There is as much difference between Adriana and Luciana as between night and day: Adriana is the absence or perversion of all that is good in Luciana. It is not the difference between dark women and fair women we find in the other comedies – Julia and Sylvia in *Two Gentlemen of Verona*, Helena and Hermia in *A Midsummer Night's Dream* – but much more like the difference in the *Sonnets* between the dark lady and the fair youth: on the one side we have all that is threatening and corruptive, while on the other there is truth and beauty. Again, all is a dream: Antipholus of Syracuse has seen Luciana before, in dreams, in madness, but then she was indistinguishable from Adriana, the two opposites bound up as one. Now, as if by the dream mechanism of decomposition they are separate, and he can love the one and avoid the other. He has overcome his fear of the overwhelming mother and projects now his image of the benevolent mother upon Luciana.

The relation between these two young women and Aemilia, the actual mother of Antipholus of Syracuse, becomes clear in the climactic scene. He has been given sanctuary in the priory, after having been locked up by Adriana and escaping her; Aemilia emerges, like the vision of some goddess, to settle all confusion. Her attention focuses on Adriana, and she upbraids her son's wife for the mistreatment she has given him. It is a tirade not unlike others in early Shakespearean comedy against the concept of equality and intimacy in marriage. We hear it from Katharina at the end of *The Taming of the Shrew*, and we see Proteus fleeing from such a marriage in *Two Gentlemen of Verona*, as do all the male courtiers in *Love's Labour's Lost*. In the later romances this antagonism between the man who would be free and the woman who would bind him home is equally apparent and more bitterly portrayed; e.g., Portia's possessiveness in *The Merchant of Venice* and Helena's pursuit of Bertram in *All's Well*. The identification of the threatening woman with the mother in the man's eyes is developed to varying degrees in these different instances – the maternal aspect of Portia is remarkable, as are Helena's close ties to the Countess – but here it is transparent: Aemilia must instruct her daughter-in-law on the proper treatment of her son, and we see this through the eyes of Antipholus of Syracuse: he has finally been able to conquer his fear of losing his identity in his mother's too close embrace because she herself tells him that this is no way for a woman to treat him:

> The venom clamors of a jealous woman
> Poisons more deadly than a mad dog's tooth.
> It seems his sleeps were hindered by thy railing,
> And thereof comes it that his head is light.
> Thou say'st his meat was sauced with thy upbraidings;
> Unquiet meals make ill digestions.
> Thereof the raging fire of fever bred,
> And what's a fever but a fit of madness?
> Thou say'st his sports were hindered by thy brawls.
> Sweet recreation barred, what doth ensue
> But moody and dull Melancholy,
> Kinsman to grim and comfortless Despair,
> And at her heels a huge infectious troop
> Of pale distemperatures and foes to life.

(V, i, 69–82)

This description of madness reminds us of the mythical monsters: Harpies, Gorgons, and Furies – all female, like Shakespeare's Melancholy and Despair – bitchlike creatures who hound men to madness. Clearly this entire race is a projection of male fears of female domination, and their blood-sucking, enervating, food-polluting, petrifying attacks are all related to pre-oedipal fantasies of maternal deprivation. By identifying this aspect of the mother in Adriana, he can neutralize it. Antipholus of Syracuse, then, finds simultaneously the two sexual objects Freud tells us we all originally have: his own benevolent and protective mother and the image of himself in his brother he has narcissistically pursued.

Psychologically it is the most satisfying ending possible, and those who ask for marriage here, or some guarantee that the existing marriage between Antipholus of Ephesus and Adriana will be revived, simply have not responded to the pattern of action Shakespeare has presented.[5] They want a 'romantic' comedy, a Menandrean comedy in which happiness is found in the person of a young person of the opposite sex who can complement the virtues of the protagonist and signify to the world that he is a mature and substantial member of the male community. The girl he marries might be a younger image of his mother, as Frye suggests, and he might even have had to compete with his father to win her, but the fact that he feels the need to possess a woman at all is in imitation of his father: this is the way grown men behave, monogamously. The situation in *The Comedy of Errors* is entirely different: the rejection of the threatening mother and the acceptance of the benevolent mother, in conjunction with the retrieval of the ideal ego or narcissistic image in the double, prepares the protagonist for marriage, but that is a separate and future action. *The Comedy of Errors* is not a romantic comedy[6] but a narcissistic comedy or egocentric comedy. In so far as comedy can revive memory traces of childhood experiences, this comedy takes us back to the pre-oedipal stage when we first emerged as creatures conscious of our own difference. By the principle of first is best, this kind of comedy can be even more satisfying than the oedipal comedy most frequent in the tradition since Menander.

Again I insist that I do not intend to add another dimension to Frye's 'fearful symmetry'. I do not believe that the stages of either literary history or psychic development are so precisely segmentable that elaborate correspondences can be drawn so as to increase significantly our appreciation of individual works. It is just as well that the conventional labels for Greek comedy are Old, Middle, and New, in that order, rather than the reverse, lest we be tempted to speak of Aristophanes as comedy's infancy and Menander as its adolescence. Systems of correspondence almost of necessity become abstract and distract us from our primary concern. I do believe that something significant happened in the comic tradition late in the fourth century B.C. and that Menander was to a large extent responsible for changing the direction of comedy for the next twenty-three hundred years. (I do not pretend to understand what is happening today on the comic stage, but I trace the Menandrean age with ease as far as Oscar Wilde.) Whereas in pre-Menandrean comedy, especially Aristophanic comedy, the goal of happiness toward which the action moves is concerned with the self as independent center of the universe, after Menander it takes two to be happy, and they have to be man and woman. The great modern comedians sometimes recreate the earlier kind of comedy, either spontaneously, as did Mozart in *Don Giovanni*, or under indirect influence from the pre-Menandrean period, as did Shakespeare in *The Comedy of Errors*.

Authors do not usually choose their models blindly. Shakespeare saw in Plautus' *Menaechmi* a pattern of action which interested him, and we see basic similarities between this play and the other early comedies: male friendship is more important than marriage and women are seen as barriers in the way of male freedom and development. The *Sonnets*, too, show the same concern,[7] while *Henry VI* is a study in misogyny and *King John* paints a rather frightening picture of mothers and wives as powers behind the throne. I must avoid, though, the suggestion that this was a major concern of Shakespeare's during his youth, lest I add the offenses of biographical criticism to a paper already burdened with the offenses of psychoanalytic and genre criticism. I do insist, finally, on but three points: comedy, as much as tragedy, requires identification between audience and protagonist, a clear point of view, and this must be based on common experience, actual or fantasized; early experiences are formative, and the effective comedian plays upon the fears and desires which we retain from infancy and childhood; romantic comedy has been in the ascendant since Menander, but there are some exceptional plays of the narcissistic type and Shakespeare's *The Comedy of Errors* is one of these.

Notes

1. T.B.L. WEBSTER, *Studies in Later Greek Comedy*, (Manchester: Manchester University Press, 2nd edn, 1970), pp. 67–74.

2. NORTHROP FRYE, 'The Argument of Comedy', in *English Institute Essays* (New York: Columbia University Press, 1948), p. 50.

3. Cf. FREDRIC JAMESON, 'Magical narratives: romance as genre', *New Literary History* 7 (1975), 135–63.

4. See R. ROGERS, *The Double in Literature* (Detroit: Wayne State University Press, 1970), pp. 126–37; LESLIE FIEDLER, 'Some Contexts of Shakespeare's Sonnets', in *The Riddle of Shakespeare's Sonnets*, ed. H. Hubler (New York: Basic Books, 1962), pp. 57–90; and *Love and Death in the American Novel* (New York: Stein and Day, 1960), pp. 205–14.

5. ALEXANDER LEGGATT, *Shakespeare's Comedy of Love* (London: Methuen, 1964), p. 9: 'The director may contrive a forgiving embrace, but nothing in the text requires

it . . . for the critic, with only the text before him, the final state of the marriage must remain an open question.' One could say the same thing – if one were a critic incapable of visualizing a stage performance of one's own direction – of the marriages in *MSND, Mer, AWell,* and *Meas.* The plays that end in secure and satisfying marriages for the major characters are few indeed, perhaps only *AYL.*

6. *Shakespearean Comedy,* ed. DAVID PALMER and MALCOLM BRADBURY (London: Arnold, 1972), pp. 7–8: 'Of the ten comedies which belong to the first half of Shakespeare's career, only *Err, Shr* and *MWW* are not given detailed discussion here: an omission which reflects less on their merits than on the volume's prevailing interest in the more "romantic" plays.'

7. See FIEDLER, 'Some Contexts'.

2   The Taming of the Shrew (1593–94)

KAREN NEWMAN '*Renaissance Family Politics and Shakespeare's The Taming of the Shrew*'*

The Taming of the Shrew is early in Shakespeare's development and might best be seen as full of contradictory possibilities, some of which were to develop more subtly in later comedies. If the farcical story of a strong man taming a headstrong woman were the whole play (or all that could be made out of it) it could easily remain a trivial piece. But many recent critics see a number of interesting contradictions arising from the material in the play. Shakespeare is perhaps not quite able to articulate what he wants to do with it; or, perhaps because of inherent contradictions in its subject matter, the play is necessarily contradictory. A broken, contradictory text is not necessarily a failure – *Measure for Measure* is a strikingly interesting play precisely because it is an 'unfinished' text – but, with *The Taming of the Shrew*, once a reader queries the story's sexual politics, the play does pose some tricky problems of interpretation.

The purely farcical reading is the traditional one. It is the view more or less espoused by the tinker Christopher Sly in the play's induction and subsequent scenes. But immediately Katherina appears there is the possibility of seeing her as more interesting than as a shrew produced by the bullying male imaginary. Are there the makings of a proto-feminist play? Or at least the anticipation of other strong Shakespearean heroines like Beatrice or Rosalind? Is the play going to degenerate into a knock-about, farcical battle of the sexes or become the study of how strong men and women adapt to the demands of a relationship in a sexist patriarchal society that in its dominant ideology of gender relations puts little store on subtlety and negotiation?

Barbara Freedman has suggested that 'traditional Western theatre offers us only two stages, comic and tragic, upon which are always playing some version of *Oedipus* or its sister play, *The Taming of the Shrew*', the stories of 'the man who discovers his own sexuality and the woman who learns to

* Reprinted from *English Literary Renaissance*, Vol. 16 (1986) pp. 86–100

disavow her[s]'.[1] While many men may say they prefer women who are strong, witty, independent, and even dominant, how many secretly wish for sexual control and even maybe wish, whether consciously or not, to return to a society where patriarchal domination was taken for granted? It is perhaps easier to be a 'liberated' man when ultimate control can be reclaimed. Such considerations which, given the controversies at the time over the roles of men and women in marriage, were familiar to Shakespeare's audience, have made the play the subject of some striking recent criticism and productions.

Katherina's final speech is always a crux in any interpretation. Even so committed a feminist as Germaine Greer reads it enthusiastically as a 'defence of Christian monogamy' that 'rests upon the role of a husband as protector and friend, and it is valid because Kate has a man who is capable of being both'.[2] But alternative readings are possible. Can it be read as Kate's acceptance of Petruchio as an equal? Or as her showing her catching on to the rhetorical situation and so showing her superiority to the other women? Does she see the opportunity to escape an oppressive family situation and the stereotype of woman as obedient and mindless, as her simpering sister Bianca presents herself? Is it delivered with a wink to the audience? Some of these readings may give the play more coherence than is justified. But Shakespeare liked to raise issues rather than provide solutions. In this case, perhaps, the solutions lay in later plays.

Using a mix of New Historicism, Feminism and (in her invocation of Althusser) making connection with Cultural Materialism, Karen Newman argues that the play both 'produces' the 'social facts of patriarchal ideology', and gives us a perspective on it. Her approach, increasingly typical of recent historical criticism in its eclecticism, starts with the characteristic anecdote of New Historicism, a discussion of domestic violence seemingly far (not just geographically, but culturally) from the world of the London theatres. She then links its implications for gender politics by means of what she terms a 'community fantasy, the shaming and subjection of a shrewish wife'. She argues that in Shakespeare's plays, conflicting social elements that point to a widespread struggle within the politics of the early modern family, are temporarily reconciled in what, quoting the Marxist critic Fredric Jameson, she calls an 'ideological mirage'. Her argument raises a recurring issue between 'New Historicist' and 'Cultural Materialist' readings of the comedies – are the oppositional social forces, especially the greater autonomy and agency of the women, finally recuperated and so controlled by the dominant, patriarchal or aristocratic powers? Newman's conclusion, consistent with the eclecticism of her approach, is a cautious one: the play's representation of gender is at once 'patriarchally suspect and sexually ambivalent, clinging to

Elizabethan patriarchal ideology and at the same time tearing it away by foregrounding or italicizing its constructed character' (see Introduction, pp. 18–22).

Notes

1. BARBARA FREEDMAN, 'Frame-Up: Feminism, Psychoanalysis, Theatre', *Theatre Journal*, 41 (1989), 58. See also her *Staging the Gaze: Psychoanalysis, Postmodernism, and Shakespearean Comedy* (Ithaca: Cornell University Press, 1990).

2. GERMAINE GREER, *The Female Eunuch* (New York: McGraw-Hill, 1971), p. 206.

Wetherden, Suffolk. Plough Monday, 1604. A drunken tanner, Nicholas Rosyer, staggers home from the alehouse. On arriving at his door, he is greeted by his wife with 'dronken dogg, pisspott and other unseemly names'. When Rosyer tried to come to bed to her, she 'still raged against him and badd him out dronken dogg dronken pisspott'. She struck him several times, clawed his face and arms, spat at him and beat him out of bed. Rosyer retreated, returned to the alehouse, and drank until he could hardly stand up. Shortly thereafter, Thomas Quarry and others met and 'agreed amongest themselfs that the said Thomas Quarry who dwelt at the next howse . . . should . . . ryde abowt the towne upon a cowlestaff whereby not onley the woman which had offended might be shunned for her misdemeanors towards her husband but other women also by her shame might be admonished to offence in like sort'.[1] Domestic violence, far from being contained in the family, spills out into the neighborhood, and the response of the community is an 'old country ceremony used in merriment upon such accidents'.

Quarry, wearing a kirtle or gown and apron, 'was carryed to diverse places and as he rode did admonishe all wiefs to take heede how they did beate their husbands'. The Rosyers' neighbors reenacted their troubled gender relations: the beating was repeated with Quarry in woman's clothes playing Rosyer's wife, the neighbors standing in for the 'abused' husband, and a rough music procession to the house of the transgressors. The result of this 'merriment' suggests its darker purpose and the anxiety about gender relations it displays: the offending couple left the village in shame. The skimmington, as it was sometimes called, served its purpose by its ritual scapegoating of the tanner, and more particularly, his wife. Rosyer vented his anger by bringing charges against his neighbors in which he complained not only of scandal and disgrace to himself, 'his wief and kyndred', but also of seditious 'tumult and discention in the said towne'.[2]

The entire incident figures the social anxiety about gender and power which characterizes Elizabethan culture. Like Simon Forman's dream of wish-fulfilment with Queen Elizabeth, this incident, in Louis Montrose's words, 'epitomizes the indissoluably political and sexual character of the cultural forms in which [such] tensions might be represented and addressed'.[3] The community's ritual action against the couple who transgress prevailing codes of gender behavior seeks to re-establish those conventional modes of behavior – it seeks to sanction patriarchal order. But at the same time, this 'old country ceremony' subverts, by its representation, its masquerade of the very events it criticizes by forcing the offending couple to recognize their transgression through its dramatic enactment. The skimmington seeks 'in merriment' to reassert traditional gender behaviors which are naturalized in Elizabethan culture as divinely ordained; but it also deconstructs that 'naturalization' by its foregrounding of what is a humanly constructed cultural product – the displacement of gender roles in a dramatic representation.[4]

I Family politics

The events of Plough Monday 1604 have an uncanny relation to Shakespeare's *The Taming of the Shrew* which might well be read as a theatrical realization of such a community fantasy, the shaming and subjection of a shrewish wife. The so-called induction opens with the hostess railing at the drunken tinker Sly, and their interchange figures him as the inebriated tanner from Wetherden.[5] Sly is presented with two 'dreams', the dream he is a lord, a fantasy which enacts traditional Elizabethan hierarchical and gender relations, and the 'dream' of Petruchio taming Kate. The first fantasy is a series of artificially constructed power relationships figured first in class relations, then in terms of gender. The lord exhorts his servingmen to offer Sly 'low submissive reverence' and traditional lordly prerogatives and pursuits – music, painting, handwashing, rich apparel, hunting, and finally a theatrical entertainment. In the longer, more detailed speech which follows at Ind., 1,100 ff., he exhorts his page to 'bear himself with honourable action. Such as he hath observ'd in noble ladies/Unto their lords'. Significantly, Sly is only convinced of his lordly identity when he is told of his 'wife'. His realization of this newly discovered self involves calling for the lady, demanding from her submission to his authority, and finally seeking to exert his new power through his husbandly sexual prerogative: 'Madam, undress you and come now to bed' (Ind., 2,118). By enacting Sly's identity as a lord through his wife's social and sexual, if deferred, submission, the Induction suggests ironically how in this androcentric culture men depended on women to authorize their sexual and social masculine identities.[6] The Lord's fantasy takes the drunken Sly who brawls with the hostess, and by means of a 'play' brings him into line with traditional conceptions of gender relations. But in the Induction, these relationships of power and gender, which in Elizabethan treatises, sermons and homilies, and behavioral handbooks and the like were figured as natural and divinely ordained, are subverted by the metatheatrical foregrounding of such roles and relations as culturally constructed.

The analogy between the events at Wetherden and Shakespeare's play suggests a tempting homology between history and cultural artifacts. It figures patriarchy as a master narrative, the key to understanding certain historic events and dramatic plots. But as Louis Althusser's critique of historicism epigrammatically has it, 'history is a process without a *telos* or a subject'.[7] This Althusserian dictum repudiates such master narratives, but as Frederic Jameson points out,

> What Althusser's own insistence on history as an absent cause makes clear, but what is missing from the formula as it is canonically worded, is that he does not at all draw the fashionable conclusion that because history is a text, the 'referent' does not exist . . . history is *not* a narrative, master or otherwise, but that, as an absent cause, it is inaccessible to us except in textual form, and that our approach to it and to the Real itself necessarily passes through its prior textualization, its narrativization in the political unconscious.[8]

If we return to Nicholas Rosyer's complaint against his neighbors and consider its textualization, how it is made accessible to us through narrative, we can make several observations. We notice immediately that Rosyer's wife, the subject of the complaint, lacks the status of a subject. She is unnamed and referred to only as the 'wife'. Rosyer's testimony, in fact, begins with a defense not of his wife, but of his patrimony, an account of his background and history in the village in terms of male lineage. His wife has no voice; she never speaks in the complaint at all. Her husband brings charges against his neighbors presumably to clear his name and to affirm his identity as patriarch which the incident itself, from his wife's 'abuse' to the transvestite skimmington, endangers.

From the account of this case, we also get a powerful sense of life in early modern England, the close proximity of neighbors and the way in which intimate sexual relations present a scene before an audience. Quarry and the neighbors recount Rosyer's attempted assertion of his sexual 'prerogatives' over his wife, and her vehement refusal: 'she struck him several times, clawed his face and arms, spit at him and beat him out of bed'. There is evidently no place in the late Elizabethan 'sex/gender system'[9] for Rosyer's wife to complain of her husband's mistreatment, drunkenness and abuse, or even give voice to her point of view, her side of the story. The binary opposition between male and female in the Wetherden case and its figuration of patriarchy in early modern England generates the possible contradictions logically available to both terms: Rosyer speaks, his wife is silent; Rosyer is recognized as a subject before the law, his wife is solely its object; Rosyer's family must be defended against the insults of his neighbors, his wife has no family, but has become merely a part of his. In turning to *The Taming of the Shrew*, our task is to articulate the particular sexual/political fantasy or, in Jameson's Althusserian formulation, the 'libidinal apparatus' that the play projects as an imaginary resolution of contradictions which are never resolved in the Wetherden case, but which the formal structures of dramatic plot and character in Shakespeare's play present as seemingly reconciled.

II A shrew's history

Many readers of Shakespeare's *Shrew* have noted that both in the induction and the play language is an index of identity. Sly is convinced of his lordly identity by language, by the lord's obsequious words and recital of his false history. Significantly, when he believes himself a lord his language changes and he begins to speak the blank verse of his retainers. But in the opening scene of the play proper, Shakespeare emphasizes not just the relationship between language and identity, but between women and language, and between control over language and patriarchal power. Kate's linguistic protest is against the role in patriarchal culture to which women are assigned, that of wife and object of exchange in the circulation of male desire. Her very first words make this point aggressively: she asks of her father 'I pray you, sir, is it your will/To make a stale of me amongst these mates?' (I, i, 57–8). Punning on the meaning of stale as laughing stock and prostitute, on 'stalemate', and on mate as husband, Kate refuses her erotic destiny by exercising her linguistic willfulness. Her shrewishness, always associated with women's revolt in words, testifies to her exclusion from social and political power. Bianca, by contrast, is throughout the play associated with silence (I, i, 70–1).[10]

Kate's prayer to her father is motivated by Gremio's threat 'To cart her rather. She's too rough for me' (1, i, 55). Although this line is usually glossed as 'drive around in an open cart (a punishment for prostitutes)', the case of Nicholas Rosyer and his unnamed wife provides a more complex commentary. During the period from 1560 until the English Civil War, in which many historians have recognized a 'crisis of order', the fear that women were rebelling against their traditional subservient role in patriarchal culture was widespread.[11] Popular works such as *The Two Angry Women of Abington* (1598), Middleton's *The Roaring Girl* (1611), *Hic Mulier*, or *The Man–Woman* (1620), and Joseph Swetnam's *Arraignment of lewd, idle, froward and inconstant women*, which went through ten editions between 1616 and 1634, all testify to a preoccupation with rebellious women.[12]

What literary historians have recognized in late Elizabethan and Jacobean writers as a preoccupation with female rebellion and independence, social historians have also observed in historical records. The period was fraught with anxiety about rebellious women. David Underdown observes that 'Women scolding and brawling with their neighbours, single women refusing to enter service, wives dominating or even beating their husbands: all seem to surface more frequently than in the periods immediately before or afterwards. It will not go unnoticed that this is also the period during which witchcraft accusations reach their peak'.[13] Underdown's account points out a preoccupation with women's rebellion through language. Although men were occasionally charged with scolding, it was predominantly a female offence usually associated with class as well as gender issues and revolt: 'women who were poor, social outcasts, widows or otherwise lacking in the protection of a family . . . were the most common offenders'.[14] Underdown points out that in the few examples after the restoration, social disapproval shifts to 'mismatched couples, sexual offenders, and eventually . . . husbands who beat their wives'.[15] Punishment for such offences and related ones involving 'domineering' wives who 'beat' or 'abused' their husbands often involved public shaming or charivari of the sort employed at Wetherden. The accused woman or her surrogate was put in a scold's collar or ridden in a cart accompanied by a rough musical procession of villagers banging pots and pans.

Louis Montrose attributes the incidence of troubled gender relations to female rule since 'all forms of public and domestic authority in Elizabethan England were vested in men: in fathers, husbands, masters, teachers, magistrates, lords. It was inevitable that the rule of a woman would generate peculiar tensions within such a "patriarchal" society'.[16] Instead of assigning the causes of such rebellion to the 'pervasive cultural presence' of the Queen, historians point to the social and economic factors which contributed to these troubled gender relations. Underdown observes a breakdown of community in fast-growing urban centers and scattered pasture/dairy parishes where effective means of social control such as compact nucleated village centers, resident squires, and strong manorial institutions were weak or non-existent. He observes the higher incidence of troubled gender relations in such communities opposed to the arable parishes which 'tended to retain strong habits of neighborhood and cooperation'. Both Montrose's reading of the Elizabethan sex-gender system in terms of 'female rule' and Underdown's explanation for this proliferation of accusations of witchcraft, shrewishness and husband domination are less important here than the clear connection between women's independent appropriation of discourse and a conceived threat to patriarchal authority contained through public shaming or spectacle – the ducking stool, usually called the cucking stool, or carting.[17]

From the outset of Shakespeare's play, Katherine's threat to male authority is posed through language; it is perceived as such by others and is linked to a claim larger than shrewishness – witchcraft – through the constant allusions to Katherine's kinship with the devil.[18] Control of women and particularly of Kate's revolt is from the outset attempted by inscribing women in a scopic economy.[19] Woman is represented as spectacle (Kate) or object to be desired and admired, a vision of beauty (Bianca). She is the site of visual pleasure, whether on the public stage, the village green, or the fantasy 'cart' with which Hortensio threatens Kate. The threat of being made a spectacle, here by carting, or later in the wedding scene by Petruchio's 'mad-brain rudesby', is an important aspect of shrew-taming.[20] Given the evidence of social history and of the play itself, discourse is power, both in Elizabethan and Jacobean England and in the fictional space of the *Shrew*.

The *Shrew* both demonstrated and produced the social facts of the patriarchal ideology which characterized Elizabethan England, but *representation* gives us a perspective on that patriarchal system which subverts its status as natural. The theatrically constructed frame in which Sly exercises patriarchal power and the dream in which Kate is tamed undermine the seemingly eternal nature of those structures by calling attention to the constructed character of the representation rather than veiling it through mimesis. The foregrounded female protagonist of the action and her powerful annexation of the traditionally male domain of discourse distances us from that system by exposing and displaying its contradictions. Representation undermines the ideology about women which the play presents and produces, both in the Induction and in the Kate/Petruchio plot: Sly disappears as lord, but Kate keeps talking.

III The price of silence

At II, i, in the spat between Bianca and Kate, the relationship between silence and women's place in the marriage market is made clear. Kate questions Bianca about her suitors, inquiring as to her preferences. Some critics have read her questions and her abuse of Bianca (in less than thirty lines, Kate binds her sister's hands behind her back, strikes her and chases after her calling for revenge) as revealing her secret desire for marriage and for the praise and recognition afforded her sister. Kate's behavior may invite such an interpretation, but another view persistently

presents itself as well. In her questions and badgering, Kate makes clear
the relationship between Bianca's sweet sobriety and her success with
men. Kate's abuse may begin as a jest, but her feelings are aroused to a
different and more serious pitch when her father enters, taking as usual
Bianca's part against her sister.[21] Baptista emphasizes both Bianca's
silence, 'When did she cross thee with a bitter word?' and Katherine's link
with the devil, 'thou hilding of a devilish spirit' (II, i, 28, 26). We should
bear in mind here Underdown's observation that shrewishness is a class
as well as gender issue – that women 'lacking in the protection of a
family . . . were the most common offenders'.[22] Kate is motherless, and to
some degree fatherless as well, for Baptista consistently rejects her and
favors her obedient sister. Kate's threat which follows, 'Her silence flouts
me, and I'll be reveng'd' (II, i, 29) is truer than we have heretofore
recognized, for it is that silence which has insured Bianca's place in the
male economy of desire and exchange to which Kate pointedly refers in
her last lines:

> What, will you not suffer me? Nay, now I see
> She is your treasure, she must have a husband,
> I must dance barefoot on her wedding day,
> And, for your love to her lead apes in hell.
>
> (II, i, 31–4)

Here we recognize the relationship between father and husband, in which
woman is the mediating third term, a treasure the exchange of which
assures patriarchal hegemony. Throughout the play Bianca is a treasure, a
jewel, an object of desire and possession. Although much has been made
of the animal analogies between Kate and beasts, the metaphorical death
of the courtly imagery associated with Bianca has been ignored as too
conventional, if not natural, to warrant comment.[23] What seems at issue
here is not so much Kate's lack of a husband, or indeed her desire for a
marriage partner, but rather her distaste at those folk customs which
make her otherness, her place outside that patriarchal system, public fact,
a spectacle for all to see and mock.

In the battle of words between Kate and Petruchio at II, i, 182ff., it is
Kate who gets the better of her suitor. She takes the lead through puns
which allow her to criticize Petruchio and the patriarchal system of
wooing and marriage. Her sexual puns make explicit to the audience not
so much her secret preoccupation with sex and marriage, but what is
implicit in Petruchio's wooing – that marriage is a sexual exchange in
which women are exploited for their use-value as producers.
Significantly, Petruchio's language is linguistically similar to Kate's in its
puns and wordplay. He also presents her, as many commentators have
noted, with an imagined vision which makes her conform to the very

order against which she rebels – he makes her a Bianca with words, shaping an identity for her which confirms the social expectations of the sex/gender system which informs the play. Their wooing can be interestingly compared with the next scene, also a wooing, between Bianca and her two suitors. Far from the imaginative use of language and linguistic play we find in Kate, Bianca repeats verbatim the Latin words Lucentio 'construes' to reveal his identity and his love. Her revelation of her feelings through a repetition of the Latin lines he quotes from Ovid are as close as possible to the silence we have come to expect from her.

In the altercation over staying for the wedding feast after their marriage, Kate again claims the importance of language and her use of it to women's place and independence in the world. But here it is Petruchio who controls language, who has the final word, for he creates through words a situation to justify his actions – he claims to be rescuing Kate from thieves. More precisely, he claims she asks for that rescue. Kate's annexation of language does not work unless her audience, and particularly her husband, accepts what she says as independent rebellion. By deliberately misunderstanding and reinterpreting her words to suit his own ends, Petruchio effectively refuses her the freedom of speech identified in the play with women's independence. Such is his strategy throughout this central portion of the action, in their arrival at his house and in the interchange with the tailor. Kate is figuratively killed with kindness, by her husband's rule over her not so much in material terms – the withholding of food, clothing and sleep – but the withholding of linguistic understanding. As the receiver of her messages, he simply refuses their meaning; since he also has material power to enforce his interpretations, it is his power over language that wins.

In the exchange between Petruchio and Kate with the tailor, Kate makes her strongest bid yet for linguistic freedom:

> Why, sir, I trust I may have leave to speak,
> And speak I will. I am no child, no babe.
> Your betters have endur'd me say my mind,
> And if you cannot, best you stop your ears.
> My tongue will tell the anger of my heart,
> Or else my heart concealing it will break,
> And rather than it shall, I will be free
> Even to the uttermost, as I please, in words.
>
> (IV, iii, 73–80)

When we next encounter Kate, however, on the journey to Padua, she finally admits to Petruchio: 'What you will have it nam'd, even that it is,/ And so it shall be so for Katherine' (IV, v, 21–2). On this journey Kate calls the sun the moon, an old man a budding virgin, and makes the world conform to the topsy-turvy of Petruchio's patriarchal whimsy. But we should look carefully at this scene before acquiescing in too easy a view of Kate's submission. Certainly she gives in to Petruchio's demands literally; but her playfulness and irony here are indisputable. As she says at IV, v, 44–8:

> Pardon, old father, my mistaking eyes,
> That have been so bedazzled with the sun
> That everything I look on seemeth green.
> Now I perceive thou art a reverend father.
> Pardon, I pray thee, for my mad mistaking.

Given Kate's talent for puns, we must understand her line, 'bedazzled with the sun', as a pun on son and play with Petruchio's line earlier in the scene 'Now by my mother's son, and that's myself,/It shall be moon, or star, or what I list' (IV, v, 6–7). 'Petruchio's bedazzlement' is exactly that, and Kate here makes clear the playfulness of their linguistic games.

In his paper 'Hysterical Phantasies and their Relation to Bi-Sexuality' (1908), Sigmund Freud observes that neurotic symptoms, particularly the hysterical symptom, have their origins in the daydreams of adolescence.[24] 'In girls and women', Freud claims, 'they are invariably of an erotic nature, in men they may be either erotic or ambitious'.[25] A feminist characterological re-reading of Freud might suggest that Kate's ambitious fantasies, which her culture allows her to express only in erotic directions, motivate her shrewishness.[26] Such behavior, which in a man would not be problematic, her family and peers interpret as 'hysterical' and/or diabolic. Her 'masculine' behavior saves her, at least for a time, from her feminine erotic destiny.

Freud goes on to claim that hysterical symptoms are always bi-sexual, 'the expression of both a masculine and a feminine unconscious sexual phantasy'.[27] The example he gives is a patient who 'pressed her dress to her body with one hand (as the woman) while trying to tear it off with the other (as the man)'.[28] To continue our 'analysis' in the scene we are considering, we might claim that Kate's female masquerade obscures her continuing ambitious fantasies, now only manifest in her puns and ironic wordplay which suggest the distance between her character and the role she plays.[29] Even though she gives up her shrewishness and acquiesces to Petruchio's whims, she persists in her characteristic 'masculine' linguistic exuberance while masquerading as an obedient wife.[30]

Instead of using Freud to analyze Kate's character, a critical move of debatable interpretive power, we might consider the Freudian text instead as a reading of ideological or cultural patterns. The process Freud describes is suggestive for analyzing the workings not of character, but of Shakespeare's text itself. No speech in the play has been more variously interpreted than Kate's final speech of women's submission. In a recent essay on the *Shrew*, John Bean has conveniently assigned to the two prevailing views the terms 'revisionist' for those who would take Kate's speech as ironic and her subservience as pretense, a way of living peaceably in patriarchal culture but with an unregenerate spirit, and the 'anti-revisionists' who argue that farce is the play's governing genre and that Kate's response to Petruchio's taming is that of an animal responding to 'the devices of a skilled trainer'.[31] Bean himself argues convincingly for a compromise position which admits the 'background of depersonalizing farce unassimilated from the play's fabliau sources', but suggests that Kate's taming needs to be seen in terms of romantic comedy, as a spontaneous change of heart such as those of the later romantic comedies 'where characters lose themselves in chaos and emerge, as if from a dream, liberated into the bonds of love'.[32] Bean rightly points out the liberal elements of the final speech in which marriage is seen as a partnership as well as a hierarchy, citing the humanist writers on marriage and juxtaposing Kate's speech with the corresponding, and remarkably more mysogynist, lines in *The Taming of a Shrew* and other taming tales.[33]

Keeping in mind Bean's arguments for the content of the speech and its place in the intersection of farce and romantic love plot, I would like to turn instead to its significance as representation. What we find is Katherine as a strong, energetic female protagonist represented before us addressing not the onstage male audience, only too aware of its articulation of patriarchal power, but Bianca and the Widow, associated with silence throughout the play and finally arriving by means, as Petruchio calls it, of Kate's 'womanly persuasion' (V, ii, 120).

Unlike any other of Shakespeare's comedies, we have here represented not simply marriage, with the final curtain a veiled mystification of the sexual and social results of that ritual, but a view, however brief and condensed, of that marriage over time.[34] And what we see is not a quiet and submissive Kate, but the same energetic and linguistically powerful Kate with which the play began. We know, then, in a way we never know about the other comedies, except perhaps *The Merchant of Venice*, and there our knowledge is complicated by Portia's male disguise, that Kate has continued to speak. She has not, of course, continued to speak her earlier language of revolt and anger. Instead she has adopted another strategy, a strategy which the French psychoanalyst Luce Irigaray calls mimeticism.[35] Irigaray argues that women are cut off from language by the patriarchal order in which they live, by their entry into the Symbolic which the Father represents in a Freudian/Lacanian model.[36] Women's only possible relation to the dominant discourse is mimetic:

To play with mimesis is . . . for a woman to try to recover the place of her exploitation by language, without allowing herself to be simply reduced to it. It is to resubmit herself . . . to ideas – notably about her – elaborated in and through a masculine logic, but to 'bring out' by an effect of playful repetition what was to remain hidden: the recovery of a possible operation of the feminine in language. It is also to unveil the fact that if women mime so well they are not simply reabsorbed in this function. *They also remain elsewhere.*[37]

Whereas Irigaray goes on to locate this 'elsewhere' in sexual pleasure (*jouissance*), Nancy Miller has elaborated on this notion of 'mimeticism', describing it as a 'form of emphasis: an italicized version of what passes for the neutral . . . Spoken or written, italics are a modality of intensity and stress; a way of marking what has already been said, of making a common text one's own'.[38]

Joel Fineman has recently observed the difficulty in distinguishing between man's and woman's speech in the *Shrew* by demonstrating how the rhetorical strategies Kate deploys are like Petruchio's.[39] But Kate's self-consciousness about the power of discourse, her punning and irony, and her techniques of linguistic masquerade, are strategies of italics, mimetic strategies, in Irigaray's sense of mimeticism. Instead of figuring a gender-marked woman's speech, they deform language by subverting it, that is, by turning it inside out so that metaphors, puns and other forms of wordplay manifest their veiled equivalences: the meaning of woman as treasure, of wooing as a civilized and acceptable disguise for sexual exploitation, of the objectification and exchange of women. Kate's having the last word contradicts the very sentiments she speaks; rather than resolve the play's action, her monologue simply displays the fundamental contradiction presented by a female dramatic protagonist, between woman as a sexually desirable, silent object and women of words, women with power over language who disrupt, or at least italicize, women's place and part in culture.

To dramatize action involving linguistically powerful women characters militates against patriarchal structures and evaluations of women in which their silence is most highly prized – which is why so many of Shakespeare's heroines, in order to maintain their status as desirable, must don male attire in order to speak: Rosalind, Portia, even the passive Viola. The conflict between the explicitly repressive content of Kate's speech and the implicit message of independence communicated by representing a powerful female protagonist speaking the play's longest speech at a moment of emphatic suspense is not unlike Freud's female patient who 'pressed her dress to her body with one hand (as the woman) while trying to tear it off with the other (as the man)'. We might even say that this conflict shares the bi-sexuality Freud claims for the hysterical symptom, that the text itself is sexually ambivalent, a view in keeping with the opposed readings of the play in which it is either conservation farce or subversive irony. Such a representation of gender, what I will call the 'female dramatizable',[40] is always at once patriarchally suspect and sexually ambivalent, clinging to Elizabethan patriarchal ideology and at the same time tearing it away by foregrounding or italicizing its constructed character.

IV   Missing frames and female spectacles

Kate's final speech is 'an imaginary or formal solution to unresolvable social contradictions', but that appearance of resolution is an 'ideological mirage'.[41] On the level of plot, as many readers have noted, if one shrew is tamed two more reveal themselves. Bianca and the widow refuse to do their husbands' bidding, thereby undoing the sense of closure Kate's 'acquiescence' produces. By articulating the contradiction manifested in the scene's formal organization and its social 'content' – between the 'headstrong women', now Bianca and the widow who refuse their duty, and Kate and her praise of women's submission – the seeming resolution of the play's ending is exploded and its *heterogeneity* rather than its unity is foregrounded. But can transgression of the law of women's silence be subversive? It has become a theoretical commonplace to argue that transgression presupposes norms or taboos. Therefore, the 'female dramatizable' is perhaps no more than a release mechanism, a means of managing troubled gender relations. By transgressing the law of women's silence, but far from subverting it, the *Shrew* reconfirms the law, if we remember that Kate, Bianca and the widow remain the object of the audience's gaze, specular images, represented female bodies on display, as on the cucking stool or in the cart, the traditional punishments for prostitutes and scolds. Representation contains female rebellion. And because the play has no final framing scene, no return to Sly, it could be argued that its artifice is relaxed, that the final scene is experienced naturalistically. The missing frame allows the audience to forget that Petruchio's taming of Kate is presented as a fiction.

Yet even with its missing frame and containment of woman through spectacle, the *Shrew* finally deconstructs its own mimetic effect if we remember the bisexual aspect of the representation of women on the Elizabethan and Jacobean stage. Kate would have been played by a boy whose transvestism, like Thomas Quarry's in the Wetherden skimmington, emblematically embodied the sexual contradictions manifest both in the play and Elizabethan culture. The very indeterminateness of the actor's sexuality, of the woman/man's body, the supplementarity of its titillating homoerotic play (Sly's desire for the page boy disguised as a woman, Petruchio's 'Come Kate, we'll to bed'), foregrounds its artifice and therefore subverts the play's patriarchal master narrative by exposing it as neither natural nor divinely ordained, but culturally constructed.

Notes

1. This would seem to be Rosyer's neighbour's duty. The *OED* cites Lupton's *Sivgila* (1580), p. 50 as an early use of *cowlstaff*: 'If a woman beat hir husbande, the man that dwelleth next unto hir sha ride on a cowlstaffe.'

2. PRO STAC 8, 249/19. I am grateful to Susan Amussen for sharing her transcription of this case, and to David Underdown for the original reference. We do not know the outcome of Rosyer's complaint since only the testimony, not the judgement, is preserved.

3. Louis Montrose, '"Shaping Fantasies": Gender and Power in Elizabethan Culture', *Representation* 1 (1983), 61–94.

4. Natalie Z. Davis, 'Women on Top', in *Society and Culture in Early Modern France* (Stanford: Stanford University Press, 1975); P. Thompson, 'Rough Music: "le Charivari Anglais" ', *Annales* ESC 27 (1972), 285–312.

5. In *Shr*, the frame tale closes the action; Sly must return home after his 'bravest dreame' to a wife who 'will course you for dreaming here tonight', but he claims: 'Ile to my/Wife presently and tame her too'. See Geoffrey Bullough, *Narrative and Dramatic Sources of Shakespeare* (London: Routledge & Kegan Paul 1957), Vol. I, p. 108.

6. See Montrose, 'Shaping Fantasies', 66–7, for a discussion of the Amazonian myth.

7. Jacques Derrida, *Response à John Lewis* (Paris: Gallimard, 1973), pp. 99–8.

8. Fredric Jameson, *The Political Unconscious* (Ithaca: Cornell University Press, 1981), p. 35.

9. Montrose, 'Shaping Fantasies', 62, after Gayle Rubin.

10. See, for example, Robert Green's *Penelope's Web* (1587), which presents the Renaissance ideal of womanhood – chastity, obedience, and silence – through a series of exemplary tales; see Linda T. Fitz, '"What Says the Married Woman?" Marriage Theory and Feminism in the English Renaissance', *Mosaic* 13 (1980), 1–22; the books examined in Suzanne Hull, *Chaste, Silent and Obedient; English Books for Women, 1475–1640* (San Marino: Huntington Library, 1982); and most recently, Lisa Jardine, *Still Harping on Daughters* (London: Croom Helm, 1983).

11. See, among others, Lawrence Stone, *The Crisis of the Aristocracy 1558–1614* (Oxford: Clarendon, 1965); Keith Wrightson, *English Society 1580–1680* (New Brunswick: Rutgers University Press, 1982), especially chapters 5 and 6. I am grateful to David Underdown for referring me to Wrightson.

12. Stone, *Crisis*, p. 137 cites Swetnam, *Family*; for references to *Hic Mulier*, see David Underdown, 'The Taming of the Scold: the Enforcement of Patriarchal Authority in Early Modern England', in *Order and Disorder in Early Modern England*, ed. Anthony Fletcher and John Stevenson (Cambridge: Cambridge University Press, 1985).

13. UNDERDOWN, 'Taming', p. 119.

14. UNDERDOWN, 'Taming', p. 120.

15. UNDERDOWN, 'Taming', p. 121, citing E.P. Thompson.

16. MONTROSE, 'Shaping Fantasies', 64–5.

17. MONTROSE, 'Shaping Fantasies', 64–5. See also DAVIS, 'Women on Top', and THOMPSON, 'Rough Music'.

18. See, for example, I, i, 65; 105–21, 123; II, i, 26, 151. For the social context of witchcraft in England, see ALAN MACFARLANE, *Witchcraft in Tudor and Stuart England* (New York: Harper and Row, 1970), and KEITH THOMAS, *Religion and the Decline of Magic* (Harmondsworth: Penguin, 1971).

19. On the importance of the gaze in managing human behaviour, see MICHEL FOUCAULT, *Discipline and Punish*, trans. Alan Sheridan (New York: Pantheon, 1977); see also the discussion of scopophilia in LAURA MULVEY, 'Visual Pleasure and Narrative Cinema', *Screen* 16 (1975), 6–18, and more philosophically, LUCE IRIGARAY, *Speculum de l'autre femme* (Paris: Minuit, 1974).

20. Kate's speech at III, ii, 18–20 makes clear this function of his lateness and his 'madbrain rudesby'. She recognizes that this shame falls not on her family, but on her alone: 'No shame but mine . . . Now must the world point at poor Katherine/And say "Lo, there is mad Petruchio's wife. If it would please him come and marry her" ' (III, ii, 18–20). Although Katherine to herself, she recognizes that for others she will be 'Petruchio's wife'.

21. See the discussion of the importance of the father and paternity in MARIANNE NOVY, 'Patriarchy and Play in *Shr*', *ELR* 9 (1975), 273–4.

22. UNDERDOWN, 'Taming', p. 120.

23. See NOVY, p. 264. For a detailed discussion of Kate's puns, animal imagery and sexual innuendoes in this scene, see M. ANDRESON-THOM, 'Shrew-taming and other rituals of Aggression: Baiting and Bonding on the Stage and in the Wild', *Women's Studies* 9 (1982), 122–43.

24. SIGMUND FREUD, *Collected Papers*, trans. Joan Riviere (London: International Psycho-analytic Press, 1948), Vol. II, pp. 51–9.

25. FREUD, *Collected Papers*, Vol. II, p. 51.

26. For a discussion of female fantasy see NANCY K. MILLER, 'Emphasis Added: Plots and Plausibilities in Women's Fiction', *PMLA* 97 (1981), 36–48.

27. FREUD, *Collected Papers*, Vol. II, p. 57.

28. FREUD, *Collected Papers*, Vol. II, p. 58.

29. See the essay on female masquerade by JOAN RIVIERE in *Psychoanalysis and Female Sexuality*, ed. H. Ruitenbeek (New Haven: Yale University Press, 1966).

30. FREUD describes a similar strategy of evasion in *Collected Papers*, Vol. II, p. 58.

31. JOHN BEAN, 'Comic Structure and the Humanizing of Kate in *Shr*', in *The Woman's Part*, ed. Carolyn Ruth Swift Lenz, Gayle Greene and Carol Thomas Neely (Urbana: University of Illinois Press, 1980), pp. 65–78. Bean quotes the 'anti-revisionist' ROBERT HEILBRUN, 'The *Taming* Untamed, or, the Return of the Shrew', *Modern Language Quarterly* 27 (1966), 147–61. For the revisionist view, see COPPÉLIA KAHN, '*Shr*: Shakespeare's Mirror of Marriage', *Modern Language Studies* 5 (1975), 88–102.

32. Bean, 'Comic Structure', p. 66.

33. Bean, 'Comic Structure', pp. 67–70.

34. For a discussion of the mystification of defloration and marriage, see Nancy K. Miller, 'Writing (from) the Feminine: George Sand and the Novel of Female Pastoral', in *The Representation of Women: English Institute Essays* (Cambridge, MA: Harvard University Press, 1983).

35. Luce Irigaray, *Ce Sexe qui n'ést pas un* (Paris: Minuit, 1977).

36. Irigaray, *Ce Sexe*, particularly pp. 282–98. Contemporary handbooks often seem an uncanny description of woman as Other: the popular preacher Henry Smith, whose *Preparative to Marriage* was published in 1591, suggests that marriage is an equal partnership, but goes on to declare that 'the ornament of the woman is silence; and therefore the Law was given to the man rather than to the woman, to shewe that he shoulde be the teacher, and she the hearer' (quoted in Novy, p. 278).

37. Irigaray, *Ce Sexe*, p. 74, quoted and translated in Miller, 'Emphasis Added', p. 38.

38. Miller, 'Emphasis Added', p. 38.

39. Joel Fineman, 'The Turn of the Shrew', in *Shakespeare and the Question of Theory*, ed. Patricia Parker and Geoffrey Hartman (New Haven: Yale University Press, 1985), p. 144.

40. See the discussion of the 'narratable' in D.A. Miller, *Narrative and its Discontents* (Princeton: Princeton University Press, 1981), especially the chapter on Austen.

41. Jameson, *Political Unconscious*, pp. 79, 56.

3   Love's Labour's Lost (?1592–94)

Louis A. Montrose '*Sport by Sport O'erthrown: Love's Labour's Lost and the Politics of Play*'*

Of all the comedies, *Love's Labour's Lost* is probably the most dated for modern readers or spectators – containing many, by now obscure, references to events, people and gossip in the 1590s – yet it has provoked some highly successful productions and provocative criticism. Modern students probably need not bother initially to decide whether Armado is a satire on a fashionable Spaniard visiting the English court, or whether the 'little Academe' refers to a group of contemporary French nobles or a radical philosophical discussion group. Better, at least initially, to delight in what Louis Montrose builds his argument upon, the verbal richness, the ease with which Shakespeare moves from one kind of humour to another, the skill of construction that sets up the audience to expect one effect and provides them with others, enabling us to draw parallels with modern foibles in love, learning, and growing up. *Love's Labour's Lost* is an extraordinarily clever comedy, in its incidental effects, in its overall conception, and in its potential for provoking its readers to consider a variety of intriguing issues.

But like the other comedies – indeed, in some ways more than most – *Love's Labour's Lost* is a very serious play. The 'play' (in many senses) of language is often seen as a major concern, but Montrose's argument extends it particularly tellingly. 'How low soever the matter', as Berowne puts it, every character (including, in his own way, Dull) delights in a great feast of language, as if the play were inviting us to display and indulge ourselves in words – high, low, new, outrageous. Costard savours his 'remuneration'; the nobles bat words back and forth like tennis balls, and even if it alludes to literary and rhetorical fashions that have long disappeared, a fast-paced production can induce a modern audience to find easy parallels today. Montrose's essay – an early one in the career of this critic whose more recent work on Shakespeare and a variety of cultural practices in the early modern period is among the most influential

---

* Reprinted from *Texas Studies in Literature and Language* v.18:4 (1977), pp. 528–552.

in contemporary Renaissance criticism – explores the multiplicity of ways through which what he terms 'purposeful play' operates, describing *Love's Labour's Lost* as an 'acute comic study of the uses to which humans at play ... put the cultural forms that they create'. Montrose's essay is typical of the early phase of New Historicism, working with a model of culture based on social anthropology, emphasizing the way a culture's games and rituals are revelatory of wider social patterns, and avoiding any explicit political or ideological critique (see Introduction, pp. 18–20).

Montrose also comments, as most critics of the play must, on the final scene, which is a striking corrective to our assumptions about comedy's inevitable happy ending. The play reaches a crescendo in a whirl of dancing, wit and music, and it seems that the love affairs will blossom into the marriages that we have been led to expect – and end the men's futile attempts to escape the temptations of the world. Then, suddenly, a character we have never seen before appears, to announce that the princess's father, the King of France, is dead. The end we have expected dissolves; the wish-fulfilment fantasy of comedy is touched by the reminder of death. We are reminded that comedy is always shadowed by tragedy – 'joy' by 'terror' – or as the common Renaissance saying had it, death is present even in Arcadia. Montrose's particular contribution to understanding the complex effects of the ending is to stress the class basis of the pair of songs presented by Armado. In pointing to 'common, rural roots' of these songs, and to their critique of 'the courtly style and aristocratic ideology that have dominated the dramatic action', Montrose anticipates recent work, such as that by Michael Bristol, that links the plays to popular rather than aristocratic ritual, play and game (see Introduction, p. 19).

I

Shakespeare's dramatic fictions are forms of purposeful play. And 'the purpose of playing', as Hamlet acutely remarks, 'is, to hold as 'twere the mirror up to nature: to show virtue her feature, scorn her own image, and the very age and body of the time his form and pressure' (*Hamlet* III, ii, 20–4). The morality of Shakespeare's art does not ultimately consist in the sententious reflections and exemplary events that can be abstracted from its fictions, but in its affirmation of the power and obligation of men and women to exercise their minds in a multivalent exploration of the ambiguous reality in which they live their lives. Shakespeare's comedies insist upon their fictive status, through which each realizes its unique and finally unanalyzable synthesis of gravity and playfulness. A work of art that professes to be no more than a play of fancy, an exploration that does not claim the sanction of a transcendent truth for what it may discover, offers its audience no easy resolutions but a way how to proceed.

In his *Treatise on Playe*, Sir John Harington (one of those Elizabethan courtiers to whose nature *Love's Labour's Lost* held up the mirror) includes 'stage-playes' along with 'enterludes, tumblers, jesting fools, and scoffers, masking and dawncing', among the actively or potentially wanton forms of play. This fundamental category of human activity called 'playe', Harington defines as 'a spending of the tyme eyther in speeche or action, whose onely end ys a delyght of the mynd or speryt'. His conception of the purpose of playing differs from Hamlet's: 'The cheefe end of play bee that which showld indeed bee the trew use of play, to recreat the speryts for a short tyme, to enable them better to seryows and wayghty matters.' Like most modern authors of treatises on play, 'Harington stresses its nature as diversion, pastime, recreation; as gratuitous, unproductive, and essentially antithetical to the substantive reality that constitutes everyday life. Shakespeare's Hamlet implies that play can be serious and that jest can be earnest; that the seeming gratuitousness of play can mask its purposiveness. As both the product of a particular place and time and the marked-off ground of critical inquiry, the play can both exemplify and anatomize the sociocultural 'nature' that it mirrors; it can, simultaneously, project the pressure of the time's body and clarify the very age's form. When the phenomena and purposes of play are understood as Hamlet – and, most assuredly, Shakespeare – understood them, then we can accept the propriety of Clifford Geertz's recent comparison of Balinese cockfights to Shakespearean dramas: each is a kind of play, set 'apart from the ordinary course of life' because 'it provides a metasocial commentary' on the world in which it is created, enacted, and experienced.[1]

In *Love's Labour's Lost*, Shakespeare experiments with a rather special case of ludic speculation: playwright, actors, and audience are engaged in the purposeful playing of a play whose fictional action is generated almost entirely by characters at play. The world of Navarre has the appearance of a playground, a special place marked off from the pressures of social reality and the unpleasant implications of a world of fallen nature. Here Shakespeare explores the dimensions of the play faculty, from charming fripperies to serious products of the imagination: dressing up, disguising, dance and song in the Masque and Pageant; flirtation and erotic play; the play of language and mind in puns, alliteration, euphuistic rhetoric, and verbal wit, as well as in the manipulated conceits of the love poetry and the tortuous logic of the set speeches; allusions to specific children's games and toys; and the game of the chase, the hunt for 'game'. Every activity in which the male quartet engages takes on the character of play, 'some strange pastime . . . Such as the shortness of the time can shape' (IV, iii, 374–5), whether it be the proposal of a 'little academe' and its solemn oath or the resolution to 'woo these girls of France'. The commons are similarly engaged: 'Away', cries Holofernes, 'the gentles are at their game, and we will to our recreation' (IV, ii, 165–7). But to see the play as tending toward a 'set exhibition of pastimes and games', its plot 'all too obviously designed to provide a resistance which can be triumphantly swept away by festivity', is to risk being so caught up in the exuberance of the activity as to lose sight of the encompassing dramatic design.[2] The atmosphere of energy and brilliance is indeed a celebration of the characters' discovery of, and delight in, their own creative powers. And it is precisely through their misdirected creative energy and verbal virtuosity that the courtiers and their low-plot counterparts captivate themselves – and threaten to captivate the audience.

The principal strategy by which Sidney and other Renaissance critics defend poetry against its detractors is to emphasize its didactic and rhetorical aspects: literature presents exemplary encomiastic and reprehensive images of virtue and vice by which it intends to move the audience to shun vice and emulate virtue. This crude mechanistic and moralistic model is perhaps appropriate to popular homiletic literature, tracts and emblem books, but it is simply inadequate to the complex structures of imagery which constitute the great literary art of the Elizabethan age. Although Shakespeare neither explicates nor moralizes (though some of his characters do), it does not follow that his plays have no didactic or rhetorical function. In *Love's Labour's Lost*, Shakespeare's intentions are no more purely recreative or aesthetic than are those of his characters. Both playwright and characters pursue significant ends through the medium of play, but those ends are usually divergent. Recent theatrical approaches to Shakespeare have rightly insisted that criticism of the plays must take into consideration their primary nature as symbolic actions directed to an audience. In a critical approach to *Love's Labour's Lost*, we must distinguish carefully between the intention of the playwright and the intentions of his characters, and try to assess the dynamics of audience response to the disjunctions that Shakespeare's ironic strategies are intended to generate. In *Love's Labour's Lost*, Shakespeare shapes a distinction between the imaginative world created by the characters *within* the fiction and the total imaginative form that is the play. The play is a fiction whose characters are motivated by their own responses to fictions. The unfolding of the play's total form exposes the self-deceptions of the characters in the process of destroying their imaginative world. The playworld constructed by the lords within which to express their creative energies goes awry when its boundaries become blurred. The ladies refuse to cooperate in the roles of passive objects or equal players in the fiction; the lords fail to discriminate their fiction's limits from the actuality that incurs with the ladies. The lords are not heroes who carry audience projections and realize themselves in objectified heroic or pastoral environments; their hyperactive fancies parody an imaginative response to the experience of reading heroic and pastoral literature.

Love's Labour's Lost is Shakespeare's acute comic study of the uses to which humans at play – Elizabethan humans, particularly those in the upper strata of the social hierarchy – put the cultural forms that they create; Shakespeare's play is a fictive critique of the ways in which its own characters use games, rituals, myths, social institutions and, fundamentally, language, as media through which to construct, explore, manipulate and protect their reality. *Love's Labour's Lost* has an intrinsic didactic and rhetorical dimension because the play is itself a manifestation of Elizabethan cultural form and because its author, actors and audience are social players engaged in the same kind of strategies as those of the characters.

II

Love's Labour's Lost employs an explicitly linguistic model of social interaction. Such a model is apposite for a play whose characters are relatively uncomplex, who are defined and exist almost exclusively in relation to other characters, forces and institutions. This can be merely another way of saying that Shakespeare's primary interest here is in theme rather than in character. But it can also mean that his interest lies not only in the dialectic of ideas but in the dialectic of characters, in the dynamics of interaction between characters – in their syntactic relation – more than in the characters themselves. The characters in *Love's Labour's Lost* are obsessed with performances, with the playing out of roles before audiences of various individual characters or groups within the fiction. Although the inherently 'theatrical' or 'dramatistic' quality of life provides a model for drama, drama may also provide models for life. The broadest perspective must include both in a reciprocal relation: drama deriving its models from actuality and, if it is efficacious, influencing the actuality of its audience in return. That a play is an imaginative analysis of interaction in the actual world is one significant implication of the *theatrum mundi* metaphor so central to the Renaissance imagination, which Shakespeare developed with unprecedented complexity and subtlety in the symbolic space of the public theatre.[3] The dynamics of social interaction are selectively analyzed, anatomized, satirized within the laboratory situation of the playworld. The play situates individuals and groups in different, interrelated contexts – characters in soliloquy and in public; as male or female; as members of a particular body politic, social status, or family group – and exhibits the differences in modes of self-presentation in characters who are alone, among their peers, or face-to-face with a sexual or social other.

The role of King has a paradigmatic status in such a drama, since he is of necessity structurally implicated in the largest and most varied number of social relationships. In *Love's Labour's Lost*, the King of Navarre is both the personification of the state *vis-à-vis* other states, and the head of a commonwealth of citizens hierarchically ordered in social statuses with a network of reciprocal rights and obligations. The role of the King's public person involves communication in the forms of negotiation, justice and courtesy. Navarre plays the negotiator in his reception of the Princess's embassy; the justiciar in Costard's trial for transgression of the royal edict; the courtier in his entertainment of the ladies and his reception of his subjects' entertainment, the Pageant of the Nine Worthies. In each role, he proves ineffectual at best. Much of the play's first scene is a delightful parody of the role of kingship, with its promulgation of laws, acceptance of petitions and dealing of equitable justice.

The duties of the King's public person are treated as intrusions into the decorum that he tries to create in the playworld of Navarre, a decorum designed to allow the maximum expression of his will as a private person. That even the most intensely private aspirations of the King and his courtiers are nevertheless conceived in exclusively public terms is immediately apparent in the striking language of his opening speech. The peculiar opposition of the grace of fame to the disgrace of death secularizes the theological import of 'grace' and the context of contemplative withdrawal by suggesting a concept of death in courtly terms, as a form of humiliation or dishonor, a consignment of one's name to oblivion.

The divine grace that the King secularizes as the grace of fame in the play's first lines is to be achieved through the 'living art' of contemplation. The Renaissance ideal of what Mazzeo calls 'the self as work of art', the refinement and integration of all personal faculties, is being parodied in a wish to refine the physical life of the self out of existence. This folly gives way soon enough to an amorous folly, in which the theological import of 'grace' is twisted into the favor that Petrarchan mistresses owe to their clamorous worshippers. Theological, Petrarchan, and courtly senses resonate ambiguously in almost all the occurrences of the world 'grace' which stud the text of the play.[4]

'Grace' is the cardinal term in aristocratic society's secular religion of courtship. 'Thy grace being gain'd cures all disgrace in me' (IV, iii, 65), writes Longaville in his sonnet to Maria. The 'grace' that the lords seek from their ladies, and are denied, is not only sexual favor but 'grace' in the larger sense of approval, the acknowledgment that they themselves

are graceful. Katherine remarks that Dumain 'hath wit to make an ill
shape good,/And shape to win grace though he had no wit' (II, i, 59–60).
This ambivalent comment suggests the dangers of deceit and pretense to
which an ideal of *sprezzatura* is subject. The Princess, having just received
her courtier's effusive posies, and being about to receive the disastrous
masque, reflects sententiously on the lords' affected attempts at grace. At
the end, Rosaline proposes to purge Berowne's 'gibing spirit' (VII, ii,
858–9). Repeated references to the King as 'your grace' accumulate an
implicit irony between the model of conduct appropriate to his elevated
social position and his personal shortcomings.

As the action progresses, the King and his company are threatened
with shame in several forms: *apocalyptic* – the final judgement of divine
powers between grace and damnation; *historical* – the judgement of
posterity between fame and oblivion; *courtly* – the consequence of
inadequacy in the deadly serious game of social maneuvers and
performances; *sexual* – both moral shame accompanying carnal desire and
the masculine shame that is precipitated by a loss to female superiority
in the game of sexual politics; *class* – public exposures of aristocratic
inadequacies, constituting a rupture in the mystique of social hierarchy.
The fear of being shamed for their wilfulness – whether by Death, by the
Ladies, by Boyet, or by the Commons – impels the lords to devise
strategies for saving face. These range from the quest for fame to 'grace us
in the disgrace of death' and its implementing oath, through the use of
specious logic and rhetorical subterfuge, to the diversionary tactics of
organized play and the ridicule of scapegoats. After repeated
humiliations, the King fears that his own foolishness will be somehow
augmented by the shortcomings of his subjects:

King	Berowne, they will shame us; let them not approach.
Berowne	We are shame-proof, my lord; and 'tis some policy
	To have one show worse than the king's and his company.

(V, ii, 511–13)

Berowne's pseudo-Machiavellian stratagem is ill-advised, for the pageant
does indeed shame the noblemen by parodying their earlier heroic
affectations.

In *Love's Labour's Lost*, Shakespeare skilfully manipulates audience
response to the courtiers through ironic strategies that discriminate levels
of awareness among the characters, and between characters and
audience.[5] The achieved effect is to put the courtiers into positions of
exposure and ridicule; they are threatened with varying degrees of the
shame they have sought to evade. Costard and the ladies disrupt the
academe and ridicule the role of ascetic scholarship. The ladies repeatedly
outwit the courtiers who woo them with words, and never let the lords

forget their violated oath. In the sonnet scene (IV, iii), Berowne, Navarre, Longaville and Dumain enter one by one wishing for 'sweet fellowship in shame!' (l. 47); each is exposed, in turn, by the one who has entered immediately before him. The brilliantly effective dramaturgy of this situation derives from a discrepancy between the illusory privacy and independence of action that each successive character believes he possesses and the highly formalized and predictable pattern of action they collectively present to the audience on behalf of the dramatist. From a position of superior knowledge, clearly realized on the stage in his spatial relation to the others, Berowne cultivates the quality of theatrical contrivance:

'All hid, all hid', an old infant play.

(l. 76)

I'll mark how love can vary wit.

(l. 98)

O, what a scene of fool'ry have I seen.

(l. 161)

'Are we betrayed thus to thy over-view?' (l. 173), asks the King in bewildered embarrassment. The audience is structurally predisposed to identify with the seemingly omniscient Berowne – until the action culminates in Costard's exposure of his self-righteousness. Costard's unanticipated entry upsets the just-completed mirror structure of disclosures and exposures, to Berowne's sudden discomfiture and our further delight. 'You were born', Berowne tells him, 'to do me shame' (l. 200). Berowne bids the King, 'dismiss this audience' (l. 206); 'Walk aside the true folk', Costard answers, 'and let the traitors stay' (l. 209). Costard has already suffered 'for the truth' of his instincts in the play's first scene (I, i, 311ff.), and now – perhaps playing to the audience – he speaks from an ironically superior moral position.

Boyet gains the upper hand by discovering the performers at their rehearsal, putting Moth 'out of his part' (V, ii, 336), and leaving the *coup de grâce* to the Princess and her ladies. In the episode of the Muscovites, the courtiers think themselves unknown to the ladies and the ladies known to them; the situation is actually reversed. The exposure is consummated when the men return in their own shapes: the ladies mock the lords, to make them 'depart away with shame' (156). Throughout the play, irony is generated by the fact that, although the lords are the focus of dramatic action, they are trapped in a position of consistently inferior awareness relative to the ladies. Throughout the play, audience awareness remains on a level equivalent to that of the Princess and her

63

entourage and superior to that of the other characters. Marcade's entry reduces all the characters and the audience to the same level. All are in an identical ironic relation to a transcendent power which is the fact of mortality in the context of the fable, the will of the playwright in the context of dramatic form. The culminating comic symbols of reunion, marriage and festivity, through which the play might have wed audience and characters with its presiding power, are denied. The King fails to separate himself from his romantic part; the Princess fails to identify with hers.

Among the gentlemen, only Berowne maintains a level of self-awareness sufficient to be fully conscious of his role-playing. This awareness is rendered more acute (and more ironic) because he is no more able than his less self-conscious companions to rid himself of a mode of role-playing that has outlived its potential value. The playground of the imagination is an ambivalent place.

The endeavors of the characters are continually undermined by the subversiveness of language; the playwright controls and uses linguistic subversion to achieve the exposure of his characters' endeavors. 'Fame'/ 'name' (I, i, 92–3); 'name'/'shame' (I, i, 117–18, 154, 156); 'game'/'shame' (V, ii, 155, 156) – rhyme associates meanings in the process of linking sounds. Fame is a secular and mundane achievement, the perpetuation of one's name registered in brass. At her hunt, the Princess reduces fame to an 'outward part' that corrupts the 'working of the heart' (IV, i, 32–3). Shakespeare subtly insinuates such a judgement in the King's very own opening declamation, by ironic verbal plays on 'brazen' (made of brass/shameless) and 'bate'/'bait' (to beat back or blunt the edge of/to persecute or harass; enticement, temptation).[6] The lords' action eventually becomes an explicit baiting (V, ii, 631) of the Worthies, and the Messenger of Death enters to effectively bate their wits' keen edge. The book-men are bound to the laws of their academe by subscribing their names. The courtier's honor, his good name, rests on the currency of his word. After the ladies' arrival, these courtiers spend much of their wit in trying to deflate the value of their own word; in so doing, they debase the names that they had wished to perpetuate in glory. Their 'grace is perjur'd much/Full of dear guiltiness' (V, ii, 790–1). They are ultimately shamed for turning an oath to a game, for profaning a ritual. The ladies, particularly the Princess, are capable of social grace; the lords, particularly the King, are not. The lords are at their most graceless during the Pageant of the Worthies, while Armado and Holofernes respond with a kind of grace beyond any that their 'betters' have demonstrated. Shakespeare seems more intent on a critique of courtly styles of social and amorous 'grace' than on an unqualified celebration of aristocratic ideals in action.

III

The text of *Love's Labour's Lost* is in large part a scenario for dramatic imitations of games and rituals – two basic cultural forms, species of organized play, which can be seen as related by inversion:

> Games . . . appear to have a disjunctive effect: they end in the establishment of a difference between individual players or teams where originally there was no indication of inequality. And at the end of the game they are distinguished into winners and losers. Ritual . . . is the exact inverse; it *conjoins*, for it brings about a union . . . or in any case an organic relation between two initially separate groups.[7]

Games move from symmetry to asymmetry; rituals move from asymmetry to symmetry. It is largely through the characters' confusions and conflations of game and ritual, contest and communion, that the play's actions and conflicts are generated. The rituals of recovery, reconciliation, marriage, and festivity, which are the culmination of romantic comedy (the kind of play the courtiers think they are in), are transformed into loss and separation because the love quest is reduced to the same level as the wit combat and becomes indistinguishable from it. The lords make the ritual goal of union with the beloved into a game whose object is to win the lady's love from her, a game that is part of a larger ritual of self-celebration.

For the Princess and her ladies, no such subtle interplay exists. They are engaged in a winning game of glittering but nonetheless quite ruthless one-upmanship, 'to make their ours and ours none but our own' (V, ii, 154). This manipulative tendency is clearest in the scene of the Muscovite masquerade. The lords have planned a surprise entertainment, but their ludicrous rehearsal has been spied upon by Boyet (V, ii, 89–118) and their efforts are foredoomed.

The sixteenth-century masque is a sophisticated form of play in which the masquers are a part of the courtly audience they entertain. Audience and masquers normally join in the masque's culminating dance, the 'revels'. As Stephen Orgel has pointed out, the Elizabethan as well as the later Jonsonian masque 'is always about the resolution of discord; antitheses, paradoxes, and the movement from disorder to order are central to its nature'.[8] The masque is art functioning very close to ritual. The Princess's intention is to turn the masque to a game that the ladies will win. Both groups are masked – the men, for the purposes of play and surprise, in order to delight; the women, for the purpose of deception, in order to mock.

The failed attempt to unite in dance is followed by an unsuccessful attempt at conversation: 'Will you vouchsafe with me to change a word?' (l. 238). The ostensibly purgative strategies of humiliation practiced by the ladies on their suitors are achieved by disruption and manipulation of the communications channel, which is both verbal – 'The tongues of mocking wenches are as keen/As is the razor's edge invisible' (V, ii, 256–7) – and visual (e.g. V, ii, 127, 134–5).

Reciprocity is severed; to use Dull's apposite terminology (IV, ii, 42ff.), collusion and pollution hold in the exchange. The frustration of the ritualistic masque structure by the ladies' deception and refusal to dance makes it a game of discord and irony, a miniature of the larger dramatic form.

This episode is a paradigm of the play's recurrent unit of action. The males initiate a hastily conceived and incompetently executed performance that not only fails to take its spectators but is rendered contemptibly inadequate by the consummate counter-performance of its audience. A comic situation of performance and counter-performance is the play's basic device for creating parodic irony. A production that seeks to capture the style of *Love's Labour's Lost* emphasizes the masque-like elements in matters of costume, music, blocking and tempo. Thematic and dramatic tensions inherent in the action can be effectively brought out to complement theatrical spectacle if the production also emphasizes the ways in which the masque is both literally and metaphorically a series of maskings and unmaskings. Incompetent role-playing is exposed and humiliated not by the unfeigned, undisguised display of an essential self but by a superior style of role-playing. In the theatre, not only the sign systems of speech and costume but also those of movement and gesture can be effectively employed to embody the agony of achieved and failed styles – the graceful and the clumsy – which generates so much of the play's social anxiety and social comedy.

The revels are ended in the mockery of a scapegoat. A production must strive to communicate both the comedy and the pathos of this play's version of unaccommodated man. Armado's playing is being made the other characters' sport at the center of their playground; at the same moment, the dark and silent figure of Marcade is breaching the playground's margins. At the opposite pole from the goal of play as freedom of the imagination is the danger of imagination's enslavement; the player may become a toy, himself the subject of play. Nor is play necessarily a gratuitous activity. 'Our sport' is described in images of business and war. Navarre and his book-men attempt to indefinitely prolong and extend the temporal and spatial limits of their playworld. Rather than a circumscribed place of the mind, a means toward the revivification of reality, the second world has become an escape and ultimate goal. The entry of Marcade disrupts the performance of the play itself. The disruptions perpetrated by the characters eventuate in the destruction of the romantic form, the form which is ideally the literary celebration of the wedding of individuals, sexes and classes. The King's last-minute plea for the Princess's grace has already been disgraced by death.

IV

When Berowne and the King conclude their discussion of the play's dramatic kind, they have closed the borders of the world of *Love's Labour's Lost* and severed its contract with the audience:

Berowne   Our wooing doth not end like an old play:
            Jack hath not Gill. These ladies' courtesy
            Might well have made our sport a comedy,
King   Come, sir, it wants a twelvemonth an' a day,
            And then 'twill end.
Berowne   That's too long for a play.

(V, ii, 874–8)

Shakespeare's insistence on an ironic relation to his characters implicates the audience in the characters' shock of discovery. In their discussion of the preceding action's dramatic form, Berowne and the King reorganize the fiction's status in complex ways. The imaginative world of study, dreams of fame, games, and courtship *within* the fiction is a counter-world to its primary, actual, and potentially tragic world of politics, finance, war and mortality. The fiction that encloses these partial, hypothetical worlds – the play itself – is a fictional counter-world to the actual world of the audience. When Berowne and the King acknowledge the illusiveness of their fanciful world of wit in explicitly dramatic terminology, the world of Navarre is now recognized as a playground bounded by a world outside; the larger context of actuality within the fiction is itself implicitly associated with the world of the theatre audience.

Within the context of the play's fictive world, the lords and their low-plot counterparts conflate the imaginative with the actual, their own 'great feast of languages' with 'the world's debate'. The Princess has a potential energy that contrasts very effectively with the kinetic energy of the males. The ladies maintain an air of detachment that keeps the imaginative and the actual firmly apart. In doing so, they perform a purgative function in the humorous world of Navarre, but they are far from embodying the spirit of romantic comedy. Theirs is not a simple, witty detachment but a sophisticated irony. They may rate the play's action 'At courtship, pleasant jest, and courtesy,/As bombast and as lining to the time' (V, ii, 78–81), while taking advantage of their courtiers' absorption in it in order to impose the priorities of the world of work upon the world of play.

The Princess and her entourage have received uncritical enthusiasm from nearly all who have written on the play. There has been a consistent tendency to endow the Princess with a normative function in the world of the play or to associate her with some ideal that is presumed to be Shakespeare's.[9] The roles that the Princess does enact in the play are both more complex and more ambivalent than the play's critics usually perceive; their bedazzlement is shared by the courtiers of Navarre.

The Princess is the practitioner of a charming power politics. Not only does she possess fully the social and personal grace that represented the quintessence of nobility to Castiglione; she also possesses a personal strength and flexibility, enabling her to control or influence the course of events, akin to the *virtù* that represented to Machiavelli the essential quality of the effective prince. The Princess masters her affects with both 'might' and 'special grace'. She possesses the courtly grace that the King attempts, with such ineptitude, to affect and the political *virtù* that he shrinks from exercising.

The darker side of the Princess's strength of character is part of a subliminal counter-theme to the gay romp that makes the play of *Love's Labour's Lost* so immediately appealing. The strategies of language and the dislocations of social bonding engendered by abuses of speech which Shakespeare anatomizes through comedy in *Love's Labour's Lost*, he explores in the harsher light of history in *The Tragedy of King Richard the Second*. Richard's solipsistic lyricism, his self-staging, and the energy with which he verbally embraces each new role thrust upon him are all characteristics that connect him to Navarre and Berowne. The agreeable faces that face so many follies in Navarre's curious-knotted garden are out-faced in a sexual combat of wits that generates laughter, not pathos. The opposition of lords and ladies in *Love's Labour's Lost* exemplifies a contrast of two linguistic modes, in which the former falls before the superior efficiency of the latter in dealing with the political strategies lurking behind social rituals.

V

The Princess's station for the hunt is a metaphor for her position in the general action. Like the ladies, once they have established themselves in the park, she is the hunter who does not pursue: her victims come to her to be shot. The focal power of the Princess and her entourage may be a sublimation of the play's origin in a female-centered court where sexual and political intrigue were inextricably bound together. The cynosural staging in Shakespeare's play and at Elizabeth's court are both designed to reflect and manipulate the rituals of courtly love and Petrarchism. Like Queen Elizabeth, the Princess successfully combines social grace with political cunning, and uses her sexuality strategically.[10]

As the play explores the relations within its own fiction, it is, simultaneously, obliquely exploring values and behaviors within the society of which its dramatic form is an imaginative projection. The Tudor humanists' ideal of a union of the decorative and persuasive functions of rhetoric in an eloquence that would move to virtuous action had faded by the 1590s as the royal court upon which it was centered persisted as an autocratic structure of neo-feudal chivalry and preferment. At the humorous court of Navarre, the practice of rhetoric is cut off from its ethical and political foundations; its function is to grace dubious actions and motives.

Walter Oakeshott has suggested, in his study of Sir Walter Raleigh's literary relations, that the lost labors of love alluded to in the play were Raleigh's adulatory *Cynthia* poems and that Armado parodies Raleigh; *Love's Labour's Lost* is claimed to be, at least in part, a topical satire on Raleigh's disgrace and banishment from court (1592) after Elizabeth's most gallant courtier was discovered to have made one of the royal maids of honor pregnant.[11]

A possibly direct relation between the play and a specific historical event is perhaps less important than the event's significance as the concrete example of a general cultural condition that is being refracted in the play's fiction. The contrary elements of refinement and crudity, decorous social forms and the ruthless pursuit of self-aggrandizement, which are characteristic of Elizabethan court society, are mirrored in Shakespeare's courtly play: an ornate and stylized artifact with a surface resemblance to the court plays of Lyly, which embodies in its fiction a disjunction between wooing artifice and sexual desire, between verbal pattern and sense experience. Such a perspective on *Love's Labour's Lost* moves logically from the play itself to the dynamics of court society. A ritualistic order of prescribed rules of decorum and deference enhanced by a profusion of symbolic pageantry and art imposes an esthetic form on the intrigue, back-biting and jockeying for prestige, wealth, and power which are the motivating forces in the life of the court. This dichotomy of outward grace and inward corruption is a recurrent theme in the poetry of Raleigh and Spenser. In Shakespeare's play, the characters' love–war imagery and games are a sublimation into courtly play of the strife that characterizes personal, social and political life in a postlapsarian world. The fallen state in which the audience exists is that in which the characters are ultimately forced to find themselves.

The indeterminacy of the ending of *Love's Labour's Lost*, the plot's open form, injects considerable ambiguity into the significance of the action. From one perspective, a new sense of relation is established between the ladies and their courtiers at the close, and the action of a romantic comedy has been initiated; from another perspective, the ladies exit the playworld as easily as they had entered it, having fulfilled their function as the collective agency of both a comic nemesis and a diplomatic coup. The follies of the men have been exposed, the illusion broken, the possibilities of self-discovery presented. In either case, the final outcome lies beyond the scope of 'our sport', the dramatic fiction of *Love's Labour's Lost*.

The characters within the play's fiction fail to perfect that equilibrium of their experience which can provide the audience with a model. *Love's Labour's Lost* demonstrates its own rhetorical logic, which is to deny a conclusion based on the logic of its characters. Rituals of verbal, sexual and social bonding are denied: the lords deny their oaths, the ladies deny the lords their 'grace', the playwright denies the audience the expected conclusion. In place of comic rituals of marriage and festivity, which would have been expected to be the culmination of the plot, we are given a pair of songs that follow the plot but are not part of it. They are not presented as an expression of the characters' vision but as a gift to them – and to the theatre audience – from the playwright. Armado styles the songs a 'dialogue' (V, ii, 885) – *discordia concors*, rather than a contest between opposing sides. The beauty of Spring is a setting for human discord as well as for the creations of art; the adversity of Winter is assuaged by homely images of human warmth among figures with common, Christian names who work, eat and play together. The sweetness and adversity so radically disjoined in the play's dramatic fiction are reintegrated by the songs. Each is an ambivalent vision in which the actual is sustained by the imaginative. The songs wed play to work, love to labor, within the larger cyclical rhythms of a human community that is harmoniously wed to nature. By celebrating the continuity of the public theatre poet's efflorescent art with his common, rural roots, the songs become a critical frame for the courtly style and aristocratic ideology that have dominated the dramatic action. Shakespeare's most courtly play holds the mirror up to the court in order to show virtue her feature, scorn her own image, and the very age and body of the time his form and pressure.[12]

By emphasizing that 'our wooing doth not end like an old play', Shakespeare is conspicuously implying that this is a new kind of play that insists that the audience take seriously the theatre's claim to hold the mirror up to the world's stage upon which the audience are the actors. Shakespeare makes a comedy by refusing to make his characters' sport a comedy. By dooming their 'old infant play' from the beginning, he creates an exhilarating and penetrating anatomy of the modes of playing.

Notes

1. See CLIFFORD GEERTZ, *The Interpretation of Cultures* (New York: Basic Books, 1973), pp. 443–53; I quote from p. 448. Harington's treatise seems to have been written late in Elizabeth's reign but was first printed in 1779: JOHN HARINGTON, *Nugae Antiquae*, ed. Henry Harington, 3 vols reprinted (Hildesheim: Georg Olms, 1968), Vol. II, pp. 154–208; I quote from pp. 157 and 173 respectively. In the present century, a pioneering study of the nature and forms of play, considered as human activity *sui generis*, is JOHANN HUIZINGA, *Homo Ludens* (Boston: Beacon Press, 1955); ROGER CAILLOIS, *Man, Play, and Games*, trans. Meyer Barash (New York: Free Press, 1961), elaborates and modifies Huizinga's perspectives and provides a detailed typology of games. The theory of play has been critically re-examined in an article of major importance: JACQUES EHRMANN, 'Homo Ludens Revisited', *Yale French Studies* 41 (1968), 31–57; Ehrmann analyzes the ideological presuppositions of the approaches of Huizinga and Caillois.

2. I quote from C.L. BARBER, *Shakespeare's Festive Comedy* (Princeton: Princeton University Press, 1959), p. 88. For a description of the atmosphere pervading the play's world, see BOBBYANN ROESEN (Ann Barton) '*LLL*', *SQ*, 4 (1953), 411–26, which was a landmark in the critical revaluation of the play and has had formative influence on much that has been written on the play in the last few years, including the present study. For a comprehensive survey of the varieties of organized play in Elizabethan England, see the articles on 'Sports and Pastimes' (including hunting, dancing, gaming – and cockfighting) in *Shakespeare's England*, 2 vols (Oxford: Clarendon Press, 1916), Vol. II, pp. 334–483.

3. Other aspects of the Renaissance *théatrum mundi* have been suggestively studied in JEAN JACQUOT, 'Le théâtre du monde de Shakespeare à Calderon', *Révue de litterature comparée* 31 (1957), 341–64; ANN RIGHTER (Barton), *Shakespeare and the Idea of the Play* (London: Chatto & Windus, 1962); FRANCES A. YATES, *Theatre of the World* (Chicago: University of Chicago Press, 1969); FRANK J. WARNKE, *Versions of Baroque* (New Haven: Yale University Press, 1972), pp. 66–89; JACKSON I. COPE, *The Theater and The Dream* (Baltimore: Johns Hopkins University Press, 1973).

4. J.A. MAZZEO, *Renaissance and Revolution* (New York: Random House, 1965), p. 146.

5. Cf. BERTRAND EVANS, *Shakespeare's Comedies* (Oxford: Oxford University Press, 1960), pp. 19–24, who gives a brief account of *LLL* IV, iii and V, ii, in terms of Shakespeare's exploitation of discrepant awarenesses.

6. See *OED*, s.v. 'Brazen', 1, 3; 'bate', v²3 (to which *OED* adds, 'Perhaps in fig. use combined with some idea of bait v.¹ 1.4 as if "to satisfy the hunger of"', and cites *LLL* I, i, 6); 'Bait', v¹ 1.4, sb.¹1.2.

7. CLAUDE LÉVI-STRAUSS, *The Savage Mind* (Chicago: University of Chicago Press, 1966), p. 32.

8. STEPHEN ORGEL, Introduction to his edition of *Ben Jonson: Complete Masques* (New Haven: Yale University Press, 1969), p. 3.

9. See e.g. RALPH BERRY, *Shakespeare's Comedies: Explorations in Form* (Princeton: Princeton University Press, 1972), p. 79: 'The Princess . . . is beyond questioning the internal arbiter of *LLL*'; CATHERINE M. McLAY, 'The Dialogues of Spring and Winter: A Key to the Unity of *LLL*', *SQ* 18 (1967), 119–27: 'The heroines represent the life force operating through Nature' (p. 122). F.P. WILSON, in the essay on 'Shakespeare's Comedies' in his *Shakespearian and Other Studies* (ed. Helen Gardner, Oxford: Clarendon, 1969), writes that the ladies are 'the fixed point of reference, the desired norm from which to some degree all the other characters depart' (p. 66). JOHN VYVYAN, in *Shakespeare and the Rose of Love* (London: Chatto & Windus, 1969), interprets the princess as a neoplatonic goddess in the Lylian manner: 'she is not only a brilliantly witty princess, but also, we must certainly infer, the allegorical figure of love and beauty' (p. 32); PAUL E. MEMMO, Jr, 'The Poetry of the *Stilnovisti* and *LLL*', *Comparative Literature*, 18 (1966), 1–15, provided a scholarly version of Vyvyan's approach: 'Shakespeare . . . brings the angelic lady of the early Renaissance down from the Empyrean . . . in a new epiphany in order to lead those who are willing to comprehend her to a new birth here on earth' (p. 15).

10. J.E. NEALE, *Queen Elizabeth I* (Garden City: Doubleday, 1934, reprinted 1957), p. 66, writes of the Queen's critical need to establish her authority in a masculine world: 'By a paradox, sex, having created the problem, itself solved it, and the reign was turned into an idyll, a fine but artificial comedy, of young men – and old men – in love . . . . It secured service, which was a monarch's function to do, and charged service with emotion, which it was Elizabeth's desire to do. Her genius rose to the game. Her royal sense, her intellectual temperament, her quick mind and gift of repartee, kept it artificial enough for safety; her humanity saved it from fatuity'. A right description of our sport.

11. See WALTER OAKESHOTT, *The Queen and the Poet* (New York: Barnes and Noble, 1961), pp. 100–27.

12. The First Quarto (1598) title page declares that *LLL* was 'presented before her Highness this last Christmas'. It has been surmised that an earlier version was acted in an aristocratic house before a private, courtly audience for whom the play's apparently pervasive topical satire was intended. The Second Quarto (1631) title page presents the play 'As it was Acted by his Maiesties Seruants at the Blacke-Friers and the Globe'. It would appear that, even if it was originally performed as a courtly entertainment, Shakespeare's comedy was intended for, or at least adapted to, a wider, public audience.

4   A Midsummer Night's Dream   (?1594–96)

'We are such stuff as dreams are made on', Prospero claims in *The Tempest*, and one of our most persistent desires is that of making coherence out of the dreams we live and which live through us, even though we may need to heed Bottom's warning that we make asses of ourselves if we go about interpreting them. A number of essays here defy Bottom's warning and address *A Midsummer Night's Dream* in suggestive ways. Since Jan Kott's essay in *Shakespeare Our Contemporary* (1964) and the RSC production by Peter Brook (1970), which was influenced by Kott's essay, *A Midsummer Night's Dream* has become central to contemporary readings of the comedies. For C.L. Barber, in *Shakespeare's Festive Comedies* (1959), the play dramatizes 'the security of make-believe'; for Louis Montrose, in an essay written some years after his piece on *Love's Labour's Lost*, printed above, play and game are no longer innocent and celebratory: 'sedimented within' the play 'are traces of those recurrent acts of bestiality and incest, of parricide, uxoricide, filicide, and suicide, that the ethos of romantic comedy would evade'.[1] Between these polarities, current debate on the play has been intense. Even critics who share a similar repertoire of assumptions may differ markedly on the play – as these two essays, by Norman Holland and Helen Golding, show.

Norman N. Holland, *'Hermia's Dream'*

Holland's analysis of Hermia's dream is an introduction to psycho-analytical criticism as well as an exemplification of its critical potency. Holland has been one of the foremost exponents of psychoanalytical criticism over a number of years. Specifically, his work uses American ego-psychology, an adaption of the psychoanalytical tradition closely aligned with clinical practice, rather than psychoanalysis as pure 'theory'. He makes no apology for 'using a psychology closer to that of the consulting room than to the increasingly abstract psychologies in contemporary literary theory'.[2] The current debate over psychoanalysis as a mode of reading frequently focuses on this issue. Holland's is perhaps the current leading voice arguing for the inescapability of the connection between textual and clinical psychoanalytic experiences, and in the development of what he terms 'transactive criticism' (for a broader discussion of psychoanalytical approaches to the comedies, see Introduction, pp. 14–7).

Second, Holland is often characterized (and widely known) as a 'subjective' reader-response critic. The classic articulation of his views was his essay, 'Unity Identity Text Self' in which he argued that readers group the themes of a text according to an 'identity theme': interpretation is thus a function of identity, whereby a reader finds a 'fantasy seemingly 'in' the work fantasies to suit their several character structures'.[3] In 'Hermia's Dream', Holland identifies the activities of the analyst and critic, using Hermia's dream in II, ii to illustrate 'someone's unconscious made conscious', to place it within 'a system of ego functions', and to 'symbolize ourselves to ourselves', arguing that finally 'we dream her dream for ourselves, and as we know ourselves so we know the dream, until its local habitation is here and its name is us'. Thus the essay unites both of Holland's critical interests, in reader-centred criticism and in providing a working psychology to account for the experiences of the reader.

HELEN GOLDING, '"The Story of the Night told Over": D.W. Winnicott's Theory of Play and A Midsummer Night's Dream'

Golding's essay also engages, from a different viewpoint, the general question Holland raises. Acknowledging that any psychoanalytic reading of a literary text raises 'endless, perhaps finally unanswerable, questions as to the validity and scope of its methodology', she avoids the common charge against psychoanalytic criticism of an ahistorical 'universalism' by arguing, in effect, for criticism as the history of the appropriation of texts within changing reading formations. For us today, she asserts, psychoanalysis makes explicit what has always 'been present' and which is now 'describable in psychoanalytical terms because these are what we have at our disposal in our own period'. She also rejects the direct application of psychoanalysis to the author or to character – the most popular kind of psychoanalytical criticism, as exemplified by most of the essays in *Shakespeare's Personality* (1990), of which Holland is coeditor. By contrast, Golding focuses on the interaction between the text and its reader or spectator, using the analogy between the clinical situation of patient and analyst that is termed 'transference'. The 'telling-over' we experience in the theatre is compared to the transferential relationship, in which in an 'as-if' situation, telling stories of ourselves and learning by 'playing' ways of communicating with ourselves and others. The transferential analogy is used very skilfully in connection with some of the ideas of the British analyst, D.W. Winnicott.

Notes

1. BARBER, p. 137; LOUIS A. MONTROSE, '*MSND* and the Shaping Fantasies of Elizabethan Culture: Gender, Power, Form', in Ferguson, Quilligan and Vickers, p. 77.

2. NORMAN N. HOLLAND, 'Introduction', in Holland, Homan and Paris, p. 3.

3. NORMAN N. HOLLAND, 'Unity Identity Text Self', *PMLA*, 90 (1975), 813–22.

NORMAN N. HOLLAND '*Hermia's Dream*'*

Literature is a dream dreamed for us.

(*The Dynamics of Literary Response*, 1968)

What could be more imaginary than a dream of a dream of a dream? Yet Hermia's dream is just that in *A Midsummer Night's Dream*. She dreams, but later decides she was dreaming that she dreamed. Then, at the very end of the play, we, the audience, are told: 'You have but slumb'red here'; we dreamed that she dreamed that she dreamed.

A dream of a dream of a dream – surely this is what the comedy means when it tells how:

... as imagination bodies forth
The forms of things unknown, the poet's pen
Turns them to shapes, and gives to aery nothing
A local habitation and a name.

(V, i, 14–17)

The psychoanalyst and the literary critic do the same. In our effort to give imaginary dreams a local habitation and a name, those of us who use psychoanalysis to talk about literature have historically used several different approaches. The first is typical of the first phase of psychoanalysis: we would use Hermia's dream as an illustration of

* Reprinted from *The Annual of Psychoanalysis*, Vol. VII (1979).

someone's unconscious made conscious. In the second phase, we would place her dream within a system of ego functions. Finally – today – we would use this airy nothing to symbolize ourselves to ourselves.

When we first hear the dream, it is still going on. That is, I think she is still dreaming when she first speaks about it. As with so many nightmares, she is having trouble waking:

> Help me, Lysander, help me! do thy best
> To pluck this crawling serpent from my breast!
> Ay me, for pity!

And only now, I think, is she beginning to come out of it:

> Ay me, for pity! what a dream was here!
> Lysander, look how I do quake with fear.
> Methought a serpent eat my heart away.
> And you sate smiling at his cruel prey.
>
> (II, ii, 145–56)

In effect, as Hermia tells the dream, she splits it into two parts. In the first, we hear the dream actually taking place. In the second, Hermia reports the dream to us after it is over. In the first part she makes a plea for help, but in the second we learn that Lysander wasn't interested in helping at all – he was just smiling and watching the serpent eat Hermia. Further, if we take the most obvious Freudian meaning for that serpent – a penis or phallus – the masculinity in the dream is split between the attacking, crawling serpent and her lover Lysander, smiling at a distance.

Among the fifty-one topics Erikson suggests considering in a full dream analysis, let me be merciful and select just one: 'methods of defense, denial, and distortion', which might be considered a variation on another topic, 'mechanisms of defense', itself a subtopic of 'ego identity and lifeplan'.[1] I see in this dream something I think is fundamental to Hermia's character.

If I go back to the first things Hermia says and look just at her speeches as an actor would, I see a recurring pattern.[2] After hearing her father, Theseus admonishes her, 'Demetrius is a worthy gentleman', and Hermia replies with her first words in the play, 'So is Lysander' (an alternative). But, replies Theseus, since Demetrius has your father's approval, he 'must be held the worthier'. 'I would my father look'd but with my eyes', answers Hermia. Next she begins a long speech by begging Theseus' pardon, wondering why she is bold, and worrying lest, by revealing her thoughts, she impeach her modesty. But, she says:

> . . . I beseech your Grace that I may know

The worst that may befall me in this case,
If I refuse to wed Demetrius.

(I, i, 62–4)

I hear in all these speeches a distinct, recurring pattern. Call it a
concern for alternatives, for other possibilities, or for an elsewhere:
Lysander as alternative to Demetrius, her judgement as an alternative to
her father's, her boldness contrasted with her modesty, or the
alternatives the law allows her. We could say that Hermia's personal style
or character consists (in the theoretical language of Heinz Kohut) of
creating self-objects.[3] Thus, after her dialogue with Theseus, the lovers are
left alone, and Hermia uses a variety of examples and legends from the
elsewhere of classical mythology to illustrate and buttress their love.
Then, to Helena, who loves Demetrius, she describes how she and
Lysander will run away, again looking for an elsewhere, an alternative to
Athens: 'To seek new friends and stranger companies'. I would phrase
Hermia's personal style as the seeking of some alternative in order to
amend something closer to herself.

Her last speeches as well as her first show this sense of alternatives.
Theseus, Egeus, and the rest have come upon the lovers and wakened
them. However, the lovers are not sure they aren't still dreaming. Says
Hermia:

Methinks I see these things with parted eye,
When every thing seems double.

(IV, i, 189–90)

Demetrius starts checking reality and asks: 'Do you not think/The Duke
was here, and bid us follow him?' And Hermia, for her last word in the
play, offers one final alternative: 'Yea, and my father'.[4]

Her dream dramatizes her 'parted eye' in all its divisions, in the double
telling, in the here and there of Lysander and the serpent, and in the very
content of the dream – her effort to save herself by getting the serpent
away and bringing Lysander closer. I think I could show the same theme
of amendment by alternative if I were to trace through the dream the
various levels of this adolescent girl's development: oedipal, phallic, anal
and oral.

Following the symbols (like that snake) and the libidinal levels of
Hermia's dream would be the first and classical way of analyzing the
dream, provided we ground the analysis on the free associations of the
dreamer. Alas, however, this being a literary dream, we do not have
associations in the way they usually float up from the couch.
Nevertheless, we can analyse the dream in the classic way by inferring
Hermia's associations.

I

We can begin by guessing at the day residue of Hermia's dream – a conversation she has with Lysander just before they lie down to go to sleep. Their conversation concerns just exactly the question of separation, as in 'lie further off', and the danger of union, Hermia's fear for her maidenly modesty if Lysander comes too close. If I think about Hermia's dream in the general framework of an adolescent girl's oedipal fears and wishes about the opposite sex, particularly in the light of this conversation, I see her imagining Lysander in two aspects. First, there is the Lysander who is physically close to her, and in the conversation they had before sleeping this is a sexual Lysander, one whom she feels is a threat to her maidenly virtue. The other is a Lysander at a distance, and him she associates with love, courtesy, humane modesty and loyalty. In the dream, she will image this distant Lysander as smiling. Not so the nearer. In the day residue, the Lysander trying to get close proclaims that 'My heart unto yours is knit,/So that but one heart we can make of it.' In the dream, this sexual union of hearts becomes a snake eating her heart away. The dream separates these two aspects of Lysander, the sexual and the affectionate, but has images of both as hostile. By her waking cry for Lysander to help her, Hermia tries to put them back together in a more benevolent, pitying way, but reality fails her in this. While she dreamed, Lysander left her for Helena.

The next time we see Hermia, she has managed to track down the missing Lysander by his voice. Lysander has been following Helena because, while he and Hermia were briefly asleep, Puck dropped on his eyes the 'love-juice' or 'this flower's force in stirring love', which made Lysander fall in love with the next being he saw. While Hermia was sleeping, Helena came in and woke Lysander. He promptly fell madly in love with her and followed her off into the forest. Thus when Hermia woke from her nightmare, she could not find him.

We have no way of knowing how much Hermia has heard through her sleep of Puck's talk about the charm for Lysander's eyes or of the ensuing dialogue between Helena and Lysander, but I am willing to assume that some of this talk has percolated into her dream. In particular I think she may have heard Puck speaking about the charm and may have drawn on the idea of a special fluid in representing the oedipal Lysander as a snake with its venom. She may also have heard Lysander declare his love for Helena, and that is why she shows him in the dream as hurting her and as a double person, that is, one who lies. This is a key word not only because his name is 'Lies-ander', but also because he made all those puns on 'lie' during the dialogue before their nap. As he said, 'for lying so [close to you], Hermia, I do not lie'. Puns and lies, in which one word carries two meanings, might have helped Hermia to split and so double her representation of Lysander, especially Lysander as a snake.

In a true free association, the next time we see Hermia, she misunderstands Demetrius and thinks he has killed Lysander while he was sleeping. She promptly compares Demetrius to a snake:

> O brave touch!
> Could not a worm, an adder, do so much?
> An adder did it! for with doubler tongue
> Than thine, thou serpent, never adder stung.

(III, ii, 70–3)

In other words, Hermia's free association for falseness while sleeping is a snake, and her free association to the snake is the doubleness of its tongue. As one of the fairies had sung earlier, 'you spotted snakes with double tongue' (II, ii, 9).

Both in the doubleness and in the tonguiness, the snake says what Hermia might well want to say about her now false Lysander. Moreover, the serpent fits Hermia's thoughts in another curious way. Twice in Shakespeare's works (although not, as it happens, in *A Midsummer Night's Dream*) we are told that the adder is deaf. So in Hermia's dream, Lysander does not seem to hear her cries for help.

In yet another way, then, Hermia applies her characteristic personal style to the sexual problems imaged in her dream. She separates the oedipal Lysander into two aspects: a sexual, hostile, intrusive being right on top of her and a milder but also hostile man at some distance. In the same way, her dream shifts its sensory mode (to return to another of Erikson's topics for dream analysis). She begins with something touching her – the serpent crawling on her breast. She shifts to looking: 'Lysander, look how I do quake with fear.' Then she looks for Lysander and does not find him: 'What, remov'd?' Then she calls to him, but he does not answer: 'What, out of hearing gone?' She has moved from the immediate sense of touch to the more distant senses of sight and hearing. Interestingly, Hermia comments on – or if you will, associates to – just this shift when next we see her. The very words she speaks when she finds her lost Lysander are:

> Dark night, that from the eye his function takes,
> The ear more quick of apprehension makes.
> Wherein it [night] doth impair the seeing sense,
> It pays the hearing double recompense.
> Thou art not by mine eye, Lysander, found;
> Mine ear, I thank it, brought me to thy sound.

(III, ii, 177–82)

Again, with her doubling and with the ear gaining what the eye loses at night, she shows her characteristic concern with alternatives, particularly one alternative compensating for another.

Sight takes on still more importance if we can imagine that Hermia has unconsciously overheard Lysander falling in love with Helena. Puck has just dropped the love-juice into Lysander's eyes. Further, when Helena comes upon the sleeping Hermia and Lysander right after Puck leaves, she is complaining that her eyes will not attract Demetrius the way Hermia's eyes do. Then, almost the first thing Lysander says when he awakes and falls in love with Helena is:

> Transparent Helena, nature shows art,
> That through thy bosom makes me see thy heart.
>
> (II, ii, 104–5)

Hermia seems to me to take this image of complete truth or candor and dream it into a snake eating her own heart, an emblem of doubleness, treachery and hostility.

If we were to limit ourselves to the old, rigid, one-to-one symbolism of early psychoanalysis, we would say simply that the snake is a symbol for a penis or a phallus. Rather than call it simply phallic, though, I would like to go beyond the symbolic code to a more human meaning for that stinging, biting snake. I can find it in Erikson's modal terms *intrusive* or *penetrating*. Hermia expresses that intrusion into her body as eating. In other words, she has built into the oedipal or phallic levels of the dream (the dream considered as an expression of an adolescent girl's attitude toward male sexuality) a regression to earlier levels of development. In yet another way, Hermia has provided an alternative – namely, anal and oral significances – to her oedipal and phallic sexuality.

For example, one of the issues raised by the serpent in Hermia's dream is possession in contrast to true love. The serpent proposes to eat Hermia's heart, to make it a prey – in other words, to possess it. Earlier that day Hermia's father, Egeus, had accused Lysander: 'With cunning hast thou filch'd my daughter's heart' (I, i, 36), just as he had given her bracelets and rings, knick-knacks and nosegays. Lysander partly replies by insisting that he has just as much money and land as Demetrius. Finally, when Hermia sees that Lysander has fallen in love with Helena, she cries:

> What, have you come by night
> And stol'n my love's heart from him?
>
> (III, ii, 283–4)

False love is treating a heart like a possession that can be stolen. In true love, by contrast, hearts fuse and become one, as in Lysander's plea for Hermia to lie down by him: 'My heart unto yours is knit,/So that but one heart we can make of it.' Similarly, Helena recalls that she and Hermia were such close friends they had 'two seeming bodies, but one heart' (III, ii, 212).

Yet it is precisely this fusion of hearts that Hermia refused when she would not let Lysander lie down with her. She left herself open to the other, possessive kind of love. Now, after her dream, she pleads to Lysander: 'Do thy best/To pluck this crawling serpent from my breast!' In other words, make an effort to get this repellent, crawling thing away – and I hear the faintest trace of an excremental metaphor here: make an effort to push this disgusting thing out of you or me.

'Crawling' she calls it, a word she uses only one other time in the play, much later, when Puck has thoroughly befuddled all four lovers, leading them on a wild goose chase through the woods. Finally, each collapses, with Hermia saying:

> I can no further crawl, no further go;
> My legs can keep no pace with my desires.
>
> (III, ii, 444–45)

Legless crawling is something less than fully human. Crawling suggests a desire for possession almost disembodied from the human, a desire that in life she has kept within 'humane modesty' but which in her dream she feels as overpowering.

At the deepest level of the dream, that desire for possession becomes eating and thus both fusing with and taking away a person's essence: 'Methought a serpent eat my heart *away*.' Phallic intrusion and possession become a hostile, consuming oral possession. The dominant image of the dream seems to me to be the mouth: the serpent's eating and Lysander's smiling. Hermia's thought moves in the direction of sublimation from the eating to the smiling, from her being the serpent's 'prey', to 'pray' in the other sense, her prayer to Lysander to help her. Similarly, in the dream she moves from being eaten to being looked at: 'Lysander, *look* how I do quake . . .' The day before, she had parted from Lysander by saying that, 'we must starve our sight/From lovers' food till morrow deep midnight' (I, i, 222–3). The sight of the beloved is lovers' food. We should perhaps hear a pun in Hermia's exclamation during her dream: 'Ay me, for pity!' 'Ay me' includes 'Eye me', look at me, as well as 'I – me', a blurting out of her dual self. Again, Hermia has defended by setting up alternatives. She deals with the nightmare by saying she is both in the dream and out of it.

In the same way, when she cannot find Lysander, she cries 'alack', and I hear the word in its original sense – just that, a lack: something is missing, taken away, dissociated. Her characteristic defense of providing an alternative can lead to a tragic separation – here it is Lysander's going off after the alternative, Helena.

Doubleness thus takes on a special charge for Hermia because it plays into her characteristic mode of defenses and adaptation: the providing of alternatives. Now, finally, I can surmise why out of all the materials that might have been important to her – her meeting with the Duke, the argument with her father, her flight by night – she dreams about the conversation she has with Lysander before they lie down to go to sleep. That conversation hinges on precisely the key issue for Hermia: one and two. Lysander wants them to have 'one turf . . ./One heart, one bed, two bosoms, and one troth', but this idea Hermia finds threatening, not only for the ordinary reasons a young girl of the gentry in the English Renaissance would, but because such a fantasy would deprive her of her customary mode of adaptation. At all levels of her dream, she is working out a theme of love within her characteristic way of dealing with inner and outer reality, namely, by finding alternatives. Union in love is one possibility, but she dreams about her fear of it as a deadly possession that would prey upon and eat away her very being. However, the other alternative, separation, leads to another kind of cruelty through distance and indifference and – alack! – a loss.

The sexual symbolism of her dream thus rests upon a far deeper doubleness, her wish and her fear that alternatives won't work, that she will have to settle for just one thing: one intrusive, penetrating, possessive lover. In a psychoanalytic context, we can guess that the adolescent Hermia is working out with Lysander a much earlier, more formative relationship with a figure never seen, never even mentioned, in this comedy: her mother.

II

When we come to mother, we come to both the beginning and the end of this kind of dream analysis. What you have just read is an analysis of this fictitious dream as if I were doing it ten years ago. I have been thinking about Hermia's dream mostly as though it were an event 'out there' in a play 'out there', wholly separate from me. I have been tracing her associations through deeper and earlier phases of her development.

In the earliest years of psychoanalysis, when people turned to invented dreams like Hermia's, they did so for two reasons. Either they were going to use the insight of the poet to confirm the views of the scientist, or they were going to use the ideas of the scientist to understand what the poet had done. One could use Hermia's dream to confirm various ideas about dreaming: that associations explain dreams, that dreams express character structure, that dreams work at a variety of developmental levels, and so on. Then one could say: 'See, Shakespeare knew this intuitively. Now psychoanalysis has shown it scientifically.' Alternatively, the psychoanalytic literary critic might say, 'Here is all this scientific knowledge about dreams. If we apply it to Hermia's dream, we shall see what an extraordinarily rich and complex thing it is.' In effect, the Shakespearean critic got a boost from psychoanalysis, and the psychoanalyst got a lift from Shakespeare.

Both these approaches, however, rest on the assumption that we can treat the dream Shakespeare invented for Hermia like a real dream. We are assuming that a play is an exact representation of reality, which obeys the same laws as reality and to which we can apply the same rules for interpretation that we would apply in real life. We can have free associations and symbols and oedipal, phallic, anal and oral levels in Hermia's dream just as in any real adolescent girl's dream.

Such an assumption is, of course, one way of relating to a play, and some psychoanalytic criticism is still written this way, but few indeed are the literary critics who would settle for this one way. For some four decades now, literary people have been insisting that literary works are not meant to be looked through so as to discover some other, imagined reality they portray. Rather, they are to be looked at as ends in themselves. They are artifacts, just like paintings or sculpture, but made of words instead. This non-representational attitude, furthermore, is part and parcel of the whole twentieth-century concept of art. As Matisse replied to a lady who complained that the arm of a woman in one of his paintings was too long: 'Madame, you are mistaken. That is not a woman, that is a picture.' So here Hermia is not an adolescent girl – she is a character in a remarkably artificial comedy, so artificial, in fact, that she states her dream in rhymed couplets. How many patients in real life do *that*?

Some ten or twenty years ago, we psychoanalytic literary critics shifted our objective. No longer did we want to treat Hermia like a literal adolescent. Instead, we wanted to understand her as one part fitted into the total play, as the arm fits into Matisse's painting. Both the character and the play are sequences of words that we understand by giving them meaning. Treating Hermia as a real person leads, of course, to one possible meaning, but a very closely limited one, and literary critics prefer to find a larger, more general meaning through themes.

I see the questions of separation and fusion that appear in Hermia's dream permeating the play. That is, *A Midsummer Night's Dream* begins with the separation of lovers. Theseus and Hippolyta have to wait out the four days till their wedding, the fairy King and Queen, Oberon and Titania, have quarreled, and, of course, the lovers have tangled up their affections and drawn down the threats of the duke and the father.

The end of the comedy brings all these lovers together and in between, what has happened is *our* dream. Puck says in the epilogue:

> Think ...
> That you have but slumb'red here
> While these visions did appear.
> And this weak and idle theme,
> No more yielding but a dream ...
>
> (V, i, 424–8)

Hermia's dream is, as we have seen, a dream within a dream, a wish therefore that what she dreams of were a wish like the dream around it, therefore the truest part of the play. What, then, is the truth she dreams? She dreams of the doubleness of lovers and the separation of the two aspects of her own lover. As in our word *duplicity*, this doubleness connotes his falseness, as perhaps his name also does: 'Lie-sander'. One part of him wishes to fuse sexually with her, and she turns to a more separate part of him for help. But, divided this way, both parts of Lysander are cruel, one more physically so than the other.

Cruelty pervades this comedy. As Theseus says to his fiancée in the opening lines:

> Hippolyta, I woo'd thee with my sword,
> And won thy love doing thee injuries.
>
> (I, i, 16–17)

You could say the same of Oberon, who humiliates Titania, or of either of our two young men, each of whom deserts and reviles and threatens his future wife. Throughout the play, the ruler, the father, the lovers, the king of the fairies, the amateur actors, and even the audience at the play within the play – all proclaim love, but they also threaten violence or humiliation. The play within the play focuses this ambivalence: it is a 'very tragical mirth' (V, i, 55), and 'the most lamentable comedy and most cruel death of Pyramus and Thisby' (I, ii, 11–12) is both the funniest and the bloodiest part of the play.

This comical tragedy within the comedy comes about because the lover Pyramus, separated from his love Thisby and confused in the dark (like our four lovers), believes a lion has eaten her. That lion in Renaissance symbology provides the opposite to Hermia's snake.[5] The royal beast takes his prey in the open, by force and grandeur. The low serpent sneaks his prey by stealth and cunning. Thus the lion in the clowns' broad farce causes right before your eyes a bloody fusion of lovers as Pyramus stabs himself over Thisby's bloody mantle and Thisby stabs herself over

Pyramus' bloody body. By contrast, the snake in Hermia's dream images a much subtler cruelty, the desertion and indifference of these not-so-courtly lovers.

This is a second way, then, to read Hermia's dream. The first way is as a clinical study of an adolescent girl. This second, larger reading sets Hermia's dream in the whole atmosphere and development of ambivalence in the comedy. We move beyond the nineteenth- and early twentieth-century concern with realism toward a more contemporary interest in theme. Instead of treating the various levels (oedipal, phallic, anal and oral) as aspects of some particular adolescent girl, I would see them all as variations on the comedy's theme of ambivalence, separations that are both loving and cruel.

Yet both these methods treat Hermia or her dream or her play as though they were 'out there', as though I were distant and indifferent to them except for a coolly intellectual curiosity. Both readings pretend the dream and the play are not connected to any me 'in here' who shapes and re-creates both the dream and the comedy to fit my own character or, as I prefer to say, my identity. Rather, an abstractly skilled interpreter finds 'the' meaning of the dream and fits it to 'the' meaning of the play.

III

In the ten years since I wrote such externalized dream analyses, most of us in literature and psychology have come to feel that new interest in the self that has quickened psychoanalytic theory throughout the world: in Paris through the writings of Lacan, in London in the object-relations theory of Milner and Winnicott and others, or in Chicago in the remarkable technical and theoretical studies of Heinz Kohut. Rather than simply look for an abstract theme 'out there' in *A Midsummer Night's Dream*, we have become more interested in how a self – my self, for example – uses the text of the play or the dream as an object to establish a self-structuring relation.

Clearly, the kind of level-by-level exegesis you have just read makes up part of that relation: working out the implications of the dream through such schemes as Erikson's for analyzing the interaction of manifest and latent content or the classic psychoanalytic scheme of developmental levels. But this kind of analysis leaves out a great deal. It ignores, for example, my feelings as I hear this dream. It ignores the personal quality of my reading.

Ten years ago, psychoanalytic literary critics cared little about the personal qualities that set one interpretation off from another, partly because we believed there was a best reading (a 'the' reading) that would rise to the top as we refined our literary ideas, and the other readings left in the pot simply wouldn't matter very much. Partly, too, we ignored the personal element because we had no way of talking about it. Now, however, we are less confident that there is some best reading, and we have a way of talking about the personal quality of a response.

That is, we have identity theory. We have a way of conceptualizing each new thing someone does as new, yet stamped with the same personal style as all the other actions chosen by that person. Each of us is a mixture of sameness and difference. We detect the sameness by seeing what persists within the constant change of our lives. We detect the difference by seeing what has changed against the background of sameness.

The most powerful way I know to think of that dialectic of sameness and difference is the one suggested by Heinz Lichtenstein: to see identity as a theme and variations like a musical theme and variations. Think of the sameness as a theme, an 'identity theme'. Think of the differences as variations on that identity theme. That is the way I have read Hermia's character, for example. She creates an alternative that will amend the original possibility. That is her identity theme, and we have seen her work out variations on it in her opening plea to Theseus, in her witty dialogue with Lysander before they lie down to sleep, and, above all, in her dream. These are all various ways by which she tries to amend through an alternative.

Now, just as Hermia develops a variation on her identity theme when she dreams, so you and I develop variations on our identity themes when we read her dream. Thus we arrive at a new kind of psychoanalytic method with literature. Our group at Buffalo called it 'transactive criticism'. We actively create, we *transact* – for example, Hermia's dream and *A Midsummer Night's Dream*. As critics, it is our job to articulate that transaction explicitly.

For me, the two images of Hermia's dream, the eating snake and the smiling lover, evoke large questions of fidelity and possession between men and women that I find puzzling and troubling as I watch my students struggling to find and maintain stable relationships or as I see in my own generation yet another friend's marriage break up. That is, Hermia's dream, her very presence in the forest with Lysander, builds on the mutual promises she and Lysander made, a contract sealed by a dangerous elopement, a pledge of faith that her lover, at the very moment of her dream, has abandoned. Her dream begins from his infidelity.

As I visualize the dream, I see a small snake at a distance – yes, like a penis in the classic Freudian symbolism – but I also remember a picture from a book of nature photographs of a snake's wide open mouth with long, curved fangs under a pink, arched palate, one demonic eye showing behind the furious jaws. The head is all mouth; really, there is so little else

besides that act of biting. Hermia describes the snake as 'crawling', and
we have already guessed at her associations. Mine are to a baby who is all
helpless, inarticulate demand. For me, then, Hermia's image of the snake
sets up the idea of possession, the way a lover or a penis can make a total
demand, much as an animal or a baby demands food.

Curiously, food comes up again when Shakespeare has the two men
explain why they switched partners. When Demetrius announces he is
back in love with Helena, he says:

> ... like a sickness did I loathe this food [Helena],
> But, as in health, come to my natural taste,
> Now I do wish it, love it, long for it,
> And will forevermore be true to it.
>
> (IV, i, 173–6)

The first time Shakespeare explains the switching of affections, it is
Lysander who has suddenly fallen in love with Helena just before
Hermia's dream. He looks at the sleeping Hermia and says:

> For as a surfeit of the sweetest things
> The deepest loathing to the stomach brings ....
> So thou, my surfeit and my heresy,
> Of all be hated, but most of me!
>
> (II, ii, 137–42)

Both times Shakespeare has his lovers refer emotional love to oral
appetite, and an appetite of total desire or total rejection, fidelity to one
girl meaning disgust at all others – at least for a time.

As we have seen, mouths appear twice in Hermia's dream, once in the
serpent's eating and once when Hermia says of Lysander, 'You sate
smiling.' For me, there is a great cruelty in that smile, just as there is in
his radical rejection of Hermia as a 'surfeit' that brings 'deepest loathing
to the stomach'. I feel hatred in that smile and in that imagery of disgust,
a hatred that psychoanalysis, in one of its hardest truths, asks us to
believe tinges every human relationship. As the tough-minded La
Rochefoucauld put it once and for all, 'In the misfortune of our best
friends we always find something that is not entirely displeasing.'[6]

In other words, if I bring my own associations to Hermia's dream and
its context, I begin to read the comedy of which it is a part as a rather
uncomfortable hovering between different views of love. In one view,
love is a total, consuming desire like a baby's for food. In the other, the
relation is less demanding: it admits a change of heart or appetite. Yet so
cool a lover may be hateful in his very smiling, just as hateful as the
snake is in his eating.

Nowadays, people reject the idea that love entitles you to possess another person. I too reject that kind of possessiveness – at least I consciously do. Yet the opposite possibility, a cool, distant love, does not satisfy me as a solution. I believe in a fidelity of mutual trust, an exchange of promises that I will be true to you and you will be true to me. I realize that contemporary patterns of marriage and sex deeply question this style of relationship. Many people believe they can and do love more than one person passionately and sexually at the same time.

No matter how contemporary I like to think myself in sexual matters, however, I have to admit that, deep down, I do not feel that the mutual pledge of loving or of sexual promises is the kind of contract one can negotiate like a lease on an apartment, with provisions for termination, renegotiation, or repairs. Nor do I believe one can hold several such leases at once. To be intimate is to risk oneself with another, and it is difficult, for me at least, to feel free to open myself up to another person without being able to feel that that opening up will be one-to-one, that neither of us will compromise our intimacy by sharing it with some third person. Somewhere inside me I deeply fear that I would be made small and ridiculous, like a child, were my lover to share our one-to-oneness with another lover. Hence I perceive Lysander's smiling as a cruel ridicule.

The comedy, however, like today's lovers, rejects possessiveness. Hermia's father states the theme: 'As she is mine, I may dispose of her.' The comedy as a whole moves away from this dehumanizing possessiveness, but what the play will substitute is not exactly clear. At the end, Duke Theseus rules:

> Egeus, I will overbear your will;
> For in the temple, by and by, with us
> These couples shall eternally be knit.

(IV, i, 179–81)

They will be married, and the power of the Duke will knit them together as couples and as his subjects.

Paradoxically, though, the comedy arrives at this knitting by a system of separations and infidelities. At first Demetrius had been in love with Helena, but at the opening of the play he has fallen in love with Hermia. Then, when Lysander's eyes are charmed, *he* falls in love with Helena. Later, the same thing happens to Demetrius: his eyes are drugged and he too falls in love with Helena. Finally, Puck uncharms Lysander, and the lovers fall into their natural pairs. The Polish critic, Jan Kott, urges us to think of this part of the comedy as a drunken switch party on a hot night, in which all the scantily clad lovers are interchangeable objects of desire who exchange with one another, finally waking up the next morning hung over, exhausted, and ashamed.[7]

Perhaps Kott takes too extreme a view, but the comedy does seem to say the lovers learn fidelity through their infidelities. Yet very little is said about how this union comes about. After they all wake up, Demetrius says of the events of the night before: 'These things seem small and indistinguishable' (IV, i, 187). And once they are reunited with their proper lovers, the two girls say not another word for the whole long last scene of the comedy.

In other words, the comedy is silent just at the point where I, with my puzzling about fidelity, am most curious. How do these lovers, who now pledge to be true to one another, derive fidelity from their previous infidelity? The play doesn't say. I feel it is up to us as readers and critics to find a solution. One distinguished Shakespearean, Norman Rabkin, writes:

> In *A Midsummer Night's Dream* Shakespeare opposes reason to the folly of lovers whose choices are often magically induced and always willful, only to make us realize that those choices are ultimately right and of the same order as that anti-rational illusion-mongering, the performing and watching of plays, which, depending on the charitable suspension of disbelief . . . nevertheless tells us truth of which reason is incapable.[8]

Rabkin suggests a parallel between the lovers falling in love and the way the rest of us give ourselves to plays. Illusions, fancies, fictions – if we can tolerate them, even lies – can lead us to a higher truth, a loving experience beyond reason. In psychoanalytic terms, I think this transcending corresponds to the basic trust we must all have developed in translating an imagining of a mother's nurturing presence into a confidence that she would really be there when needed. By not being there, she is unfaithful, but out of that first infidelity, most of us made the most basic of fidelities.

Thus I read Hermia's dream as having three parts. First, the snake preys on a passive Hermia's heart in an act of total, painful, destructive possession – hard on Hermia, but satisfying to that masculine snake. That possessiveness is one possibility open to me in relating to a woman or a play.

Second, Lysander smilingly watches the woman he so recently loved being possessed by another. His smile signals to me another kind of cruelty – dispassion, distance, indifference – another way of relating to a play or a lover. The snake is fantastic and symbolic, whereas Lysander presents a far more realistic lover whom I can interpret all too well through our century's alternatives to romantic commitment.

Then there is a third aspect to the dream, as I view it. It is a nightmare. The dream has aroused anxieties too great for Hermia to sleep through. She wakes, and we never learn how she might have dreamed that a loving Lysander plucked away a possessive snake. Instead, we are left with his deserting her for another woman.

For me, the sense of incompleteness is particularly strong, because I very much need to see a coherence and unity in human relations. I want a happy ending for this comedy. I want these couples married at the end, but I don't see – I don't trust, really – the way the comedy gets them together. Out of infidelity comes fidelity – but how? Hermia trusts Lysander, but he is unfaithful and leaves her alone and terrified: 'I swoon almost with fear.' It is hard for me to trust that there will be a happy outcome despite his cruel and contemptuous abandonment.

When I confess my uneasiness because the dream is incomplete and the play is silent on the creation of trust, I am working through something about myself I have faced many times before. It's hard for me simply to trust and to tolerate uncertainty or absence or silence. I question both Hermia's dream and the sexual revolution of our own time because I need to *know* things, particularly about human relations. I need to feel certain.

None of this, of course, do Lysander or the other lovers say. They talk about feelings of love and jealousy we can all share, but they do so within the conventions of Renaissance marriage. You and I, however, read what they say from a perch in our own culture, with its many marital and nonmarital and extramarital possibilities, all challenging the traditional limits on relations between the sexes. Where Shakespeare's lovers proceeded in their own day to a sure and socially structured Renaissance conclusion, now I feel they are opening up all kinds of twentieth-century uncertainties without, naturally, saying much about them. In particular, Hermia's dream images the tension between possessiveness and distance and the – to me at least – unknown way trust will resolve that tension.

Often, I think, we Shakespeareans teach Shakespeare as though we were ourselves unaffected by any of the changes in the relations between men and women that have happened since the days of Queen Elizabeth or A.C. Bradley. We are reading Shakespeare's romantic comedies in the middle of a sexual revolution. It would make sense to come to grips with the way our own feelings about that revolution shape our perception of episodes like Hermia's dream (or, even more drastically, Kate's anti-feminist speech at the end of *The Taming of the Shrew*). That assertion of ourselves is the new direction psychoanalytic literary criticism has begun to take.[9]

In acknowledging my role in bringing these twentieth-century issues to this comedy of 1594, I am discovering through Hermia's dream how I am unconsciously or half-consciously possessive, even though I consciously aspire to an ethic of mutual trust. More generally, I am discovering that Hermia's dream takes its life not from some fictitious dreamer, but from my own concern with relations between men and women in my own time and my own hopes for those relations. I read Hermia's dream as an emblem of two human problems. One is an American problem of the 1970s and 1980s. Can one separate love from trust? The other is a universal human question: how can we establish trust with another being whom we partly trust and partly mistrust? Reading Hermia's dream this way, I – or you and I, if you will go along with me – can go beyond the earlier relationships with literature that psychoanalysis made possible.

At first we treated the unconscious processes in literary characters as though they were fact, not fiction, happening 'out there', separate from us dispassionate observers. Then we set the character into an ego process embodied in the play as a whole. We began to acknowledge that we were included in that process, too, as we lent ourselves to the play. Now we have begun to make explicit the self-discovery that was only implicit and silent in those two earlier methods.

We can learn how each of us gives life to Shakespeare's imaginings 'out there' through our own times and lives, our wishes and fears and defenses 'in here'. Through psychoanalytic identity theory, we can understand how we are able to talk about the words of another through ourselves and, in doing so, talk about ourselves through the words of another – even if they are as airy a nothing as dream of dream of dream. When we do, we each continue Shakespeare's achievement in and through ourselves. Just as self and object constitute each other in human development, so in the literary transaction the reader constitutes text so that text may constitute its reader. In this mutuality, Hermia's dream is not simply a dream dreamed for us. Rather, we dream her dream for ourselves, and as we know ourselves so we know the dream, until its local habitation is here and its name is us.

Notes

1. Erik H. Erikson, 'The Dream Specimen of Psychoanalysis', in *Psychoanalytic Psychiatry and Psychology: Clinical and Theoretical Papers, Austen Riggs Center*, ed. R.F. Knight and C.R. Friedman (New York: International University Press, 1954), pp. 131–70, 144–5.

2. For a more elaborate example of this method, see Norman N. Holland, 'A Touching of Literary and Psychiatric Education', *Seminars in Psychiatry* 5 (1973), 287–99.

3. H. Kohut, *The Analysis of the Self: A Systematic Approach to the Psychoanalytic Treatment of Narcissistic Personality Disorders* (New York: International University Press, 1971), p. xiv–xv and *passim*.

4. Most Shakespeareans regard Hermia and Helena as interchangeable, except for height and hair colour (III, ii, 290ff. and II, ii, 114). Reading their 'sides', however, though, as an actress would (see note 2 above), I detect a characterological difference. As in the text, Hermia speaks and acts through

'amendment by alternative' (to compress her identity into a theme). Helena tries to cope (I think) by establishing a contradiction or opposition and then seeking to become that opposite. See, for example, her speeches in I, i: 'Call you me fair? That fair again unsay', and 'O that your frowns would teach my smiles such skill'. She would give everything, she tells her rival Hermia, 'to be you translated'. And she adds: 'How happy some o'er other some can be'. All these lead to her explication of the emblem of Cupid in terms of reversals, and her decision at the end of the scene to convert Demetrius' pursuit of Hermia in the wood to his presence with herself. Compare her last words in the play, 'And Hippolyta' (Theseus's opposite) to Hermia's, 'and my father' (Theseus's parallel).

5. See the similar juxtaposition of lion and snake threatening a sleeper in *AYL* IV, iii, 106–18.

6. LA ROCHEFOUCAULD, *Maximes*, ed. F.C. Green (Cambridge: Cambridge University Press, 1946), maxime 583, p. 138 (my translation).

7. JAN KOTT, *Shakespeare our Contemporary*, trans. B. Taborski (Garden City: Doubleday, 1964), pp. 210–16.

8. NORMAN RABKIN, *Shakespeare and the Common Understanding* (New York: Free Press, 1967), p. 74; see also pp. 201–5 and 234n.

9. For a particularly fine example of this new mode, applied to a number of Shakespearean plays, see MURRAY SCHWARTZ, 'Shakespeare through Contemporary Psychoanalysis', in Schwartz and Kahn, pp. 21–32.

HELEN GOLDING ' "The story of the night told over": D.W. Winnicott's Theory of Play and A Midsummer Night's Dream'*

I Interpretation, object relations, transference

A psychoanalytic reading of a literary text raises endless, perhaps finally unanswerable questions as to the validity and status of its methodology. A protracted examination of these questions is beyond the scope of this study: the reading itself must validate or find against the approach taken. Yet these questions must at least be acknowledged; since psychoanalytic doctrines are so diverse it may be helpful to state the particular orientation from which the exploration proceeds. It must also be stressed that the argument is heuristic rather than dogmatic, for psychoanalysis is itself such a speculative business that its connection with literature must necessarily be made tentatively. The problems facing anyone trying to understand such a connection are three-fold; they concern the nature, location and philosophical status of psychoanalytic literary criticism.

---

* Reprinted from *Ideas and Production* 8 (1988) 'Drama in theory and performance' edited by Edward E. Esche.

Some of Freud's applications of psychoanalysis to works of art[1] are properly dismissed by critics as outmoded, but his capacity for bold speculation remains admirable. We in our sophistication, reading in the late twentieth century, some time since threw out the notion of the authorial voice in the text: hence any attempt to psychoanalyse the author is futile, and more heinously, naive. Similarly, playing spot-the-neurosis in fictional characters has rightly been scorned as at worst, philosophically untenable, or at best tautological. So at what point can psychoanalysis and literature illuminate one another? Peter Brooks argues for the text itself as the only proper object of literary –psychoanalytic study.[2] He identifies the transference relationship as the means whereby a textual, rhetorical psychoanalytic criticism can be illuminating of both literature and psychoanalysis.

'Transference' is the term applied to the peculiar quality of the relationship which exists between patient and analyst. By projecting onto the analyst elements of figures from the past life, the patient transfers entrenched and unconscious patterns and expectations into the present relationship with the analyst. In the context of this restaging, their particular nature becomes apparent and they are uniquely accessible to interpretation, understanding and acceptance, or modification. The patient at various times may treat the analyst as father, mother or sibling, which reveals the nature of the relationship with the introjection of these figures. Transference is made possible through the deliberate withdrawal by the analyst of the usual demands in a one-to-one relationship for attention and recognition of oneself. In the early days of psychoanalysis, Freud treated the phenomena of projection and transference as a hindrance, but came to realise that they are crucial to the success of the analysis.

Brooks's thesis takes further the model of literature as transference proposed, but ultimately relegated to the sphere of fantasy, by Meredith Anne Skura,[3] and the approach he advocates actually has more in common with her controlling model of literature as psychoanalytic process, because of the degree to which the transference dictates what happens. Fantasy should not be understood as 'mere' regression, but as an alternative way of apprehending experience: 'fantasy provides a dynamic model of intratextual temporal relations and of their organization according to the plot of wish, or desire. We might thus gain a certain understanding of the interplay of form and desire.'[4] It is the understanding of literature and transference by means of one another that leads on to the work of the British psychoanalyst and child psychiatrist, Donald Winnicott (1896–1971).

Winnicott's most original contribution to psychoanalytic thought was in the sphere of pre-Oedipal development and object relations theory, building on the work of Melanie Klein and Ronald Fairbairn. Classical psychoanalysis is an instinct theory: it identifies satisfaction of instinctual drive, or libido, as the earliest and primary aim of the psyche. Object relations theory by contrast assumes that relationship (that is, emotional contact with a real object) is what the psyche seeks above all for its development and well-being. The two theories are not wholly discrete, insofar as instinctual drive always requires an object, and an object can only have value for a subject with a drive to relate to it. However, the distinction has various implications in which a difference is apparent. For example, instinct theory holds that an infant is at the beginning entirely narcissistic and pleasure-seeking, and only develops a capacity to relate to objects through ego development at the Oedipal phase, while object theory maintains that the infant's capacity to relate is innate, and that it is born into relationship with the mother.

The transference relationship is real and not-real; it is a phenomenon in the present life of patient and analyst, yet it draws its power and peculiar character from the past, and exists to facilitate the future. In certain ways it defies the usual temporal constraints upon relationship, yet is also rigorously contained within the analytic hour: an hour which is figuratively and literally a space as well as a time. This seemingly rigid structure paradoxically allows a loosening of psychic set to occur, and a playing around with ideas of past, present and, eventually, the future. The nature of a transference relationship and its healing potential emerge not so much in what is said, but more in how it is said and in the act of saying at all. Winnicott described a potential space, in the first instance between the mother and the baby, where play can begin to happen: play which fosters the development of the capacity to live in creative rather than merely compliant relation to the world. At the beginning of life the infant is not capable of conceptualizing and differentiating 'me' and 'not-me', nor has it the capacity for objective perception. It requires almost complete adaptation by its mother, whom it cannot distinguish from itself. Winnicott did not think maternal perfection possible or even desirable as an aspiration. In his terms a 'good-enough' mother is one who adapts almost entirely to her baby's needs at the beginning, thereby allowing the infant to experience the illusion of creating the world that meets its demands. As time passes the mother must progressively fail to adapt to just the degree which enables the child to begin to experience external reality in manageable amounts. Without the initial illusory experience of 'creating' the breast, the infant cannot move from her to relationship with an objective world. Part of this development is effected by the opening up of a potential space between the mother and the infant in which the child begins to play, at first with a transitional object, because this allows the child to be united with the mother in her absence, or to be alone in her presence. He suggests that the basis for the capacity to be alone is the experience of being alone *in the presence of someone*.[5]

The transitional object is a concrete external symbol of its 'transition from a state of being merged with the mother to a state of being in relation to the mother as something outside and separate'.[6] By extension, because play happens in a potential space, the infant can be both joined with and separated from the world of objects. The relationship between objective perception and subjective conception is one that continues to concern us throughout our lives, and in order to maintain our capacity for creative rather than reactive living in later life, we fill this potential space with cultural experience.

This potential space seems to share certain features and enabling possibilities with the transference relationship, and also with the text of *A Midsummer Night's Dream*. Shakespeare's play is ostensibly about romantic love and the obstacles encountered in its development towards mature and satisfying expression. The text metaphorically opens up space after space, all of them potential spaces within the provisional space of the theatre. The uncertainty of this arena is made explicit in Puck's closing speech, when the audience is directly addressed as audience for the first time:

If we shadows have offended
Think but this and all is mended,
That you have but slumbered here
While these visions did appear.

(V, i, 409–12)

So an examination of the temporal–spatial relations of the text may actually reveal as much of its significance as the play content.

There is yet the question of whether it is erroneous and unhelpfully idealist to apply Freudian values and concepts to English literature of the Renaissance. History is what we make of what happened rather than what did happen, but it is one of the ways (and these ways include psychoanalysis and literature) in which we know and give ourselves form as human subjects. Just as psychoanalysis cannot make a person what he has not the potential to become, psychoanalytic insight into the work of Shakespeare need not be judged as superimposing something wholly extraneous. It is the business of making explicit the implicit, describable in psychoanalytic terms because these are what we have at our disposal in our own period. This is perhaps particularly relevant to the study of a theatrical text, because of the peculiarities of theatre as an art form. These are well defined by Michael Bristol: his discussion is concerned with the relevance of Elizabethan cultural history to its literary texts, but the implications of his argument extend to the present, and to current consideration. Theatrical business is 'historically contingent within a specific culture, so that theater continually redefines itself in relation to other closely related social, cultural, and artistic orders'.[8] Our perceptions as audience or actors are shaped by, among other things, psychoanalytic thought, and to bring this influence as fully as possible to consciousness seems the most constructive response to it. We are probably more self-consciously aware than ever before of ourselves in relation to a text, as readers, or to plays as audience and actors. This returns us to the relevance of the transference and what we are doing when we read, enact and watch plays. It perhaps does no more violence to a Renaissance text to look at it in terms of psychoanalysis than by way of any other form of literary criticism, whose apparatus was no more part of contemporary apprehension than Freud's conceptual framework.

Finally, before turning to the text itself, I would draw attention to some of Peter Fuller's observations which have relevance to the historical moment of *A Midsummer Night's Dream*.[9] I shall not pursue all the implications but cite them as one more perspective on the question of historical validity. Bristol repudiates too facile an acceptance of the notion of development in literary form, claiming that his view imposes a false teleology.[10] Although his point is a serious one, it is surely not possible to abandon altogether the concept of historical development in artistic expression. In his account, 'The Rise of Modernism', Fuller persuasively gives this a psychoanalytic gloss, which, as it treats the development from the mediaeval period to the Renaissance in terms of object relations theory, leads on naturally enough to a discussion of Winnicott and *A Midsummer Night's Dream*.[11] The change between mediaeval and Renaissance art can be characterised in grossly general terms as a move from two-dimensional, stylised and ornate symbolism to a greater naturalism, consciousness of perspective and three-dimensional representation. In the theatrical arts, the allegorical figuration and theological themes of miracle and mystery plays gave way to drama of humanly-centred conflict. This increasingly human focus ranged widely from the most publicly political sphere to familial intimacy and commanded a style of representation which in its apparent realism required the new term *personation*.[12] A historical account of this movement would refer to the revival of classical learning and the humanities, the new scientific discoveries. In very broad terms this led to an increased secularization of human constitution. It was not that classical themes and motifs were a wholly new discovery: interest in them is discernible in mediaeval art, expressed in its own particular idiom. Rather, what changed in the Renaissance, and increased as the span of time lengthened from classical times, was the awareness of its attitudes and their expression as something to be reconsidered and consciously reintegrated into the Christian tradition bequeathed by the Middle Ages. Divine creator and providential plan continued to hold sway through the Renaissance, but human agency assumed more prominence, as did the increasingly tensioned nature of the human–divine relationship.

The psychoanalytic view that Fuller brings to bear does not replace, but complements the historical account, opening a broader field of vision. He describes mediaeval stylization as not merely symbolic of the disconnection of spiritual subjects from the material world, but rather as an expression of the real world as experienced by mediaeval consciousness, which was 'much more mixed up with [its] objects than were painters of the Renaissance [and] made much less distinction between internal and external space'.[13]

The conventions of the Renaissance – perspective, outline and the third dimension, and in drama a certain realism albeit highly self-conscious – can thus be read in terms of the growing recognition of space and distance between self and object, of separateness within relationship which Winnicott describes as part of the development of the healthy infant towards individuality. My purpose in quoting Fuller was two-fold: to exemplify how psychoanalysis is compatible with other narrative accounts, and to indicate the general relevance of the work of Winnicott to the art of the Renaissance. The worth of the connection made must be tested in a reading of *A Midsummer Night's Dream* itself.

II Psychoanalysis in the text

In watching a play at all we engage in something like the transference. We suspend the rules of quotidian relationship and enter the space of the theatre, real and not-real, where we can meet via one another as actors and audience the elusive sense of the other in the text. By cooperation with it, in re-working, re-interpretation, our reality is changed. The words are written, immutable marks on the page, just as the events of the past are unchangeable: what changes, through performance or transference, is their present discourse. What happens to us is what Hippolyta describes in response to the lovers:

> But all the story of the night told over,
> And all their minds transfigur'd so together,
> More witnesseth than fancy's images
> And grows to something of great constancy;
> But howsoever, strange and admirable.
>
> (V, ii, 23–7)

A 'telling over' is what audience and actors have been participating in during their night in the theatre, and the enabling, transfiguring power of this is acknowledged along with the finally mysterious nature of the process.

These lines are a response to Theseus's comment on the power of imagination, and it affords a moment aside, a brief retrospective on the process. A closer examination of elements of the first scene may elucidate some of the workings of this activity. From the very beginning our playful collaboration is enlisted, in the opening exchange between Theseus and Hippolyta. Their 'nuptial hour' is signalled as the resolution towards which we will proceed through the delays of the play, our reward being the delays as much as the resolution. We are told that four days of stage time will pass in the three hours or so of 'real' time, but we are in fact doubly challenged on entering this play world, as the stage time before the nuptials is actually only two nights, not four. Yet the play is coherent: thus we have involuntarily to relax our usual notions of temporality and the meaning obtaining to them. Furthermore, Theseus experiences four days passing as slowly and tediously, Hippolyta as quickly, which alerts us to their possibly different levels of desire. That they both invoke the moon in such entirely different terms, as a 'step-dame or a dowager' and 'a silver bow new bent in heaven' reinforces this difference. Throughout the text references to the moon, metaphors around it, and the fact that a large part of the drama is enacted by moonlight plays with the concept of the external concrete world and the tenuous nature of our objective relationship to it. The moon is a phenomenon of the externally observable world, but so notoriously mutable that it has become symbolic of fluctuation. It is another reminder to the audience of its own implication in the reconstruction: the travail of the mechanicals to bring the moonlight into a chamber makes us reflect on the whole play's doing precisely this.

It is from such textual pointers, in metaphor and temporal–spatial constructions, that we infer the transference and perform our reconstructive work. Similarly in one moment of real time, Theseus links past and future with his moment of fantasy in the play's present:

> Hippolyta, I woo'd thee with my sword,
> And won thy love doing thee injuries;
> But I will wed thee in another key,
> With pomp, with triumph and with revelling.

> (I, i, 16–19)

This is how the illusion of a space for meaning within real theatre-going time is created. It is also how the intermediate space of the transference is opened, between neurosis and psychic health, which facilitates the passage from the one to the other. It has its own reality, but its provisional 'as-if' quality is an essential part of that reality. Egeus also shapes the fantasy of reworking the past in the present moment of the text, wishing but in fact unable to blot out, to repress what has happened

in the violence of 'As she is mine I may dispose of her' (l. 42). The
shaping power of relationship is forcefully suggested by Theseus's rather
ghastly metaphor of Hermia's father as one

> To whom you are but as a form in wax
> By him imprinted, and within his power
> To leave the figure, or disfigure it.
>
> (49–51)

Many sons and daughters must have learnt via the release afforded by
the transference what they could not learn in any other way: how true in
another sense this has been when their present behaviour and perception
is constrained by the relationship with the past introjected father. The
temporal injunction imposed on Hermia, again in terms of the moon,
emphasizes the doubts already set up in the tension between Theseus and
Hippolyta's differing construction on this same space of time, and it taints
their projected relationship by association:

> Take time to pause; and by the next new moon,
> The sealing-day betwixt my love and me
> For everlasting bond of fellowship,
> Upon that day either prepare to die
> For disobedience to your father's will,
> Or else to wed Demetrius, as he would,
> Or on Diana's altar to protest,
> For aye, austerity and single life.
>
> (83–90)

The stichomythic exchange between Hermia and Lysander (II, 135–40)
is another textual representation of the work of the transference: they look
back, repeat, reconstruct, telling over where things have gone wrong,
hoping for a different outcome. The other example of stichomythia in this
scene (II, 194–201) performs a related function, as Hermia and Helena
struggle with and try to re-work in their own terms concepts such as love,
hate, fault, folly and the meaning of the oppositions smiling and
frowning, praying and cursing. Hermia's words following on her earlier
stichomythic exchange with Lysander counselling patience in their trial,
embody by extension the psychic truth that not without a measure of
acceptance can a trouble be resolved: just as a baby cannot be weaned
unless it has a real experience of the breast, be this a literal or metaphoric
one.

All through the play a sense of place is evoked very specifically. This is
first signalled by Lysander when he proposes the woods as the means
whereby he and Hermia can transform their troubled circumstance:

> And in the wood, a league without the town
> (Where I did meet thee once with Helena
> To do observance to a morn of May),
> There will I stay for thee.
>
> (165–8)

This idea of place as a space which enables experience to arise within it, together with the provisional and changeable quality that this entails, is taken up by Hermia:

> Before the time I did Lysander see,
> Seem'd Athens as a paradise to me.
> O then what graces in my love do dwell,
> That he hath turn'd a heaven unto a hell!
>
> (204–7)

She follows this with an even more specific invocation of past and future in terms of place:

> And in the wood, where often you and I
> Upon faint primrose beds were wont to lie,
> Emptying our bosoms of their counsel sweet,
> There my Lysander and myself shall meet....
>
> (214–17)

This kind of spatial construction permeates the play and is a crucial feature of the way in which the text is enactive of transference. It is not simply that place is continually and vividly evoked,

> I know a bank where the wild thyme blows,
> Where oxslip and the nodding violet grows ...
>
> (II, i, 249–50)

thus gaining significance from being so privileged, but powerful emotion is also textualised and worked through in terms of place, as when Titania accuses Oberon of infidelity, 'but I know/When thou hast stol'n away from fairy land' (II, i, 64–5) and then goes on to her long speech concerning the effects of their rift in which emotional discord is externalized onto their surroundings by projection. The most prominent use of textual–spatial device is the wood itself, which affords an expansion of space within the stage world: very much a potential space, as the same area is made different use of by the three different sets of characters – fairies, lovers and mechanicals. This is on one level a formal device to forward the narrative by enabling an interlocking of plot elements. But the variation of the meaning held by the wood as place for the different characters gives it some quality of the transferential space across which resolution can be achieved. This same quality characterizes the potential space posited by Winnicott and which is neither inner psychic reality nor external reality.

This much the Athenian wood shares with the Forest of Arden in *As You Like It*, and Prospero's island in *The Tempest*, and this sense of an enabling potential space was brought out in Adrian Noble's 1985 Royal Shakespeare Company production of *As You Like It*. The suggestion was made that the two worlds of court and country were not straightforwardly separate places. The banished Duke's furniture covered in dust-sheets in the first part of the play reappeared in the forest from under a much larger dust-sheet suggestive of harsh winter hardship facing the characters, and the difficulty and pain of beginning self-transformation. The furniture remained, though it mellowed with the rest of the set as the other world became a more conventionally pastoral green. A full-length mirror made all this explicit: in a doubling of the roles Duke Frederick steps through it to explore the moral implications of the character of his opposite, Duke Senior. Within this conceptual framework the illusion of diametric oppositions was exposed. The antagonistic separation of courtly from rustic life, and of men from women, was questioned, and these pairings were allowed to approach integration, or at least relationship, by means of the facilitating environment of the forest, which is neither external concrete reality nor wholly inner psychic reality. In a related manner Prospero's island is not a space that meets the expectations of mundane law: it is the space which allows reconciliation and reparation to happen, but is also informed to some extent by the dispositions of those inhabiting it.

> *Gonzalo*   How lush and lusty the grass looks! how green!
> *Antonio*   The ground, indeed, is tawny.
>
> (II, i, 51–2)

This is not to repudiate Prospero's shaping influence: the different views are not mutually exclusive.

These two plays share also with *A Midsummer Night's Dream* the spatial device of the play or masque within the play. It is a common enough feature of Renaissance drama, and in many of Shakespeare's plays there is comment or joking about theatricality, from the 'poor player,/That struts and frets his hour upon the stage' (*Macbeth*) to 'If this were played upon a stage now, I could condemn it as an improbable fiction' (*Twelfth Night*).

This self-consciousness about illusion and reality in the theatre can be viewed in more than one light. Gurr attributes such textual interplay to staging conventions before the introduction of the proscenium arch which was accomplished during the period, and when the lines between actor and audience, and between actor-as-character and actor-as-individual were less distinguishable.[14] But it can equally well be construed as drawing attention to the creative use of play-space, and to how finally the responsibility rests with actors and audience to make use of a play-text in order to realise the potential of the convention. The concentric movement in *A Midsummer Night's Dream* draws audience and actors from the theatrical space and implicates them in that of the fairy world looking in on the space of the mortal world:

> Shall we their fond pageant see?
> Lord, what fools these mortals be!
>
> (III, ii, 114–15)

Within the mortal world the lovers look in on the mechanicals' play within the play, which opens up in its ironic distancing a space from which can emerge the possibility of knowing – without being overwhelmed – how precarious the development of love and relationship can be. The laborious literal-mindedness of the mechanicals' stagecraft again allows the actors and audience of *A Midsummer Night's Dream* to play with their playing in its difference from but connection with

> A tedious brief scene of young Pyramus
> And his love Thisbe, very tragical mirth.
>
> (V, i, 56–7)

The uncertainty, the provisional nature of the theatrical space, and its creative possibilities are similarly brought home to us by the mechanicals in their use of the wood as potential space whereby to relate to external reality: the same reality of theatrical space that in fact confronts the actors playing the 'hempen homespuns':

> This green plot shall be our stage,
> this hawthorn-brake our tiring-house. . .
>
> (III, i, 3–4)

The fairies' masque performs a related task for that in effect is the generic function of the last scene of the play. Again, the masque element can be understood as a matter of fad and fashion: popular taste demanding novelty and spectacle. Court patronage, and the shift in the early seventeenth century from open, legally unconfined theatrical space to enclosed, private theatre, also favoured the convention. But its meaning is not confined to historical causation. The heightened illusion of the masque reinforces the reality, albeit symbolic reality, of the rest of the play. It presents life as an idealized moment. Agnes Latham makes a clear statement of this function in her discussion of the masque at the end of *As You Like It*:

> The emphasis on reality is particularly important at the end, when Shakespeare is anxious to clarify the relation of his fable to life as it is lived. . . . The nearer the story comes to fairy tale, the deeper the intuitive truth it conveys. At the moment when the masque formalizes it we become aware of two things simultaneously, that life *is* and *is not* like that.[15]

This is to say no less than that playing 'the play' gives us a key to the creation of meaningful experience of ourselves, our lives. The integral relationship between illusion and reality is more explicitly, more sombrely expressed in *The Tempest* as the masque breaks up:

> These our actors
> As I foretold you, were all spirits, and
> Are melted into air, into thin air:
> And, like the baseless fabric of this vision,
> The cloud-capp'd towers, the gorgeous palaces,
> The solemn temples, the great globe itself,
> Yea, all which it inherit, shall dissolve,
> And, like this insubstantial pageant faded,
> Leave not a wrack behind.
>
> (IV, i, 148–56)[16]

Latham's comment on Shakespeare's use of couplets in masque and for all supernatural phenomena is also helpful, pointing out that its very purpose is its distance from natural speech. In *A Midsummer Night's Dream* this creates a linguistic gap between the fairies and the mortals, another space which is played in by the lovers, when they are most privately besotted and, most noticeably, when they are in the depth of their entanglement in the fairy world and lapse into rhyming couplets.

Michael Bristol's article on carnival identifies some of the areas of connection between psychoanalysis and *A Midsummer Night's Dream* that I have tried to convey:

> . . . theater is a place in which a pragmatically liminal or illicit time (idleness) coincides with the illicit representation of time (juxtaposition of past and present). In the theater an audience has an experience that is an alternative to regular social discipline. . . . The actor's work is not at all like work in the ordinary sense: it is a professional liminality – play and experimentation.[17]

Psychoanalysis and literary texts are both ways in which we tell stories about ourselves, ways in which we know ourselves, our human nature, and as subjects relating to objects. This notion is explicit in Winnicott's writing, when he says

> . . . it is play that is the universal, and that belongs to health: playing facilitates growth and therefore health; playing leads into group relationships; playing can be a form of communication in psychotherapy; and lastly, psychoanalysis has been developed as a highly specialized form of playing in the service of communication with oneself and others.[18]

These connections seem to be particularly apparent in *A Midsummer Night's Dream* and must explain in some measure its enduring appeal to audiences, as we turn to it to experience ourselves playing and to be reminded of our capacity for something more than mere reactive compliance: for creative living.

Notes

I would like to acknowledge with thanks the help and encouragement of Nigel Wheale (Anglia Higher Education College, Cambridge) in the preparation of this essay.

1. Helpfully collected in *Pelican Freud Library*, vol. 14, *Art and Literature*, ed. ALBERT DICKSON (Harmondsworth: Penguin, 1985).

2. PETER BROOKS, 'The Idea of a Psychoanalytic Literary Criticism', *Critical Inquiry* 13/2, Winter 1987, *The Trial(s) of Psychoanalysis*, 334–48.

3. MEREDITH ANNE SKURA, *The Literary Use of the Psychoanalytic Process* (New Haven: Yale University Press, 1981).

4. SKURA, p. 339.

5. D.W. WINNICOTT, 'The Capacity to be Alone' in *The Maturational Process and the Facilitating Environment* (London: Hogarth Press, 1965).

6. D.W. WINNICOTT, 'Transitional Objects and Transitional Phenomena' in *Playing and Reality* (Tavistock Publications, 1971).

7. WILLIAM SHAKESPEARE, *A Midsummer Night's Dream*, ed Harold F. Brooks (London: Methuen, 1979). All subsequent references are to this edition.

8. MICHAEL BRISTOL, 'Carnival and the Institutions of Theatre in Elizabethan England', in *English Literary History* 50/4 (1983), 637.

9. PETER FULLER, *Art and Psychoanalysis* (London: Writers and Readers, 1980).

10. BRISTOL, op. cit.

11. FULLER, op. cit., p. 130.

12. For a discussion of this and other Renaissance developments in stage business, see ANDREW GURR, *The Shakespearean Stage, 1574–1642*, 2nd edn (Cambridge: Cambridge University Press, 1980).

13. FULLER, op. cit., p. 151.

14. GURR, op. cit., p. 119.

15. AGNES LATHAM, (ed.) *As You Like It*, 'Introduction' (London: Methuen, 1975), p. xxii.

16. WILLIAM SHAKESPEARE, *The Tempest*, Frank Kermode, (ed.) (London: Methuen, 1954; 6th edn with corrections, 1962).

17. BRISTOL, op. cit.

18. WINNICOTT, *Playing and Reality*, p. 48.

5 The Merchant of Venice (1596–97)

Along with *The Taming of the Shrew*, and perhaps *Measure for Measure*, *The Merchant of Venice* is the comedy that has produced the greatest critical controversy in recent years. Its popularity right to the present has unquestionably centred on the confrontation between the Jew, Shylock, and the Christian mercantile world, the Venice–Belmont alignment of Portia, Antonio and Bassanio. But how that conflict has been interpreted has varied enormously, with the different readings inevitably bringing issues of gender, class and, most especially, race starkly to the foreground. The dominant assumptions of Shakespeare's age did not include liberal attitudes to racial any more than to gender or class differences, and while twentieth-century Western societies may not be able to make great claims for racial tolerance or equality, the acceptance of racial differences has more official sanction today than in the late sixteenth century. All the more interesting, therefore, that Shakespeare's play should so easily lend itself – and not only in this, supposedly racially more sensitive, century – to readings that see Shylock as a victim, the marginalized 'other' of a rapacious, exploitative and belligerent dominant group. As Clifford Williams, who directed an interesting production for the RSC in 1965, put it in his programme notes, in Shakespeare's England a Jew was 'thought of – at worst – as a Bogeyman. In the twentieth century the Bogeyman has been infinitely multiplied: as well as Jews there are Black Men, Catholics, Communists, Yellow Men, White Men and Buddhists. The world has crazily and incredibly divided itself into camps of bogeymen.'

Recent productions have tended away from the romantic to such serious and satiric concerns – and most centre attention on Shylock rather than on the romantic story. The 1988 Phoenix Theatre production (transferred in 1989 to Broadway) starred Dustin Hoffman in a superficial but unambiguously sympathetic portrayal of Shylock. Similarly, Laurence Olivier's 1970 and (adapted for American television) 1974 productions for the National Theatre emphasized Shylock's humanity and saw the basic conflict of the play as economic, not religious. The setting was heavily materialistic Victoriana, with the (usually) incredulous bargain around which the play centres portrayed as a believable part of the rivalry of nineteenth-century capitalism. The BBC television production (1980) stars Warren Mitchell in a brilliant and sympathetic portrayal of Shylock, moving between stock comic Jewish accent and deep-seated anguish. The production brought out the play's examination of prejudice among all ethnic groups, inviting us to consider all prejudice to be wrong, regardless of its source. Suffering, as Shylock puts it, is 'the badge of all our tribe'. That observation and his question, 'Hath not a Jew eyes?' becomes applicable to all men and women.

Thus the play can be read as an appeal for tolerance of the 'other' as representing part of 'us', anticipating Prospero's (perhaps) reluctant 'this thing of darkness I acknowledge mine' in *The Tempest*. We learn the ferocity of prejudice, the way both the rational and violent protests of marginalized classes and groups are provoked and produced by the dominant forces within a society. One common reading not only sees Shylock as a victim (and his enforced conversion to Christianity as an arrogant act of triumph by the Christians), but Antonio as mean-spirited and discontented, Portia as cynically ruthless in her manipulation of the caskets as in her behaviour in the trial, and Bassanio as a superficial fortune-hunter. Such a reading makes the play highly satirical, undercutting the audience's expectations of a comic situation and ending (handsome, risk-taking hero, desirable, clever heroine, and marriage at the end) against the distasteful means by which the 'harmony' is achieved.

FRANK WHIGHAM, 'Ideology and Class Conduct in The Merchant of Venice'

There is no doubt that there is much in the play that encourages such a reading. And yet it is certainly not the dominant one in the play's history, which, as summarized by Whigham, has been that 'Bassanio becomes solvent, Portia is married to a fit mate, and Antonio is to be repaid, after which all are to live happily ever after.' According to such readings (less prevalent now than thirty years ago) Portia is not only a desirable romantic heroine, beautiful, rich and intelligent, but she represents superior moral values – friendship, trust, even (for some psychoanalytical critics) idealized mother-love, or (for some feminist critics) the strength of a woman to assert herself in what are traditional masculinist areas of commerce, law and the choice of a marriage partner. The rejection of Shylock thus becomes the justifiable expulsion of disruption and evil. An extreme, but once very common, version of this reading was to see the play asserting the triumph of specifically 'higher' Christian values. It is this reading that has made many uneasy about racism in the play, concerned about canonical texts that seem to reinforce rather than question racism. Whigham locates another, sceptical reading challenging the dominant one.

COPPÉLIA KAHN, *'The Cuckoo's Note: Male Friendship and Cuckoldry in The Merchant of Venice'*

Kahn's essay, by contrast, returns to Barber's influential view of the comedies: they centre, she argues, 'on courtship, a holiday of jokes, disguisings, songs, wordplay, and merriment of many kinds'. However, her reading connects the play to the darker fears such a reading smoothes over, focusing both on the 'psychological needs' the play satisfies, and the interconnections between male friendship and male fears that she sees the play examining. Her succinct approach, juxtaposing 'homoerotic wish' with 'heterosexual anxiety' is a sharp and useful contrast with Whigham's in both methodology and underlying assumptions about the ways texts articulate the contradictions of 'ideology' and 'personality'.

FRANK WHIGHAM, *'Ideology and Class Conduct in The Merchant of Venice'**

One of the most significant issues in *The Merchant of Venice* is the rhetorical assertion of social status. Shakespeare locates this activity in a context of social mobility and class conflict, where language and other modes of self-projection serve as both enabling and repressive forces. The styles of the Christians and of Shylock are calculated: each aims to manipulate its audience, to secure access to the society's resources of power and privilege. In each case the movements of wooing and assault constitute ideological assertion. Insofar as the play presents an examination of political or class interaction, the normative aristocratic style is not simply the medium of presentation, nor even the harmonious sign of authorial approval; it is itself a subject for scrutiny. To accept these words and actions 'in the rainbow hues of romance', as some interpreters suggest,[1] is to accept without question a mode presented for questioning, to surrender to the imperatives of the style itself.

Contemporary records attest to a widespread fascination with the uses of stylized identity as a social tool. Queen Elizabeth and Prince Hal carefully constructed public images of magnificence in order to defuse

---

* Reprinted from *Renaissance Drama* (1979), pp. 93–115.

their inheritance from problematic forebears. Othello and Sir Henry Sidney artfully purchased élite status, the former with exotic tales, the latter with a false pedigree.[2] Tamburlaine and Coriolanus declaimed their transcendent excellence. Sir Christopher Hatton, eventual lord chancellor, was accused of dancing his way to office and his queen's heart.[3] Sir Fridericke Frigoso proposed to define the ideal courtier in order 'to disgrace therefore many untowardly Asseheades, that through malapartnesse thinke to purchase them the name of a good courtier'.[4] The analyst might thus focus on the individual action, or on its representative status, or on its audience. Praise and blame for achievement or imposture, fiction or perception, were distributed according to the ideological stance of the viewer.

The Merchant of Venice anatomizes this social rhetoric through parallel focuses of inclusion and exclusion. As style reveals relation with one's equals and discrimination from one's inferiors, so the plot enacts these concepts in linear fashion. The marriage plot chronicles Bassanio's courtship of and assimilation into the élite; the trial plot depicts Shylock's critical invasion of their preserve of power. These actions are parallel, because each focuses on the promulgation of instrumental style, culminates in an interpretive trial, and results in the clarification of social identity.

I

The marriage plot takes place in a context where insecurity is held at bay by reassuring assertions of class solidity and value. In the choric dialogue of the first scene Salerio and Solanio respond to Antonio's sadness with a practiced flattery supportive of his social value, and, by reflection, their own. References to the magnificence of his tonnage overcome any sense of anxiety and vulnerability through the force of weighty dignity. Commercial and social superiority are fused:

> There [on the sea] where your argosies with portly sail,
> Like signiors and rich burghers on the flood,
> Or as it were the pageants of the sea,
> Do overpeer the petty traffickers
> That cur'sy to them (do them reverence)
> As they fly by them with their woven wings.[5]

The social imagery embodying the values of the life of commerce expresses their ideological status: material and aesthetic distinctions take on almost moral force. This accretion owes something to the Marlovian excess of Barabas's world-girdling trade empire in *The Jew of Malta*. However, the emphasis here is not on a heroic imperialism of the sea, with implications of self-determining social mobility and disrespect for established boundaries, but on the solid value of those who are impregnably dignified within those bounds. These first lines go far to suggest the world of the play, where appearances govern reality, money governs appearances, and class expectations and mystifications govern the use of money.

However, the threats of the sea question the security Salerio has invoked. He describes them in terms of social degradation (to 'see my wealthy Andrew dock'd in sand/Vailing her high top lower than her ribs/To kiss her burial', I, i, 27–9) and apocalyptic misdirection and usurpation of Antonio's luxury imports ('rocks,/Which touching but my gentle vessel's side/Would scatter all her spices on the stream,/Enrobe the roaring waters with my silks' I, i, 31–4). For Salerio thoughts of pleasurable security inescapably arouse fears for its loss; he thus voices the other of the play's twin subjects – the invasion, usurpation, or loss of security and privilege. The safety of position and wealth is continually embattled, not given but achieved, and always requiring vigilant defense. The complexity of the play's treatment of these issues is latent in the fact that the tools of assault and defense are the same – stylized assertion and its enabling force, money.

When Bassanio makes his request for funds to Antonio, his ornate style belies the humility of its content. The comparison of his 'project' of obtaining Portia's hand to Jason's search for the Golden Fleece makes his plan a quest, magnificent and dangerous (and more deserving of underwriting). The parallel with Jason has a shady side, however, since Jason and Medea were both associated with untruth and deception, and since the Golden Fleece image was frequently used to signify the goal of commercial enterprise, monetary profit.[6] Bassanio's language also has a specifically commercial vocabulary: he frequently uses such terms as 'rate', 'owe', 'hazard', 'richly', 'undervalu'd', 'worth', 'means', and 'thrift'. The intermixture of heroic and mercantile language emphasizes their relation to each other; the tonal disjunction suggests an ironic reading, since in romantic heroics financial foundations are usually suppressed as tawdry. Bassanio's request is for the 'means to hold a rival place' with the other suitors; this turns out to consist of 'rare new liveries', 'gifts of rich value', and followers with 'courteous breath'. Bassanio romanticizes in heroic terms the pragmatic web of technique, effort and self-interest which baser men work with more openly.

Antonio makes it clear that Bassanio shall have the money for friendship's sake rather than for the art of his appeal. That he should feel the need to make the appeal, and insist on delivering it in full, despite clear signs from Antonio that it is superfluous, suggests his insecurity in the friendship. Such covert alienation informs many relationships in this play. The purest expression of this occurs in Act III, where Solanio tells Salerio the rumor of the loss of Antonio's shipping. The brief conversation is mired in rhetorical cleverness:

I would she [Report] were as lying a gossip in that, as ever knapp'd ginger, or made her neighbours believe she wept for the death of a third husband: but it is true, without any slips of prolixity, or crossing the plain highway of talk, that the good Antonio, the honest Antonio; – O that I had a title good enough to keep his name company!

(III, i, 8–14)

The disjunction of style and content in the obtrusively witty conveyance of fearful rumor for their friend and patron suggests the tenuous nature of attachment and regard in this society, where tragic news is an occasion for gratuitous self-display.

In scene ii Shakespeare presents aristocratic life from another angle, the boredom of country-house life, where the only activity of interest for a daughter is speculation regarding marriage. Portia's stylized and petulant world-weariness is put in perspective by Nerissa's observation of its origin in surfeit and idleness. Her rebuke does not really register with Portia, who chafes under the curb of a dead father's will. Nerissa soothingly assigns the government of the suitors to heaven, the casket device being sacramental, the inspiration of a holy man. However, the casket device in fact functions with quite secular effectiveness to select, by stylistic tests, a man of just the right sort of awareness, ultimately reaffirming and supporting a particular class-oriented definition of value. Lawrence Stone provides an equation for the relation between money and status:

Money was the means of acquiring and retaining status, but it was not the essence of it: the acid test was the mode of life, a concept that involved many factors. Living on a private income was one, but more important was spending liberally, dressing elegantly, and entertaining lavishly. Another was having sufficient education to display a reasonable knowledge of public affairs, and to be able to perform gracefully on the dance-floor, and on horseback, in the tennis-court and the fencing-school.[7]

Shakespeare presents such items in emblematic moments and small touches, placing at the center of his plot the crucial element implicit in Stone's catalogue: the ability to judge as well as manifest style. Castiglione had stressed the import of this in general; Shakespeare creates an emblematic test conceived specifically on stylistic lines.

The emphasis on such criteria is central from the first mention of the casket device. All the suitors who are unwilling to risk their futures on such a test are shown to be, in Portia's eye, defective in style. Her mockery of them allows her to demonstrate her own impeccable credentials. Their weaknesses range from innocence of proper styling to obsessive concern with it. The Neapolitan prince seems to have been persuaded to wish himself a horse. The Country Palatine is never merry, and Monsieur le Bon is infirm of image ('every man in no man'). Falconbridge, the English baron, is ill-educated (having neither Latin, French, nor Italian) and ill-clothed, with a hodge-podge of fashions from around the world. The German, out of regard for tradition, is a drunkard. The Scottish lord fares most poorly of all, being only a mark for Portia to shoot wit-cracks at. Portia's mockeries deal primarily with external manifestations of style; as she judges others, she reveals herself.

Shakespeare's comic observation of Portia deepens into irony at the end of the scene, where the two most important suitors, Morocco and Bassanio, are brought together. Of the latter there is a bare mention, revealing at least a visual impression made on his last visit. (Here, presumably, were given the 'speechless messages' which led Bassanio's mind to 'presage thrift' (I, i, 175) in his venture.) Morocco too is considered (and condemned) in visual terms, as having 'the complexion of a devil'. Throughout the scenes with Morocco the element of complexion provides a measure of the exclusive implications of courtesy in Portia's society.

The remainder of the casket action is divided into three segments: the failures of Morocco and Arragon and the success of Bassanio. The failures provide criteria by which to examine Bassanio's success. The action of Morocco opens with his statement of defiant insecurity regarding his skin color. He dresses in white, and declares that his blood is as red as that of any blond's, asserting inner virtue over outward defect. He converts his color to a virtue by assimilating it to fierceness: 'I tell thee lady this aspect of mine/Hath fear'd the valiant' (II, i, 8–9). In this, as in many other ways, he reminds one of Tamburlaine.[8] His imagery of martial exploit and confrontation is in the style of early Elizabethan rant, which is ineffective with this young sophisticate. The world of physical action and martial valor, the natural violence of the she-bear and the lion, are all unwelcome in Belmont, legitimate only as figurative language. Morocco finds that what he sees as his 'own good parts' gain scant credit with Portia. Unlike Desdemona, she does not love the Moor for the dangers he has passed, but seems to find him something of a barbarian. (Portia is not a rebel against her culture; she is its judgemental representative.) She alludes to his color when she remarks that he stands 'as fair/As any comer [she has] look'd on yet' (II, i, 20–1). He seems, in sum, to be handicapped by his race, his lack of sophistication, and his outmoded style. The attribute of his style most relevant here is his lavish claims made for his own desert. In the early days of Elizabethan drama the non-European setting and character, presented with extensive rhetorical ornament, gave the exotic an incantatory power over Elizabethan audiences. In the courtly context, however, the imperialistic titanism of Tamburlaine is ill-adapted to purposes of wooing. In *The Merchant of Venice* the requirements for success have moved into a lower key, more civilized and guileful. A polished Bassanio may succeed where a Morocco weighted with golden attributes will fail. The conqueror no longer spins Fortune's Wheel with his hand, but plays the odds and wins with a 'system'.

Shakespeare further exposes these patterns in the scene of Morocco's choice, which sets up a major irony for the casket action. Morocco is governed by two assumptions, of his own worth and of the validity of appearance in displaying value. Like Tamburlaine he insists on correct ranking for himself: 'A golden mind stoops not to shows of dross' (II, vii, 20). He also assumes, like Tamburlaine, that the world dare not deceive him; shows of dross must contain only dross: 'Is't like that lead contains her? – 'twere damnation/To think so base a thought, it were too gross/To rib her cerecloth in the obscure grave' (II, vii, 49–51). So, of course, he chooses the best exterior, and loses. His judgement is rooted in a simpler world, with a more linear scale of value, less obscure and demanding less of one in the way of training and education. It is a world in which men are still intoxicated with the thrill of power attendant upon might, and less concerned to exercise that power within society's complexities. A more discriminating member of a more differentiated society, Portia rejoices because she is not to be allied to an image so primitive and out of place. The displacement of typical Elizabethan ethnocentrism to Italy, where one of the victims is an Englishman, emphasizes the focus on the exclusive motive itself. Portia requires one of her own sort, with whom she can share assumptions and jokes, and her father's device skilfully excludes the unfit. Virtue without appropriate external appeal has no traction in this world.

Unlike Morocco, Arragon recognizes the possible falsity of externals, yet he ignores lead. Gold he condemns as the choice of the many:

> The fool multitude that choose by show,
> Not learning more than the fond eye doth reach,
> Which pries not to th' interior, but like the martlet
> Builds in the weather on the outward wall,
> Even in the force and road of casualty.

> (II, ix, 26–30)

Here is the sense that judging by externals is risky, and that the wise man will look inward to avoid hazard. The hazard Arragon fears is to be ranked with the barbarous multitude (a class-oriented objection that never occurs to Morocco). He laments the corrupt derivation of place:

> O that ...
> 　　　　　　　　　　　clear honor
> Were purchas'd by the merit of the wearer! –
> How many then should cover that stand bare! ...
> How much low peasantry would then be gleaned
> From the true seed of honor!
>
> 　　　　　　　　　　　　　　　　(II, ix, 42–47)

The primary impact of Arragon's speculations is a stress on the disjunction between surface and inner value, and on the frequent misreadings of externals. This complication of Morocco's interpretive approach serves to heighten our awareness of the stylistic character of Bassanio's entry, which follows at once. His gifts of rich value, his retinue with courteous breath, and his resemblance to costly summer manifestly impress Portia and Nerissa, but we should be aware of the reflection of Arragon's words on this flashy entry.

Bassanio's choice of the leaden casket is the culmination of all the motifs suggested so far: by the demonstration of stylistic class affinities Bassanio wins marital bliss, a splendid fortune, and a solid class grounding. The scene is set with a series of allusions to artistic signs of harmony. They conduct a witty duet, cleverly playing variations on the Petrarchan theme of love torture, creating an effect not dissimilar to the sonnet spoken by Romeo and Juliet. As they test and reveal their verbal affinity, they establish social congruence and foreshadow a decorous love match. Each builds on the other's remarks in a fashion reminiscent of the witty games of repartee depicted in *The Book of the Courtier* or Guazzo's *The Civile Conversation*, with the same effect of mutual reinforcement.

Bassanio's meditation on his choice concerns the deceptiveness of appearance, especially ornamental appearance. He finds it in law, in religion, in assertions of valor and beauty. Of all these elements he says that 'ornament is but the guiled shore/To a most dangerous sea: the beauteous scarf/Veiling an Indian beauty (III, ii, 97–99).[9] There is no reason to question these familiar perceptions (though the racial stereotype is a revealing term for evil: he casts it as dark and non-European). However, when he concludes sententiously, 'Therefore, thou gaudy gold, Hard food for Midas, I will none of thee,/Nor none of thee thou pale and common drudge/'Tween man and man' (III, ii, 101–104), one may wonder how to take his reflections. For we can hardly forget Bassanio's borrowing from Shylock through Antonio, his rare new liveries and costly gifts, all of which, bred from Shylock's gold (as Sigurd Burckhardt notes),[10] were meant to nurture his chances for success in Belmont. Maybe

Bassanio is so unreflective as to be unaware of the irony of his words; even his meditations may be so rhetorically ordered as to preclude self-consciousness. Insofar as he may be imagined to conceive the self as a configuration of public gestures, the perception of irony may be somewhat anachronistic. He may be unconcerned with the tension between the artful form of his meditation and its moral content; aesthetic and moral perspectives often seem askew from one another in this play. Perhaps some such compartmentalization, and the instrumental utility it implies, are part of Shakespeare's point here.

Indeed, in *The Book of the Courtier* troublesome moral matters regarding deception are often suppressed or obscured by the proponents of the aestheticized personality. When lord Gasper Pallavicino, the book's chief devil's advocate, labels a certain rhetorical stratagem 'a very deceite,' Sir Fridericke Frigoso replies in defense that it is 'rather an ornament . . . than a deceite: and though it be a deceite, yet it is not to be disallowed.'[11] One might suggest here that Bassanio speaks against falsehood to disguise his own operations, but this would assume an unlikely degree of intellectual self-consciousness on the courtier's part. Perhaps we can only say that an excessive concern for the rhetorical projection of self somehow works against self-knowledge. The irony in *The Merchant of Venice* seems most explicable if placed in the gray area between deception and self-deception, rhetorical conspiracy and illusion.[12]

The actual choice of the leaden casket results logically from this meditation on the implications of appearance. Bassanio seems to act on the basis of stylistic *sententiae* derived from Castiglione. The interlocutors of *The Book of the Courtier* repeatedly enjoin us to hide art with art, to underplay our attributes in order to generate greater impact when the truth is revealed. When Bassanio decides to trust the least prepossessing casket, he assumes it promises reward by the principle of *ars celare artem*. He imputes this paradigm to the test itself; it is the intuition that constitutes passage, into marriage and membership.

Portia, chosen rightly, proceeds to wish herself, her beauty, and her money arithmetically multiplied, that 'only to stand high in [his] account,/[she] might in virtues, beauties, livings, friends/Exceed account' (III, ii, 155–7). The elaboration of this quantitative imagery belies the 'unlesson'd . . . unschool'd, unpractised' girl, whose modesty is an art of ostentation. Her surrender of self emphasizes her own value and its accompanying material benefits almost as strongly as Bassanio did in seeking her:

Myself, and what is mine, to you and yours
Is now converted. But now I was the lord
Of this fair mansion, master of my servants,
Queen o'er myself: and even now, but now,

This house, these servants, and this same myself
Are yours.

(III, ii, 166–71)

At this, Bassanio is bereft of words. He would seem to agree with Francis Osborne, who advised his son that 'as the fertilitie of the ensuing year is guessed at the height of the river Nilus, so by the greatness of a wive's portion may much of the future conjugall happiness be calculated'.[13] Bassanio becomes solvent, Portia is married to a fit mate, and Antonio is to be repaid, after which all are to live happily ever after.

To many this is an adequate reading of the entire play. The hero meets the test and wins the rich and beautiful lady who is the prize. As often happens in fairy tales, beauty, goodness, and right-feeling intelligence have been assimilated to one another; the achievement of the lady is the achievement of the comedy. However, Shakespeare has written a more complex play than this model suggests. Several matters remain to be integrated with what has gone before; some are quite critical, even subversive, of the dominant ideology articulated in the marriage plot. But criticisms are tucked safely out of sight, and we are left with what appears to be an entertaining play. (The Elizabethan political climate was hostile to playwrights who meddled with matters beyond their proper sphere. Obtrusive neatness is thus often legalistic camouflage, a sign of prohibited criticism underneath.)

When one reads *The Merchant of Venice* as a study of courteous ideology, a different sort of coherence is revealed: the trial plot, far from simply providing an antagonistic movement, *mirrors* the marriage plot. The collective rituals of language and style reaffirm the dominant ideology not only by the induction of consonant suitors, but also by the expulsion of 'malapart asseheades'. Both actions rest upon assumptions of the revelation of natural hierarchy.

II

The narrative structure of the trial plot parallels that of the casket plot in that they are both organized by the social rituals surrounding a bid for power. Bassanio and Shylock both seek power in a social context where the old feudal hierarchy is being reordered by the pressures of capitalism. Bassanio's procedure was perceived as reaffirming the model of sanctified natural hierarchy, and thus the bulwarks between the élite and its inferiors. As we have seen, however, his assertion of the natural distinction of the élite is itself positive, in the sense that it is in fact posited, created by the human powers of imagination and money. He therein implicitly represents one major version of disruptive social mobility.

Shylock represents another. Unlike Bassanio, he does not seek membership in the power-wielding class. (Indeed, his contempt for their ways matches theirs for his; both sides endorse the structure of exclusion and the self-righteous perception of élitism.) Shylock does aim at the achievement and exercise of power, and like Bassanio denies the natural status of class distinction. Shylock's overt version of positivism leads him to a disruption of the courtly ideology apparently quite unlike Bassanio's affirmations of it, but the implicit positivist threat to social rigidity is the same. Shylock is also subjected to trial, and is finally punished for his heterodox self-assertion. And just as Bassanio's reward (marriage and enrichment) is fitting to his courtly mode, Shylock's punishment and reduction to insignificance grow out of his legal and commercial mode of self-definition. This portion of the play then reveals the alternative to Bassanio's successful quest: the exclusion and baffling of the unsuccessful impostor or poacher.

The mode of Shylock's bid for power is first registered stylistically. In dealing with Bassanio and Antonio, he strives to demystify their power and prestige, to strip to essences what is romantically obscured. He takes the incantatory terms with which Solanio and Salerio sang Antonio's reputation and stands them on their feet.

> . . . His means are in supposition: he hath an argosy bound to Tripolis, another to the Indies, I understand moreover on the Rialto, he hath a third at Mexico, a fourth for England, and other ventures he hath squand'red abroad, – but ships are but boards, sailors but men, there be land-rats and water-rats, water-thieves and land-thieves, (I mean pirates), and then there is the peril of waters, winds, and rocks.
>
> (I, iii, 15–23)

Shylock's epistemology threatens their heroic self-concept (and the supremacy it implies), revealing adventure as risk, dangerously akin to weakness. The Christians prefer to control the frame of their public image, needing to be witnessed rather than inspected. Their right to power and privilege will not bear Shylock's demystifying examination.

Similarly, they are unwilling or unable to use Shylock's observations to re-examine themselves from a new perspective. This is revealed as Antonio, with the force of public morality behind him, humiliates Shylock in the marketplace for his 'Jewish' business practices: 'he rails/. . . On me, my bargains, and my well-won thrift/Which he calls interest' (I, iii, 43–6). The divergent vocabularies suggest a gap in communication, combining in Antonio's case an inability to perceive the object with a readiness to judge it. Shakespeare reveals the social impact of this communication gap in the reception of Shylock's tale of the 'scientific' manipulation of Laban's sheep.

Shylock tells the tale to justify his taking of interest. The precedent is obscure, and Antonio's overready interpretation emphasizes the rigidity of his conceptual vocabulary, under which Shylock stands condemned. Before he can even complete the tale of Jacob, Antonio demands to know 'And what of him? did he take interest?' (I, iii, 70), moving instantly to interpret in the terms of his predetermined code. Shylock responds that his example works in other terms: 'No, not take interest, not as you would say/Directly int'rest, – mark what Jacob did' (I, iii, 71–2). Antonio's reductive stock response to the obscure story makes clear that he perceives only in his own derivative vocabulary:

> This was a venture sir that Jacob serv'd for,
> A thing not in his power to bring to pass,
> But sway'd and fashion'd by the hand of heaven.
> Was this inserted to make interest good?
> Or is your gold and silver ewes and rams?

Shylock's response, 'I cannot tell, I make it breed as fast' (I, iii, 86–91), attempts to cut across the arbitrary terms of Christian philosophy to a pragmatic standard that reveals Antonio's response as predetermined and conventional. The latter is unwilling or unable to make the venture of thought required by Shylock's irony; he blatantly ignores Shylock's 'But note me signior', turning to Bassanio with a series of complacent *sententiae*:

> Mark you this Bassanio,
> The devil can cite Scripture for his purpose, –
> An evil soul producing holy witness
> Is like a villain with a smiling cheek,
> A goodly apple rotten at the heart.
> O what a goodly outside falsehood hath!
>
> (I, iii, 92–7)

These lines demonstrate Antonio's dismissive prejudgement of Shylock's Mosaic tale, which Antonio sees as an attempt to use a Christian argument. Shylock's explanation in biblical terms is seen as *prima facie* proof of falsehood, an illegitimate assumption of (Christian) image: the book is their book, and can only legitimately reveal their truths. His attempt to enlist their language in order to be taken seriously is doomed to confusion.

It is significant that Shylock is condemned in terms of having a false outside: a double attitude toward assumed surfaces is revealed here. The creation of an attractive image can be regarded as a deception when one dislikes the perpetrator, while the same sort of performance by an ally is regarded either as laudable decoration or revelation of consonance of inner and outer value. The flexibility of this attitude allows for any convenient labeling of artificial surface, from moral falsehood to aesthetic accomplishment.

The rest of the third scene, and indeed of the entire bond story, revolves around the assumption that those excluded from the élite circle of community strength are powerless to change their state or affect those within. Shylock speaks bitterly of the contradiction between their normal debasement of him and their suit to him for money, with its implicit trivialization of any resentment he might feel. When he complains of a previous humiliation, Antonio says, 'I am as like to call thee [dog] again,/ To spet on thee again, to spurn thee too' (I, iii, 125–6), inviting all the ruin he believes Shylock can offer. Shylock, more responsively aware of the ambiguity of language and experience than Antonio, conceives a revenge that is primarily a gesture that will evidence his existence as a figure of significance to those who feel safe inside the circle. The plan for revenge is couched in language whose threat is unreal to Antonio. It is more apparent to Bassanio, whose experience on the periphery has perhaps taught him more of life's unfunny jokes. Shylock's 'merry sport', like Morocco's she-bear, is so violently and barbarically alien to Antonio's world that he regards it as absurd, and therefore trivial. Shylock has clearly counted on this, and to silence Bassanio, he shows how profitless the pound of flesh is from a mercantile point of view:

> If he should break his day what should I gain
> By the exaction of the forfeiture?
> A pound of man's flesh taken from a man,
> Is not so estimable, profitable neither
> As flesh of muttons, beefs, or goats, – I say
> To buy his favour, I extend this friendship.

> (I, iii, 159–64)

By trivializing the bond in commercial terms and casting himself in the role of suitor, of 'petty trafficker', Shylock suggests his comparative insignificance and the accuracy of the flattering social model earlier proposed for Antonio. Remaining orderly and insignificant in Antonio's eyes will enable Shylock to reduce him to the status of powerless and trivial tool, to be the definer instead of the defined.

In using the law for his own purposes of dominance and self-expression, Shylock performs an act of invasion formally parallel to Bassanio's – both attempt to engineer a change in status through the use of an ideologically weighted language. Bassanio's goal is participation in the group conferring identity, and in the attendant social and financial privileges. He compels desert by the manipulation of the systems of courtesy. Shylock desires not community with but dominance over his social superiors. He wants to invert the hierarchy, using the powers of authentication himself to spite the principles of reciprocity falsely asserted by the aristocratic ideology. This he aims to accomplish by precipitating out another ideologically affiliated system – the law – from its particular social and historical context, and positing it to be objective and available for use by all. In other words, he insists, in his literalist fashion, on taking the law at its face value. He insists on accepting as authentic and natural the law's claim to universality. He sees that his hope of power and parity rests on the separation of the law from single factional affiliation. He fails in the end precisely because the law is itself an ideological expression of the imperatives of the élite. In a most literal way, the ruling ideas here are the ideas of the ruling class; the law remains finally in the sole employ of its owners. The duke (a partial judge) has striven to recall Shylock to subordination through his own positive powers, 'generously' attributing to him the 'Christian' qualities of mercy and gentleness, contrasting him with 'stubborn Turks, and Tartars never train'd/To offices of tender courtesy' (IV, i, 32–3).[14] Shylock refuses these proffered signs of social inclusion because they would return him to hierarchical submission.

His power rests on his assertion of the law's absoluteness; admission of the possibility of interpretation or compromise would return him to the realm of the contingent, and place his status in the determination of others. He insists on staying beyond their reach, refusing to justify his acts in their terms. He replies instead in language which to them is irrational, beyond the pale of intelligibility, a language of other inexplicable acts, of cats and pigs and hatred which, long denied entrance to the system of civilization, now refuses to be domesticated. Shylock is no longer bound to communicate at all, for he now sees himself as not bound to the hierarchical social body, but to the law. He is therefore not bound to confer upon them the commensurate status that conversation implies.

Shylock has engineered a figure-and-ground reversal by forcing the élite to accept the sort of diminution of identity and social stature which grows directly from their own systematic oppression. In this way he universalizes his own plight as dehumanized tool and disposable slave of order:

> You have among you many a purchas'd slave,
>   Which (like your asses, and your dogs and mules)
> You use in abject and in slavish parts,
> Because you bought them, – shall I say to you,
> Let them be free, marry them to your heirs?

Why sweat they under burthens? let their beds
Be made as soft as yours, and let their palates
Be season'd with such viands? you will answer
'The slaves are ours', – so do I answer you:
The pound of flesh which I demand of him
Is dearly bought, 'tis mine and I will have it:
If you deny me, fie upon your law!
There is no force in the decrees of Venice:
I stand for judgement, – answer, shall I have it?

(IV, i, 90–103)

At the moment of his greatest power, Shylock presses his audience to
recognize the implications of the ideology of universal harmony by
redirecting its oppressive faculties onto one of their own, thereby forcing
them to confront an example they cannot ignore. In demonstrating its
oppression of one, he reveals its oppression of many, demystifies the
universal harmony of the dominant ideology, and stops the dance. It is an
arresting moment in Elizabethan literature.

It is also very brief, for the play shifts its tone from tragicomic insight
to saturnine *deus ex machina*: ironically named Portia, the voice of
inequity[15] enters to restore the imbalance after Shylock's profound
demystification. Her famous 'quality of mercy' speech is specifically
presented as a *compulsion* ('on what compulsion must I be merciful', he
has asked); mercy itself is presented as an attribute of power. Portia also
offers Shylock apparent membership in the class establishment in return
for his assent to a vocabulary that would wash away the foundation of
his power. She argues that they are governed by a Christian rule of
mercy, and that Shylock is one of them:

Though justice be thy plea, consider this,
That in the course of justice, none of us
Should see salvation: we do pray for mercy,
And that same prayer, doth teach us all to render
The deeds of mercy.

(IV, i, 194–8)

Therefore, she reasons, 'must the Jew be merciful'. Shylock scoffs at her
concern for his salvation ('my deeds upon my head!') and insists on the
solidity of his claim at written law, rather than trust in the law his
opponents call divine. He knows they are not bound by this law, and he
cannot bind them with it either. His power is contingent upon the escape
from the positive into the putatively natural.

Bassanio sees this, and seeks to have the duke take this weapon from
Shylock by setting aside the law. But this, of course, would involve

setting aside its claim to be natural rather than positive. Shylock, as Burckhardt notes, would be forcing them to espouse publicly the mode of positivism which he shares with them, but which they deny.[16] To admit the law's flexibility would call the fictive ground of their power into question; they dare not do so, and Shylock knows it.

Portia has, of course, a prepared solution to the problem, and the way she implements it shows, as A.D. Moody observes, that her goal is not just saving Antonio, but 'putting Shylock at the mercy of his enemies'.[17] By repeated ironic demonstration of the irreducible nature of the stated law she leads Shylock to be utterly confident in it, and to reveal his murderous urge to destruction and revenge; in so doing she creates an emotional setting, ideal for his destruction.

This she accomplishes with great economy by means of two graceful strokes of positive power. First, she reveals that the objective certainty of the law, by means of which Shylock thought to bind its makers, is still subject, despite all his efforts, to creative interpretation. When she finds no mention of a jot of blood, she reveals the language of the law as infinitely interpretable, as the ongoing creation of its native speakers, who maintain their power precisely by 'ad libbing' with it. Portia discovers the necessary escape clause in the white spaces between the lines, where no strict construction is possible.

Though the reading regarding the blood is sufficient for Shylock's destruction (loss of lands and goods and – according to line 328 – life), Portia adduces a second legal weapon (Shakespeare's own creation, not in the sources) which not only renders Shylock's defeat irrevocable, but places it in an explicitly ideological perspective. It seems that any *alien* who plots against the life of a citizen loses his goods and places his life at the mercy of the duke. As W.H. Auden observes, the effect of this is to show that factional bias is built in even in law, that Shylock was excluded by definition as alien to begin with.[18]

The ideology is redeemed, and the aristocratic identity reaffirmed, through Shylock's destruction. Portia's speech on mercy functions precisely as an ideological weapon. The final driving-home of this irony is Shylock's forced conversion. Blatantly a mockery and punishment (here an alternative only to death), compulsory conversion is associated historically with confiscation of goods by the state.[19] Shylock is denied his wealth, his original means to power, which excludes him thoroughly from creative activity in the world of significance.[20] In this light the brilliance of the solution to the Shylock problem is evident even now: it still has such power to bend the perception of observers to its will as to lead some readers to say, with Nevill Coghill, that 'Shylock [has] at least been given the chance of eternal joy'!²¹ This issue of generosity is a phantom, however; Shylock has simply been rendered totally powerless in the secular world of the play (the only world there presented – real

Christian transcendent options are completely absent). He equates his impoverishment with death: 'you take my life/When you do take the means whereby I live' (IV, i, 372–3). Spiritual generosity to Shylock is in fact a guise for material generosity to Antonio, the state, and Lorenzo and Jessica. The dissonance of this ironic windfall of goods with the traditional schematic access of joy and riches in comic resolution suggests that Shakespeare began earlier than is usually thought to test the implications of genre (and the awareness of his audiences) as he later did in the 'problem comedies'. The resolution fits in letter but not in spirit, as is appropriate for its legalistic content.

Shylock's defeat concludes with one last reminder of positive power. If Shylock refuses to submit to the proposed conversion, the duke says he will withdraw the pardon just offered. The immutably natural law of Venice is shown again to be open to interpretation and revision whenever it is advantageous to its own. The trial finally crushes Shylock between the law's immutability and its fluid capacity to redefine itself at will. Shylock cannot maintain his heterodox identity; he is stamped into the mold designed for him.

III

The deflation of Shylock is the enabling event for the fifth act's generically typical articulation of harmony. The denseness of Shakespeare's resolution of the play's issues goes beyond the concerns of this essay, but certain of his uses of traditional symbols for harmony enfold and bring to summation the problem of class invasion and the ideological hedges which render it so difficult. The obtrusive references to art and the folk motif of the ring are the two chief such tools.

Lorenzo and Jessica effect a counterpoint to the actions of Bassanio and Portia which provides a context for the allusions to artful harmony. In each case an outsider enters the privileged group by means of manipulated appearance. Jessica's entry recasts Bassanio's in such a way as to reveal much more openly the strategic nature of the venture and the rewards at its end.

> She hath directed [says Lorenzo]
> How I shall take her from her father's house,
> What gold and jewels she is furnish'd with,
> What page's suit she hath in readiness.
>
> (II, iv, 29–32)

Jessica has prepared to direct and act in her own drama, the fictional status of which is appropriately offensive to her father on various

123

grounds. His mode of dealing with Christian assertions of status has been shown to be that of demystification. He objects repeatedly to the public legitimation of licensed display and disguise ('varnish'd faces') embodied in Lorenzo's masque; the creative and interpretive mode which governs the wooing plot is contemptible to him. He condemns this prominence of style as merely superficial, as 'shallow fopp'ry', under which hide the same selfish motivations belied by the élite's abstract claims to law and honor. These motivations are made quite clear during the actual 'theft' of Jessica: 'Here catch this casket, it is worth the pains', she says; 'I will make fast the doors and gild myself/ With some moe ducats, and be with you straight': 'Now, by my hood, a gentle, and no Jew', Gratiano observes; Lorenzo judges that 'true she is, as she hath prov'd herself' (II, vi, 33, 49–51, 55). Jessica proves her truth by falsehood to her father, and she is finally a more faithless Jew than he. She is true, however, to the canons of truth of the class she has joined, both in her acquisition of her financial inheritance and in her celebration with Lorenzo in Genoa, where they display their credentials by lavish spending and revelry, trading Leah's ring for a monkey. True love, exploitation and the demonstration of identity here coalesce.

They continue this demonstration in Belmont, trading classical allusions and reflexively apostrophizing the music of the spheres, praising its reduction to order of the 'wild and wanton herd'. 'The man that hath no music in himself', Lorenzo says, 'nor is not moved with concord of sweet sounds,/Is fit for treasons, stratagems, and spoils' (V, i, 83–5). Given the ideological connotations of art already established in earlier acts, Lorenzo's assimilation of himself and Jessica to the celestial harmony is suggestive. While his lines do assert Shylock's unmusical discontinuity with the romantic world of Belmont, as has often been noted, their underlying reference here is to the 'treasons, stratagems, and spoils' of the elopement of Lorenzo and his bride. The familiar redemptive force of the harmonious consciousness is questioned here. The imagination is turned to competitive uses, the 'concord of sweet sounds' is chiefly a stratagem, and the spoils accrue to those who artfully elevate private urges to the status of universal harmony. The comic decorum of Act V is achieved with many of the same tools of poetic assertion which make the endings of happier plays glow with warmth and love, but their earlier use for gain, and to maim Shylock, render their full credibility suspect in this play. The mythic glow of the final circle's inclusiveness is founded upon the suppressed factional benefit of its exclusions.

The ring motif with which the play ends makes this concrete. In the first place, it presents the resolution of the trial (in the destruction of Shylock) as a comic matter for the Christians, in the risible as well as beneficent sense. Portia had always found it so, laughing from the start in Act III about the fun she and Nerissa should have at their play-acting. During the trial there are repeated comic asides and ironies, and after Shylock is expelled Portia institutes the practical joke of taking the rings as payment. Auden has noted in his analysis of Iago, another Venetian, how the practical joke depends on the contemptuous objectification of its victim.[22] This principle underlies Iago's destruction of Othello, and Portia's defeat of Shylock in this play. Her game with the ring echoes the trial in a comic key, judging Bassanio's transgression to be insignificant and including the victim in the final mutuality. The risk of the loss of community emphasizes its value: the social fabric is intentionally torn and then re-established by the revelation of the threat's ludic status. The strategy is similar to the use made of Shylock: the threat is made ludicrous (as Gratiano's graceless laughter shows), and the shared joke again confirms the group's identity.

The play closes on a final note of joking anxiety combining the major themes of sharing and exclusion: 'Well, while I live, I'll fear no other thing/So sore, as keeping safe Nerissa's ring' (V, i, 306–7). The comedy ends not with the departure for a wedding, since that has already taken place, but with an anticipation of future anxiety. The obsessive Elizabethan cuckoldry joke was founded on both fear of and delight in the burglar. Here its application to the play's themes of inclusion and exclusion, invitation and invasion, wooing and assault, allows Shakespeare to synthesize the erotic and class-oriented aspects of his purposes in one image. The fascination with cuckoldry seems to have arisen from the conjunction not primarily of sexes, but of classes: the typical cuckold is bourgeois, his burglar a socially elevated or pretentious rake. If in this play the lower enters through the front door, and gains rank and status as well as sex, he still partakes of the scheming trickster. He must still pick Portia's locks with the keys of courtesy, while Lorenzo, his masked *alter ego*, steals daughter, stones and ducats alike. Both circumvent the safeguards of possessive old men. Gratiano, Bassanio's most figural alternate, is most given to blunt signals; his itch and his fear, on the way to the marriage bed, close the play with a carefully infolded emblem of these major themes of class interaction. For, as Kenneth Burke suggests, 'the relations between classes are like the ways of courtship, rape, seduction, jilting, prostitution, promiscuity, with variants of sadistic torture or masochistic invitation to mistreatment'.[23] If the audience delights in the cuckoldry joke, if the climber, the social second-storey man, cannot think of enjoying his bride without crossing himself with the talismanic invocation of the housebound husband, *The Merchant of Venice* must simply be seen to end with, and arouse in its audience, the contradictions of the socially mobile culture it reflects.

IV

Lawrence Stone provides a convenient summary of the nature and function of the dominant ideological patterns of late-sixteenth-century England. They

> ... present a picture of a fully integrated society in which stratification by title, power, wealth, talent, and culture are all in absolute harmony, and in which social mobility is consequently both undesirable and unthinkable. Reality, however, is always somewhat different.
>
> This ideological pattern and ... measures designed to freeze the social structure and emphasize the cleavages between one class and another were introduced or reinforced at a time when in fact families were moving up and down in the social and economic scale at a faster rate than at any time before the nineteenth and twentieth centuries. Indeed it was just this mobility which stimulated such intensive propaganda efforts.[24]

Carefully restricted social and sexual intercourse played major roles in this ideology of harmony, which presented itself as a natural model of reciprocal interaction while exploiting the less artful. Despite his investment in the discrimination of hierarchy, Castiglione provided 'conventions of enrichment and fantasy'[25] both to those who would freeze the class structure and to those who would invade its upper reaches from below. At the same time Elizabethan jurists were energetically elaborating a legal system which came increasingly to be used as a major weapon in the war between those who sought and those who denied. The outcry against law-mongering from all sides reveals its universal employment. These pursuits of power through stylistic nuance and verbal complexity had by the century's end generated profound disorder among the supposedly mutual and well-beseeming ranks of the Elizabethan polity. Yet the pursuit of status and privilege was always coated with the necessary legitimating colors – for which the justification of another charming Shakespearean thief may stand: 'Why, Hal, 'tis my vocation, Hal, 'tis no sin for a man to labour in his vocation', (*I Henry IV*, I, ii, 101–2).

Notes

1. A.R. HUMPHREYS, *Shakespeare: Mer* (London: Arnold, 1973), pp. 62–3.

2. ROGER HOWELL, *Sir Philip Sidney: The Shepherd Knight* (London: Hutchinson, 1968), p. 18.

3. NORMAN WILLIAMS, *Elizabeth I. Queen of England* (London: Collins, 1967, reprinted 1971), pp. 185–6.

4. BALDESSARE CASTIGLIONE, *The Book of the Courtier (1528)*, trans. Sir Thomas Hoby (London: Everyman, 1561, reprinted 1928), p. 29.

5. Regarding the social moralization of the sea we may also note Morocco's reference to 'the watery kingdom, whose ambitious head/Spits in the face of heaven' (II, vii, 44–5).

6. ELIZABETH S. SKLAR, 'Bassanio's Golden Fleece', *Texas Studies in Language and Literature* 18 (1976), 502–3.

7. STONE, *Crisis*, p. 50.

8. See M.C. BRADBROOK, *Shakespeare and Elizabethan Poetry* (London: Chatto and Windus, 1951), p. 175.

9. The verbal parallel with Salerio's earlier description of the threats to Antonio's luxury trade invites us to note the suggestions of danger and falsehood specifically.

10. SIGURD BURCKHARDT, '*Mer*: the Gentle Bond, In *Shakespearean Meanings* (Princeton: Princeton University Press, 1968), p. 215.

11. CASTIGLIONE, p. 132.

12. For this distinction see KENNETH BURKE, *A Rhetoric of Motives* (Berkeley: University of California Press, 1950, reprinted 1969), p. 114.

13. Quoted in STONE, *Crisis*, p. 613.

14. The function of the Duke's intervention may be unfolded by reference to an analytic statement by MAX WEBER regarding the residual presence of such behaviour in the nineteenth century, when Shylock's perception of the law (though not his use of it in *Mer*) had become normative:

'The modern capitalist concern is based inwardly above all on *Calculation*. It requires for its survival a system of justice and an administration whose workings can be *rationally calculated*, at least in principle, according to general fixed laws, just as the probable performance of a *machine* can be calculated. It is as little able to tolerate the dispensing of justice according to the judge's sense of fair play *in individual cases* or any other irrational means of principles of administering the law ... as it is able to endure a patriarchal administration that obeys the dictates of its own caprice, or sense of mercy and, for the rest, proceeds in accordance with an inviolable and sacrosanct, but irrational tradition. ... What is specific about modern capitalism as distinct from age-old capitalist forms of acquisition is that the strictly *rational organization of work* on the basis of rational technology did not come into being *anywhere* within such irrationally constituted political systems, nor could it have done so. For these modern businesses with their fixed capital and their exact calculations are much too sensitive to legal and administrative irrationalities. They could only come into being in the bureaucratic state with its rational laws where ... the judge is more or less an automatic statute-dispensing machine in which you insert the files together with the necessary costs and dues at the top, whereupon he will eject the judgement with more or less cogent reasons for it at the bottom: that is to say, where the judge's behaviour is on the whole *predictable*.

Quoted in Georg Lukacs, 'Reification and the Consciousness of the Proletariat' in *History and Class Consciousness*, trans. Rodney Livingstone (Taunton: Merlin Press, 1971), p. 96.

127

15. Regarding the discussion of equity in relation to *The Merchant of Venice*, see E.A. ANDREWS, *Law Versus Equity in Mer* (Boulder: University of Colorado Press, 1965); W. MOELWYN MERCHANT, Introduction to *Mer* (Harmondsworth: Penguin, 1967); W. NICHOLAS KNIGHT, 'Equity, *Mer*, and William Lambarde', *Shakespeare Survey* 27 (1974), 93–104.

16. BURCKHARDT, pp. 229–30.

17. A.D. MOODY, *Shakespeare, The Merchant of Venice* (London: Edwin Arnold, 1964), p. 43.

18. W.H. AUDEN, 'Brothers and Others', *The Dyer's Hand* (London: Faber and Faber, 1963), pp. 218–37.

19. See WILBUR SANDERS, 'Appendix A: Barabas and the Historical Jew of Europe', in *The Dramatist and The Received Idea* (Cambridge: Cambridge University Press, 1968).

20. It is interesting to note a sexual parallel here with the unsuccessful suitors for Portia's hand, who are forbidden to wive, to build a family. Shylock, whose loss of his bags and stones has already been mocked in implicitly sexual terms, and whose 'gentle' daughter has (been) stolen away, is here financially castrated, rendered impotent. In yet another way Bassanio and Shylock ventured for similar rewards, and ran similar risks.

21. NEVILL COGHILL, 'The Basis of Shakespearean Comedy,' *Essays and Studies* n[ew] s[eries] 3 (1950), quoted in MOODY, p. 18.

22. AUDEN, 'The Joker in the Pack', *The Dyer's Hand*, pp. 246–68.

23. BURKE, p. 115.

24. STONE, *Crisis*, p. 36.

25. HUMPHREYS, pp. 62–3.

COPPÉLIA KAHN *'The Cuckoo's Note: Male Friendship and Cuckoldry in The Merchant of Venice'**

Shakespeare's romantic comedies center on courtship, a holiday of jokes, disguisings, songs, word play, and merriment of many kinds, which culminate in marriage, the everyday institution which both inspires holiday and sets the boundaries of it. Shakespeare doesn't portray the quotidian realities of marriage in these comedies, of course. He simply lets marriage symbolize the ideal accommodation of eros with society, and the continuation of both lineage and personal identity into posterity. Yet at the same time he never fails to undercut this ideal. In *The Merchant of Venice* he goes farther than in the other comedies to imply that marriage is a state in which men and women 'atone together', as Hymen says in *As You Like It*. Rather than concluding with a wedding dance as he

---

* Reprinted from *Shakespeare's Rough Magic* edited by P. Erickson and C. Kahn.

does in *A Midsummer Night's Dream* or *Much Ado About Nothing*, a wedding masque like that in *As You Like It*, or a combination of family reunion, recognition scene, and troth plighting as in *Twelfth Night*, he ends *Merchant* with a combat of wits between men and women, a nervous flurry of accusations and denials, bawdy innuendos and threats of castration, which make up the final episode of a subplot rather than rounding off the main plot by celebrating marriage. Commonly referred to as 'the ring plot', this intrigue may seem trivial, but is actually entwined with the main courtship plot from the middle of the play, and accomplishes more than one darker purpose on which the romantic moonlight of Belmont does not fall.[1]

To begin with, Shakespeare structures the ring plot so as to parallel and contrast Antonio and Portia as rivals for Bassanio's affection, bringing out a conflict between male friendship and marriage which runs throughout his works.[2] As Janet Adelman points out in her penetrating essay on the early comedies, same-sex friendships in Shakespeare (as in the typical life cycle) are chronologically and psychologically prior to marriage. 'The complications posed by male identity and male friendship', she argues, rather than heavy fathers or irrational laws, provide the most dramatically and emotionally significant obstacles to marriage in *The Comedy of Errors*, *The Two Gentlemen of Verona*, *The Taming of the Shrew*, and *Love's Labour's Lost*.[3] In these plays, Shakespeare tends toward what Adelman calls 'magical solutions', facile twists of plot and changes of character in which the heroes are enabled to pursue friendships with other men while also contracting relationships with women, even though these relationships jeopardize or conflict with their earlier ties with men. *Merchant*, I think, is perhaps the first play in which Shakespeare avoids this kind of magical solution and gives probing attention to the conflict between the two kinds of bonds, and to the psychological needs they satisfy.

Second, the ring plot comes to rest on the idea of cuckoldry, a theme as persistent in the comedies as that of male friendship. Bonds with men precede marriage and interfere with it; cuckoldry, men fear, follows marriage and threatens it. I wish to demonstrate the interdependence of these two motifs. First, though, it may be helpful to summarize the ring plot.

Articulated in three scenes, it begins at the very moment of Portia's and Bassanio's betrothal, after he has correctly chosen the lead casket. As Portia formally surrenders lordship over her mansion, her servants, and herself to Bassanio, she gives a ring, enjoining him not to part with it. If he does, she cautions, he will bring their love to ruin and give her cause to reproach him. The next turn of the plot occurs during Shylock's trial. When there appears to be no recourse from the payment of the pound of flesh, Bassanio declares that though his wife be dear to him 'as life itself', he would sacrifice her (and his own life) to save his friend. Portia in her lawyer's robes drily remarks, 'Your wife would give you little thanks for that/If she were by to hear you make the offer' (IV, i, 28–85). Thus Shakespeare establishes a motive for the trick the wives play on their husbands: they want to teach them a lesson about the primacy of their marital obligations over obligations to their male friends. Next, the rings reappear at the end of the trial scene. When Bassanio offers the lawyer 'some remembrance' for his services, the disguised Portia asks for the ring, and persists in asking for it even when Bassanio protests,

> Good sir, this ring was given me by my wife,
> And when she put it on, she made me vow
> That I should neither sell, nor give, nor lose it.
>
> (IV, i, 437–9)

At this point, it would seem that Bassanio has passed the test his wife devised: he knows how to value her ring. A moment later, though, at Antonio's urging he gives the ring away. Finally, reunited with their husbands, Portia and Nerissa demand the rings (which, of course, they still have) as proof of fidelity. Pretending to believe that Bassanio and Gratiano gave the tokens to Venetian mistresses, while the men try to defend themselves the women threaten retaliation in the form of cuckoldry. All the while, we as audience are in on the joke, titillated, but reminded by numerous *double entendres* that the doctor and his clerk, whom Portia and Nerissa pretend to regard as fictions concocted by their guilty husbands, are in fact the two wives, who know better than anyone that their husbands are blameless.

Two complementary anxieties run through this intrigue: that men, if they are to marry, must renounce their friendships with each other – must even, perhaps, betray them; and that once they are married, their wives will betray *them*. Each anxiety constitutes a threat to the men's sense of themselves as men. In Shakespeare's psychology, men first seek to mirror themselves in a homoerotic attachment (the Antipholi in *The Comedy of Errors* offer the best example of this state) and then to confirm themselves through difference, in a bond with the opposite sex – the marital bond, which gives them exclusive possession of a woman.[4] As I have argued elsewhere, the very exclusiveness of this possession puts Shakespeare's male characters at risk; their honor, on which their identities depend so deeply, is irrevocably lost if they suffer the peculiarly galling shame of being cuckolded.[5] The double standard by which their infidelities are tolerated and women's are inexcusable conceals the liability to betrayal by women. In fact, the ring plot as a whole can be viewed as a kind of cadenza inspired by a bawdy story in a Tudor jestbook, the point of which is that the only way a jealous husband can be wholly assured of not being cuckolded is to keep his finger in his wife's 'ring'. The joke stresses both the intense fear of cuckoldry of which men are capable, and the folly of such fear.[6]

Until the trial scene, it might seem that Shakespeare is preparing for a fairy-tale conclusion, in which both Antonio's and Portia's claims on Bassanio could be satisfied. Though they are paralleled and contrasted with each other (for example, both enter the play with a sigh expressing an inexplicable sadness, Antonio puzzling 'In sooth I know not why I am so sad', and Portia declaring, 'By my troth, Nerissa, my little body is aweary of this great world'), neither the friend nor the beloved behaves competitively at first.[7] When Bassanio needs money to court Portia, Antonio's purse is his; when he needs it (as it seems at one point) to rescue Antonio, Portia's wealth is at his disposal. But when Antonio's ships fail to return and his bond with Shylock falls due, he sends a heartrending letter to Bassanio which arrives, significantly, just when he and Portia are pledging their love, and prevents them from consummating their marriage. Bassanio's two bonds of love, one with a man, the other with a woman, are thus brought into conflict. Portia immediately offers Bassanio her fortune to redeem his friend, but remarks, 'Since you are dear bought, I will love you dear' (III, ii, 312), calling attention to her generosity and his indebtedness. In contrast, Antonio's letter reads,

> Sweet Bassanio, ... all debts are clear'd between you and I, if I might but see you at my death: notwithstanding, use your pleasure, – if your love do not persuade you to come, let not my letter.

> (III, ii, 317–20)

As others have noted, the generosity of both rivals is actually an attempt 'to sink hooks of gratitude and obligation deep into the beneficiary's bowels'.[8]

At the trial, Bassanio's implicit conflict of obligations comes out in the open when, in language far more impassioned than that he used when he won Portia, he declares he would give her life for his friend's:

> Antonio, I am married to a wife
> Which is as dear to me as life itself,
> But life itself, my wife, and all the world,
> Are not with me esteem'd above thy life.
> I would lose all, ay sacrifice them all
> Here to this devil, to deliver you.

> (IV, i, 278–83)

How neatly ironic that, in successfully urging Bassanio to give away Portia's ring, Antonio actually helps her to carry out her plot against her erring husband: again, the two claims are irreconcilable, and the friend's gives place to the wife's. 'Let . . . my love withal/Be valued 'gainst your wife's commandement', pleads Antonio, making the contest perfectly explicit (IV, i, 445–46). In the final scene, Shakespeare maintains the tension between the friend's claim and the wife's until Antonio offers to pledge a pound of his flesh that his friend 'Will never more break faith'; only then does Portia drop her ruse, when Antonio offers to sacrifice himself once again. Thus Shakespeare suggests that marriage will triumph over friendship between men.

Nevertheless, it takes a strong, shrewd woman like Portia to combat the continuing appeal of such ties between men. At first, her power derives from her father; the wealth he bequeathed and the challenge he devised make her a magnet, drawing nobles from all over Europe who hazard all to win her. Though in her opening scene Portia sees herself as caught in the constraints of her father's will, Shakespeare soon makes it clear that she has a will of her own. In her merrily stinging put-downs of the suitors, wit and verbal force substitute for sexual force and prerogative – as they also do when she prompts Bassanio to choose the right casket, when she manipulates the letter of the law, and when she uses the ring to get the upper hand over her husband.

Portia's masculine disguise, however, also produces the suggestion that she is not just a clever woman, but something of a man as well.[9] For example, when Bassanio protests concerning the ring, 'No woman had it, but a civil doctor' (V, i, 210), or when Portia jokes, 'For by this ring the doctor lay with me' (V, i, 259), it is as though images of her as male and as female are superimposed. When Portia shares her plans for disguise with Nerissa, she says their husbands 'shall think we are accomplished with that we lack' (III, iv, 61–2), slyly suggesting not a complete physical transformation from female to male, but the discrete addition of a phallus to the womanly body. The line carries two implications, at least. One is that the phallus symbolizes not just masculinity *per se* but the real power to act in the world which masculinity confers. The arguments she presents as Dr Bellario would have little force if she delivered them as Portia, a lady of Belmont. Another implication is that Portia as androgyne is a fantasy figure who resolves the conflict between homoerotic and heterosexual ties, like the 'woman . . . first created' of sonnet 20, who is also 'pricked out'. As the concluding episode of the ring plot proceeds, however, the *double-entendres* about Portia's double gender become mere embellishments to the action, in which she uses her specifically female power as wife to establish her priority over Antonio and her control over Bassanio.

That power is based on the threat of cuckoldry, the other strand of

meaning woven into the ring plot. When Portia gives the ring to her
future husband, she says,

> This house, these servants, and this same myself
> Are yours, – my lord's! – I give them with this ring,
> Which when you part from, lose, or give away,
> Let it presage the ruin of your love,
> And be my vantage to exclaim on you.
>
> (III, ii, 170–4)

Portia's gift limits the generosity of her love by a stringent condition.[10]
She gives all to her bridegroom; he in turn must keep her ring, or their
love will turn to 'ruin'. This ominous note recalls another Shakespearean
love token, the handkerchief Othello gives Desdemona. He calls it a
'recognizance and pledge of love', but as he describes its history, it seems
not so much the symbol of an existing love as a charm on which the
continuation of that love magically depends. The handkerchief was first
used to 'subdue' Othello's father to his mother's love, and Othello hints
that it should have the same effect on him when he warns, in lines
reminiscent of Portia's, 'To lose, or give't away were such perdition/As
nothing else could match' (III, iv, 65–66). However, Portia's ring has less
to do with magic than with rights and obligations. Unlike Othello, she is
concerned more with 'vantage', which the *OED* defines as gain or profit,
than with some vaguer 'ruin'. She sees marriage as a contract of sexual
fidelity equally binding on both parties, for their mutual 'vantage'.

On one level, the ring obviously represents the marriage bond, as it
does in the wedding ceremony. But on another, it bears a specifically
sexual meaning alluded to in the play's final lines, spoken by Gratiano:
'Well, while I live, I'll fear no other thing/So sore as keeping safe
Nerissa's ring' (V, i, 306–7). Rings, circles, and Os are frequently, in
Shakespeare's works and elsewhere, metaphors for female sexual parts.
In the last scene, speaking to Bassanio, Portia refers to the ring as 'your
wife's first gift' (V, ii, 166), that is, her virginity. In giving Bassanio her
'ring', Portia gives him her virginity, and a husband's traditionally
exclusive sexual rights to her. In *All's Well That Ends Well*, Diana voices
the same metaphorical equation when Bertram compares his masculine
honor to the ring he wears: 'Mine honor's such a ring', she replies; 'My
chastity's the jewel of our house' (IV, ii, 45–6). When Bassanio accepts the
ring from his bride, he vows to keep it on his finger or die. Again, the
two meanings, proper and bawdy, come into play. He promises to be
faithful to his wife, and also to keep her sexuality under his control – by
keeping her 'ring' on his 'finger'.

When Bassanio's passionate outburst in the trial scene reveals the
intensity of his friendship with Antonio, Portia feels threatened, and later

retaliates with the only weapon at a wife's command: the threat of infidelity. In a turnabout of the conventional metaphor for female chastity, she declares that her supposed rival 'hath got the jewel that I love' – the ring, representing her husband's sexual favors and his fidelity. She continues with an even more unorthodox assertion of sexual equality:

I will become as liberal as you,
I'll not deny him anything I have,
No, not my body, nor my husband's bed:
Know him I shall, I am well sure of it.

(V, i, 226–9)

Refusing to honor the double standard on which the whole idea of cuckoldry depends, and refusing to overlook her husband's supposed sexual fault, she threatens to seize a comparable sexual freedom for herself. One facet of Shakespeare's genius is his perception that men don't see women as they are, but project onto them certain needs and fears instilled by our culture. He and a few other writers stand apart in being critically aware that these distorted but deeply felt conceptions of women can be distinguished from women themselves – their behavior, their feelings, their desires. From Portia's point of view, women aren't inherently fickle, as misogyny holds them to be; rather, they practice betrayal defensively, in retaliation for comparable injuries.

The ring plot culminates in fictions: though Bassanio did give Portia's ring away, in fact he wasn't unfaithful to her as she claims he was, and though she threatens revenge she clearly never intends to carry it out. This transparent fictitiousness makes the intrigue like a fantasy – a story we make up to play out urges on which we fear to act. In terms of fantasy, Bassanio does betray Portia, both by sleeping with another woman and by loving Antonio. Portia, in turn, does get back at him, by cuckolding him. At the level of fantasy, Shakespeare seems to imply that male friendship continues to compete with marriage even after the nuptial knot is tied, and that men's fears of cuckoldry may be rooted in an awareness that they deserve to be punished for failing to honor marriage vows in the spirit as well as in the letter.

René Girard has argued that the binary oppositions on which the play seems to be built – Christian versus Jew, realism versus romance, the spirit versus the letter, and so on, collapse into symmetry and reciprocity. Girard holds that, though 'The Venetians appear different from Shylock, up to a point. . . . They do not live by the law of charity, but this law is enough of a presence in their language to drive the law of revenge underground, to make this revenge almost invisible. As a result, this revenge becomes more subtle, skillful, and feline than the revenge of Shylock.'[12] By trivializing serious issues into jokes which rest on playful fictions, the ring plot serves to disguise the extent to which the Venetians do resemble Shylock. But it also articulates serious issues; in it as in the main plot, ironic similarities between Jew and Christian abound. Portia's gift to Bassanio seems innocent, like Shylock's 'merry bond', but it too is used to catch a Venetian on the hip and feed a grudge. Her vow of revenge through cuckoldry parallels Shylock's in his 'Hath not a Jew eyes?' speech: both justify revenge on the grounds that what their adversaries denounce they actually practice. Just as in the trial Portia pleads for the spirit of mercy but actually takes revenge against Shylock through the letter of the law, so her original professions of boundless love are undercut by her later desire to even the sexual score. As Shylock says, 'These be the Christian husbands!' (IV, i, 291). He was once a husband, too, and pledged his love to Leah with a ring – a pledge dishonored (so far as we know) only by his daughter when she turned Christian.

Finally, though, the ring plot emphasizes sexual differences more than it undercuts social and moral ones. It portrays a tug of war in which women and men compete – for the affections of men. Bassanio's final lines recapitulate the progression from homoerotic bonds to the marital bond ironically affirmed through cuckoldry which the action of the ring plot implies:

> Sweet doctor, you shall be my bedfellow, –
> When I am absent then lie with my wife.

> (V, i, 284–5)

Similarly, the very last lines in the play, spoken by Gratiano, voice the homoerotic wish, succeeded by the heterosexual anxiety:

> But were the day come, I should wish it dark,
> Till I were couching with the doctor's clerk.
> Well, while I live, I'll fear no other thing,
> So sore, as keeping safe Nerissa's ring.

> (V, i, 304–7)

Notes

1. NORMAN RABKIN has written perceptively about the ring plot as one of many 'signals' in *Mer* which 'create discomfort, point to centrifrugality'. See *Shakespeare and the Problem of Meaning* (Chicago: University of Chicago Press, 1981). Interesting essays on the ring plot are: MARILYN L. WILLIAMSON, 'The Ring Episode in *Mer*', *South Atlantic Quarterly* 71 (1972), 587–94; J.E. SIEMON '*Mer*: Act V as Ritual Reiteration', *Studies in Philology* 67 (1970), 201–9. For an interpretation centring on Portia's power and how the ring plot resolves its threat to male dominance, see A. PARTEN, 'Re-establishing the Sexual Order: the

Ring Episode in *Mer*', in *Women's Studies 9: Special Issue on Feminist Criticism of Shakespeare II*, ed. GAYLE GREENE and CAROLYN SWIFT (1982), 145–56. While I share her view that cuckoldry is 'a particularly disturbing spectre which is bound up with the idea of female ascendancy' (149–50), we disagree about how the ring plot represents this spectre. She holds that, by making explicit the male anxieties which cuckoldry inspires and then exposing them as '*only* a game' (150), it dispels those anxieties; I believe that by voicing them loudly, in the final scene, in lieu of conventional conclusions which celebrate marriage, the ring plot seriously undermines any comic affirmation of marriage. For a reading of the final scene as Portia's way of getting back at Antonio, see LESLIE FIEDLER, 'The Jew As Stranger', in *The Stranger in Shakespeare* (New York: Stein and Day, 1972), especially pp. 134–6.

2. Others have commented on the triangulated rivalry which the ring plot brings out. In her introduction to *Mer* in *The Riverside Shakespeare*, ed. G.B. EVANS et al. (Boston: Houghton Mifflin, 1974), ANNE BARTON notes that the ring plot is 'a test which forces Bassanio to weigh his obligations to his wife against those to his friend and to recognize the latent antagonism between them' (p. 253). LEONARD TENNENHOUSE, 'The Counterfeit Order of *Mer*', in *Representing Shakespeare: New Psychoanalytic Essays*, ed. MURRAY SCHWARTZ and COPPÉLIA KAHN (Baltimore: Johns Hopkins University Press, 1980), observes that 'This test of Bassanio's fidelity to Portia becomes, at Antonio's insistence, a test of Bassanio's love for Antonio' (p. 62). LAWRENCE W. HYMAN, 'The Rival Loves in *Mer*', *SQ* 21 (1970), 109–16, sees the main action of the play as a struggle between Portia and Antonio for Bassanio, and interprets Antonio's bond with Shylock as a metaphor for the bond of love between him and Bassanio. See also R.W. HAPGOOD, 'Portia and *Mer*: The Gentle Bond', *Modern Language Quarterly* 28 (1967), 19–32; on the ring plot, pp. 26–9. SHIRLEY N. GARNER, 'Shylock, His Stones, His Daughter, and His Ducats', *The Upstart Crow* 5 (1984), 35–49 argues that the play is structured not by a rivalry between Antonio and Portia for Bassanio's affection, but rather by a power struggle between Antonio and Shylock in which each wants to destroy the other's manliness.

3. JANET ADELMAN, 'Male Bonding in Shakespeare's Comedies', In *Shakespeare's Rough Magic: Renaissance Essays in Honor of C.L. Barber*, ed. PETER ERICKSON and COPPÉLIA KAHN (Newark: University of Delaware Press, 1985), pp. 73–103.

4. For an extensive treatment of the psychology of homoerotic bonds in Shakespeare, see PETER ERICKSON, *Patriarchal Structures in Shakespeare's Drama* (Berkeley: University of California Press, 1985). See also the interesting treatment of the theme in SHIRLEY N. GARNER, '*MSND*: "Jack shall have Jill;/ Nought shall go ill"' in *Women's Studies 9: Special Issue on Feminist Criticism of Shakespeare I* (1981), 47–64.

5. See COPPÉLIA KAHN, *Man's Estate: Masculine Identity in Shakespeare* (Berkeley: University of California Press), 1981 *passim*, but especially chapter 4.

6. The story can be found in C. WHITTINGHAM, *Tales and Quick Answers* (1530), reprinted in *Shakespeare's Jestbook* (Chiswick, 1814) p. 14.

7. There is a hint, however, that Antonio's sadness is caused by the prospect of Bassanio's marriage. When noting Antonio's mood, Gratiano comments that he is 'marvelously chang'd' (I, i, 76), and a few lines later we learn that Bassanio had earlier promised to tell him about a vow to make a 'secret pilgrimage' to a certain lady (I, i, 119–20).

8. The phrase comes from HARRY BERGER, 'Marriage and Mercifixion in *Mer*: The Casket Scene Revisited', *SQ* 32 (1981), 161, and describes what he regards as Portia's attempt to control Bassanio by giving him the ring. Regarding the secret agenda behind Antonio's generosity, see HAPGOOD, p. 261: 'Antonio is at

once too generous and too possessive. . . . He wants Bassanio to see him die for his sake'.

9. In connection with Portia's disguise as a learned doctor, see LISA JARDINE, 'Cultural Confusion and Shakespeare's learned Heroines: 'These are old paradoxes', *SQ* 38 (1987), 1–18. She argues that the ring plot exemplifies the cultural contiguity of female learnedness with socially penalized sexual knowingness, when Portia and Nerissa pretend to have cuckolded their husbands.

10. Three articles published after this one first appeared view the play in terms of gift exchange, and interpret the ring plot as an aspect of it. KAREN NEWMAN, 'Portia's Ring: Unruly Women and Structures of Exchange in *Mer*', *Shakespeare Quarterly* 38 (1987), 19–33, argues that 'Portia gives more than Bassanio can ever reciprocate, first to him, then to Antonio, and finally to Venice itself. . . . In giving more than can be reciprocated, Portia short-circuits the system of exchange and the male bonds it creates, winning her husband away from the arms of Antonio'. In substantial agreement with NEWMAN, L. ENGLE, 'Thrift is Blessing: Exchange and Explanation in *Mer*' SQ 37 (1986), 20–37, views the ring plot as the final transaction in a play structured as a chain of financial transactions, one 'which binds both men in obligation to Portia' as 'a woman triumphing over men and male systems of exchange'. R.A. SHARP, 'Gift Exchange and the Economies of Spirit in *Mer*', *Modern Philology* 83 (1986), 250–66, thinks that the passage of the ring from Portia to Bassanio, back to Portia as the 'clerk' and finally to Bassanio again 'implicates Antonio in her union with Bassanio, bringing him into the force field of their magic circle'.

11. See DAVID WILLBURN, 'Shakespeare's Nothing', in Schwartz and Kahn, and the story cited in n. 2.

12. RENÉ GIRARD, 'To Entrap the Wisest: A reading of *Mer*', in *Textual Strategies: Perspectives in Post-Structuralist Criticism*, ed. JOSUÉ A. HARARI (Ithaca: Cornell University Press, 1979), pp. 100–19.

13. LYNDA BOOSE, 'The Comic Contract and Portia's Golden Ring', *Shakespeare Studies* 20 (1987), 241–54, agrees that the play ends by questioning the marriage bond, characterizing Gratiano's speech as 'an anxiously defended hostility directed against something that has come to represent the social bond itself'. S. KLEINBERG, '*Mer*: the Homosexual as Anti-Semite in Nascent Capitalism', in *Literary Visions of Homosexuality*, ed. S. KELLOGG (New York: Haworth Press, 1983), disagrees, remarking 'the happy ending of the play is the triumph of heterosexual marriage and the promise of generation over the romantic but sterile infatuation of homoeroticism. In this competition, Shakespeare as ever is conservative'. As always, Shakespeare's text is a site of political contest.

6   Much Ado about Nothing (1598)

CAROL THOMAS NEELY *'Broken Nuptials: Much Ado about Nothing'**

Although *Much Ado about Nothing* seems to many readers to be the least romantic of Shakespeare's comedies, with little of what the traditional romantic readings see as their characteristic benevolent wish-fulfilment, it has proved enormously popular in the theatre, largely because of the exchanges between Beatrice and Benedick, who are richer, more developed and well-matched versions of Petruchio and Katherine in *The Taming of the Shrew*. While there are two love-plots, neither fulfils the fantasy expectations of the romantic pattern: Hero and Claudio are contracted in a mixture of business and sentimentality, Beatrice and Benedick seem to be manipulated into each other's arms, even though we are probably delighted that it should work out so well. A number of psychoanalytic critics have offered valuable comments upon the play, especially on the interaction of violence and love, idealization and degradation, in Claudio's attraction to and then rejection of Hero. Citing Melanie Klein, Westlund argues that he idealizes her, and in doing so, denies her sexuality. When it emerges, he feels deceived and insecure, and repudiates her.[1]

Neely's approach – representative of her important work on Shakespeare – links the psychoanalytic approach with feminism. In focusing what she terms 'the broken nuptials' that shadow the comedies, she suggests that Shakespeare brought out the intermingling of misogyny, idealization, sexual anxiety and social convention by which both men and women feel commitment as a loss of power. Such an approach points to the dark underside of a play whose appeal has usually rested on the attractiveness of Beatrice and Benedick in combination with (perhaps as articulations of) the play's seeming realism. The traditional view is that both are presented as prisoners of conventional attitudes, one masculinist and cynical, the other sophisticated and aggressive, both relying on

---

* Reprinted from *Broken Nuptials in Shakespeare* (Yale: University Press, 1985), pp. 27–57.

keeping other people at a distance. The world they inhabit – most usefully characterized as a brittle, upper-class, post-war society – has given them values dominated by a sterile, militaristic indifference, and we are delighted that they can be persuaded to look to the buried roots of emotional commitment, even with a little help from their friends. The play hints at prior involvements between the two, and so it is possible to romanticize them as two wary lovers brought to realize their 'true' natures. On such a reading, popular in the theatre, the play can be brought closer to other romantic comedies. Neely does not discount the lovers' surface attractiveness, nor their desire for independence, but focuses on the repressions of a society where gender is assigned through a series of social roles and obligations, most of which are determined by a society characterized by patriarchy and militarism, where the assumption is that nuptials are an unchallengeable ritual whereby the order of that society can be preserved. Her argument shows that other social possibilities are at work in the play.

Note

1. JOSEPH P. WESTLUND, *Shakespeare's Reparative Comedies: A Psychoanalytic View of the Middle Plays* (Chicago: University of Chicago Press, 1984), pp. 37–8.

Marriage, no one doubts, is the subject and object of Shakespeare's comedies, which ordinarily conclude with weddings celebrated, recelebrated, or consummated. But throughout these plays broken nuptials counterpoint the festive ceremonies, revealing male and female antagonisms and anxieties that impede the movement toward marriage.

Leo Salingar finds broken nuptials the distinctive feature of a number of Shakespeare's plays that have Italian *novelle* as sources.[1] I extend the implications of the expression, using it to refer to all of the parodic, unusual, or interrupted ceremonies and premature, postponed, or irregular consummations that occur in nearly every comedy from *Love's Labour's Lost*'s deferred weddings to *Measure for Measure*'s premature consummations. The centrality of the motif is reinforced by the fact that Shakespeare added broken nuptials when they are absent from his sources and altered and enlarged those he found there, imbuing them with more complex and wide-ranging functions and significance than they originally had.

The broken nuptials express a couple's anxieties and are a means of achieving the release of emotion moving toward clarification which C.L.

Barber has explored in the festive comedies. I shall argue, extending Barber's insights, that release of emotion is necessary in all of the comedies, as is some transformation of released emotion, although not precisely the sort that Barber finds characteristic of the late romances. Within the continuity of the comedies which the motif manifests, overall development is likewise apparent. In earlier comedies, irregular nuptials identify and release conflicts, engendering their resolution. In later comedies in which conflicts are severe and anxieties deeply rooted, nuptials are more severely disrupted and resolutions increasingly strained.[2]

Much Ado About Nothing contains the most clear-cut example of broken nuptials – Claudio's interruption of his wedding ceremony to accuse Hero of infidelity. Poised at the center of the comedies (7th of 13) the play looks backward to the romantic comedies and forward to the problem comedies. In the Beatrice/Benedick plot, the mutual mockery, double gulling, and Benedick's acceptance of Beatrice's command to "Kill Claudio" function, as do mockery and parody in the festive comedies, to break down resistance and release desire and affection. In the Claudio/ Hero plot, the anxieties underlying romantic love are expressed and contained by the broken nuptials, Hero's vilification and mock death, and Claudio's penitent acceptance of a substitute bride. While critics are generally in agreement that the Claudio/Hero story is the main plot and the Beatrice/Benedick story the subplot, they also concur that the subplot couple is dramatically more interesting, and psychologically more complex than the mainplot couple. Discrepancies in the sources, and tone, of the two plots have generated charges of disunity that have been countered by claims that the two are unified by one or another theme: giddiness, moral complacency, the deceptiveness of appearances. Varied, hesitant, or inadequate attempts to categorize the play also suggest that the relationship between the two plots has not been fully understood and confirm and illuminate *Much Ado's* affinities with both festive and problem comedies.[3]

The two plots are played out against a backdrop of patriarchal authority, which is protected by the extensive bawdy, especially the cuckoldry jokes, and contained by the ineffectuality of the men's exercise of power, especially when exaggerated in the Dogberry subplot. The play's lighthearted, witty bawdy expresses and mutes sexual anxieties; it turns them into a communal joke and provides comic release and relief in specific ways. It manifests sexuality as the central component of marriage and emphasizes male power and female weakness. Its clever, inventive innuendo emphasizes the anatomical 'fit' between sexes: 'Give us our swords; we have bucklers of our own' (V, ii, 19).

The bawdy persistently views sex as a male assault on women. Men 'board' (II, i, 138) women, 'put in the pikes' (V, ii, 20), and women cheerfully resign themselves to being 'made heavier . . . by the weight of a man', and 'stuff'd' (III, iv, 26, 62–3). The women counterattack by mocking the virility that threatens them: the 'blunt foils' (V, ii, 14), 'short horns' (II, i, 22), and 'fine little' wit (V, i, 161) of the men. They do not, however, see their own sexuality as a weapon. They joke about female 'lightness' (III, iv, 36, 43, 45) to warn each other against it, not to threaten men; even the term itself identifies women with weakness rather than strength.

But women's proverbial 'lightness' is also a source of power. Women fear submission to men's aggressive sexual power. Men, likewise perceiving sexuality as power over women, fear its loss through female betrayal. They defend themselves against betrayal in three ways: they deny its possibility through idealization, anticipate it through misogyny, or transform it, through the motif of cuckoldry, into an emblem of male virility. As Coppélia Kahn shows, cuckoldry is associated with virility through the horn, which symbolizes both.[4] The reiterated motif 'In time the savage bull doth bear the yoke' (I, i, 254) emphasizes the bull's potency as well as his submission to dull domestic life and inevitable cuckoldry. Similarly, to be 'horn-mad' (I, i, 262) is to be both furious with jealousy and sexually voracious; both halves of the pun imply aggressiveness. The defensive function of these jokes is especially apparent in the extended one that precedes the couples' pledge to marry. In it the scorn due the cuckold is ingeniously swallowed up in the acclaim awarded the cuckolder for his 'noble feat' by which he attains power over both the woman and the husband:

> *Claudio* Tush, fear not, man! We'll tip thy horns with gold,
> And all Europa shall rejoice at thee,
>
> (V, iv, 44–57)

All rejoice with the woman. The cuckold is crowned, the cuckolder is noble, and even the illegitimate calf will be proud of, if intimidated by, his father's virility – and may even inherit it.[5]

> *Benedick* Bull Jove, sir, had an amiable low.
> And some such strange bull leaped your father's cow
> And got a calf in that same noble feat
> Much like to you, for you have just his bleat.
>
> (V, iv, 48–51)

Here Benedick implies that Claudio, like his putative father, may become a cuckolder, and Claudio subsequently jokes that Benedick, too, may be a 'double-dealer' (V, iv, 114). Cuckoldry has thus been deftly dissociated from female power and infidelity and identified instead with masculine virility and solidarity, which are emphatically reasserted on the eve of the weddings.

Marriage and cuckoldry, both potentially threatening to male bonds and power, have become assurances of them. But male authority in the play remains lame and diffused. Leonato is a weak father; Claudio, a passive protagonist; Don John, a conventional villain. Don Pedro is potentially the most powerful man in the play by virtue of his age, rank and multiple connections with the others. But this potential remains subdued. He phrases himself out of the plots he initiates, is moved from the center of the action to the periphery, and is curtailed as a rival suitor. His illusory competition with Claudio for Hero is abruptly dropped, and what could become a courtship of Beatrice – 'Will you have me, lady', (II, i, 314) – when politely dismissed by her as a joke, is immediately abandoned in favor of the project of uniting her with Benedick. The men's rivalry evaporates, and their violence is defused. First Leonato's and Antonio's attempts to avenge Hero are comically presented, and then Benedick's challenge is laughed off.

Male power in the play also remains benign because it is blunted by its ineffectuality and rendered comic by Dogberry's parody of it. Most of the men's schemes – Pedro's to woo Hero, the Friar's to reform Claudio, Don John's and Leonato's to get revenge, Benedick's to kill Claudio, the Watch's first to 'offend no man' (III, iii, 80) and later to bring wrongdoers to justice – are botched, backfire, or fall apart. But though none of the schemes works as it is supposed to, they all achieve their goals. Dogberry's bungling attempts to arrest Borachio and Conrade on some charge or other mirror and parody the inept strategy and good luck of the other men. Whereas at the end of the church scene Beatrice and Benedick transcend melodrama and create witty romance, in the following scene (IV, i) Dogberry transform melodrama downward into farce, parodying the perversions inside the church. The arraignment precedes any examination of the evidence, malefactors and benefactors are confused with each other, and judges as well as accused have charges brought against them. When, at the end of the scene, Dogberry defends himself; he becomes a comic spokesman for his betters. He endearingly articulates the men's testy response to insults real or imagined, their reliance on conventions – of dress, rank, wit, institutions – to protect and confirm their self-importance, and the potential for assininity that goes along with their desires for swaggering and safety:

I am a wise fellow; and which is more, an officer; and which is more, a householder; and which is more, as pretty a piece of flesh as any is in Messina, and one that knows the law, go to! And a rich fellow enough,

go to! And a fellow that hath had losses; and one that hath two gowns
and everything handsome about him.

(IV, ii, 80–6)

The play's presentation of male power is further symbolized by the
sheerly linguistic invention, 'the Prince's officer Coxcomb' (IV, ii, 72),
whose denomination suggests deference and pride, elegant arrogance
and assinine folly, but also embodies comfortable security. Such security
is threatened by those outsiders who wish to usurp legitimate authority
and who are perhaps symbolized by Coxcomb's antithesis, the 'thief
Deformed': ''a has been a vile thief this seven year; 'a goes up and
down like a gentleman' (III, iii, 125–7). Yet in spite of the men's rivalry,
ineffectuality and silliness, all of the play's plot-generating deceits
and revelations are controlled by them, and it is they who fit women
with husbands. Their authority and solidarity are confirmed in the
play's conclusion, which reconciles male power and alliances with
marriage.[6]

But first conflicts disrupt both the male bonds and the two couples. The
Claudio/Hero alliance is thinly sketched as a conventional one in which
the functions of romantic idealization are made clear. Claudio protects
himself from Hero's sexuality by viewing her as a remote, idealized love
object who is not to be touched or even talked to: 'she is the sweetest lady
that ever I looked on' (I, i, 183).[7] Patriarchal marriage customs
conveniently coalesce with romantic rhetoric, enabling him to maintain
Hero as an object of social exchange and possession: 'Lady, as you are
mine, I am yours', he cautiously vows (II, i, 296).[8] He lets Don Pedro do
his wooing for him. He scarcely acknowledges Hero's sexual
attractiveness, and his only reference to his own desires seems oddly
passive and gynocentric in a play crammed with aggressively phallic
innuendo: 'But now I am returned and that war-thoughts/Have left their
places vacant, in their rooms/Came thronging soft and delicate desires,/
All prompting me how fair young Hero is' (I, i, 294–7).[9] Claudio thus
alleviates his anxieties about marriage by viewing it both as a romantic
ideal and as a conventional social arrangement that will occupy the time
between battles. Once married, he intends to go off to Aragon
immediately with Don Pedro, their companionship uninterrupted (III, ii, 3).

Hero's willingness to be the passive object of her father's negotiations,
Don Pedro's decorous wooing, and Claudio's low-keyed proposal provide
her with a parallel defense against sexuality. She is as unforthcoming as
Claudio at their first exchange, and perhaps she welcomes his silence, for
she asks Don Pedro as he begins his wooing to 'say nothing' (II, i, 83).
Her own uneasiness about sex is suggested in her unhappiness on her
wedding day, and the one bawdy innuendo that she contributes to the
banter, 'There, thou prickest her with a thistle' (III, iv, 74) is as tentative

as Claudius's allusion. Hero is the perfect object of his 'delicate' desires: modest, chaste, virtuous, silent.

The witty verbal skirmishes comprising Beatrice's and Benedick's 'merry wars' explicitly express the anxieties about loss of power through sexuality, love and marriage that lie beneath Claudio's and Hero's silent romanticism. Their verbal wars fill up the silence of the Hero/Claudio plot and reveal the fundamental asymmetry of the battle of the sexes. Benedick expressly equates loving with humiliation and loss of potency; he imagines it as a castrating torture: 'Prove that ever I lose more blood with love than I will get again with drinking, pick out mine eyes with a ballad maker's pen and hang me up at the door of the brothel house for the sign of blind Cupid' (I, i, 243–7). He likewise fears being separated from his friends by marriage and loss of status with them if he must 'sigh away Sundays' or, feminized, 'turn spit' like Hercules (I, i, 196; II, i, 244). He defends himself against a fall into love and marriage and against fears of female betrayal by distrust of women – 'I will do myself the right to trust none' (I, i, 237). Distrust, coupled with the claim that all women dote on him, allows him to profess virility without putting it to the proof. Mocking Claudio's romantic idealization, he is similarly protected by misogyny; the parallel function of the two poses is evident in Benedick's admission that, could he find an ideal woman, he would abandon the pose: 'But till all graces be in one woman, one woman shall not come into my grace' (II, iii, 27–9). As he continues his description of the ideal woman, it is clear that she, like Claudio's Hero, meets the conventional prescriptions for a suitably accomplished and submissive wife: 'Rich she shall be, that's certain; wise, or I'll none; virtuous, or I'll never cheapen her; fair, or I'll never look on her; mild, or come not near me; noble, or not I for an angel; of good discourse, an excellent musician' (II, iii, 29–33). Benedick's misogyny puts him in a position of unchallengeable power; his wit is consistently belligerent, protective and self-aggrandizing. But his bawdy incorporates, as romantic rhetoric does not, the aggressiveness and urgency of desire even while defending against it.

Instead of defensively asserting power and certainty, Beatrice's sallies often directly reveal weakness and ambivalence; her wit, in contrast to Benedick's, is consistently self-deprecating. Her mockery of marriage and men poignantly reveals her desire for both. The fear of and desire for women's roles that generate her merry mask are suggested in her description of her birth and her mother's response to it – 'No, sure, my lord, my mother cried; but then there was a star danced, and under that was I born' (II, i, 322–3) – and in Leonato's similarly paradoxical description of her – 'She hath often dreamt of unhappiness and waked herself with laughing' (II, i, 333). Her repartee, like that of the others, embodies anxiety about being unmarried, as it does about being married: 'So, by being too curst, God will send you no horns' (II, i, 23). She does not mock Hero's marriage plans as Benedick does Claudio's but only urges her to marry a man who pleases her. Hero's engagement does not engender smug self-satisfaction in her but a sense of isolation: 'Thus goes everyone in the world but I, and I am sunburnt. I may sit in a corner and cry "Heigh-ho for a husband!" ' (II, i, 306–8). Even her allusion to 'living as merry as the day is long' in heaven 'where the bachelors sit' shows her desire to continue to share equally in easy male camaraderie rather than a desire to remain single (II, i, 45–7).[10]

Beatrice's ambivalence about marriage is rooted in her fear of the social and sexual power it grants to men. Her bawdy jests manifest both her desire for Benedick and her fear of the potential control over her which her desire gives him. In the first scene it is she who quickly shifts the play's focus from Claudio's deeds of war to Benedick's deeds of love. She refers to him as 'Signior Mountanto', suggestively initiates dialogue by asking, 'Is it possible Disdain should die while she hath such food to feed it as Senior Benedick?' (I, i, 29, 117), and from behind the safety of her mask admits to Benedick (of him) – 'I would he had boarded me' (II, i, 137). But her jesting about the unsuitability of husbands with beards and those without them both mocks Benedick's beard and reveals her ambivalent attitude toward virility: 'He that hath a beard is more than a youth, and he that hath no beard is less than a man; and he that is more than a youth is not for me, and he that is less than a man, I am not for him' (II, i, 34–7). Because she is apprehensive about the social and sexual submission demanded of women in marriage and wary of men's volatile mixture of earthly frailty with arrogant authority, Beatrice does not want a husband

> Till God make men of some other metal than earth. Would it not grieve a woman to be overmastered with a piece of valiant dust? To make an account of her life to a clod of wayward marl? No, uncle, I'll none. Adam's sons are my brethren, and truly I hold it a sin to match in my kindred.
>
> (II, i, 56–61)

Neither hating nor idealizing men, she does not wish to exchange kinship with them for submission to them. Given the play's dominant metaphor of sex as a male assault, the subordination demanded of Renaissance women in marriage, and the valiant cloddishness of many of the men in the comedies, Beatrice's fear of being 'overmastered' seems judicious. But her anxieties, like Benedick's, grow out of pride and fear of risk as well as out of justified wariness.

Beatrice and Benedick, both mockers of love, cannot dispel these anxieties or admit to love without intervention. The asymmetrical gulling perpetrated by their friends (the 'only love-gods' in this play, II, i, 372) resemble the ceremonies mocking men and the attacks on female recalcitrance already examined. These garrulous deceits follow upon and displace Hero's and Claudio's silent engagement and confront anxieties there left unspoken. As male and female anxieties are different, the two deceits are contrasting. The men gently mock Benedick's witty misogyny while nurturing his ego. Their gentle ribbing of Benedick's 'contemptible spirit' is tempered with much praise of his virtues; he is proper, wise, witty and valiant 'As Hector' (II, iii, 180–7). They alleviate his fears about Beatrice's aggressiveness by a lengthy, exaggerated tale of her desperate passion for him: 'Then down upon her knees she falls, weeps, sobs, bears her heart, tears her hair, prays, curses – "O sweet Benedick! God give me patience" ' (II, iii, 148–50). The story dovetails perfectly with his fantasy that all women dote on him (and presumably it gratifies the other men to picture the disdainful Beatrice in this helpless state). The men also reassure Benedick that Beatrice is sweet and 'out of all suspicion, she is virtuous' (160–1). The gulling permits Benedick to love with his friends' approval while remaining complacently self-satisfied. Even these protective assurances of his power win from him only a grudgingly impersonal acknowledgment of his feelings: 'Love me? Why, it must be requited' (II, iii, 219). This he must justify by relying, like Claudio, on friends' confirmations of the lady's virtue and marriageability, and by viewing marriage not personally but conventionally as a social institution designed to control desire and ensure procreation: 'the world must be peopled' (236).

The women's gulling of Beatrice is utterly different in strategy and effect. They make only one unembroidered mention of Benedick's love for her, and even that is interrogative – 'But are you sure/That Benedick loves Beatrice so entirely?' (III, i, 36–7). They praise *his* virtues, not Beatrice's. Instead of treating sex with detachment, as the men do with their joke about ' "Benedick" and "Beatrice" between the sheet' (II, iii, 139), the women include an explicit, enthusiastic reference to it: 'Doth not the gentleman/ Deserve as full as fortunate a bed/As ever Beatrice shall couch upon?' (III, i, 44–6). Throughout most of the staged scene, they attack at length and with gusto Beatrice's proud wit, deflating rather than bolstering her self-esteem. The men emphasize Beatrice's love whereas the women emphasize her inability to love as a means of exorcizing it: 'She cannot love,/Nor take no shape nor project of affection,/She is so self-endeared' (54–6). Beatrice, accepting unabashedly the accuracy of these charges – 'Contempt, farewell! And maiden pride, adieu!' (109) – is released into an undefensive and personal declaration of love and of passionate submission to Benedick: 'Benedick, love on; I will requite thee,/Taming my wild heart to thy loving hand./If thou dost love, my kindness shall incite thee/To bind our loves up in a holy band' (111–14). She views marriage not as a social

inevitability but as a ritual expressing affectionate commitment.
Benedick's 'love' will be requited with 'kindness', not merely with
the production of 'kind'. And, unlike Benedick, she trusts her own
sense of his worth more than her friends' praise: 'For others say
thou dost   deserve, and I/Believe it better than reportingly'
(115–16).

The effect of the gullings is to engender parallels between the two
women and the two men and to emphasize differences between the men
and women, manifesting in this way the connections between the two
plots. Hero asserts herself for the first time during the gulling of Beatrice.
She zestfully takes the lead in the mockery, parodying Beatrice's
contemptuous wit and scorning her scorn; her vehemence perhaps reveals
some resentment of Beatrice's domination and shows her own similar
capacity for aggressiveness, realism and wit. In their next scene together
on her wedding day, Hero for the first time expresses her own
apprehensiveness about marriage by being heavy of heart and refusing to
join in the sexual banter of the other women. Like Hero, Beatrice is now
'sick' with love, and her wit is out of tune.[11] Claudio welcomes Benedick's
love-sickness even more gleefully than Hero does Beatrice's. During the
gulling, his comic descriptions of the doting Beatrice and the valiant
Benedick are caricatures of his own romantic ideals, while his description
of Beatrice dying for Benedick (II, iii, 173–7) hints at the violence, anxiety
and desire for female submission that lie beneath the romantic veneer.
Benedick in love is, like Claudio, 'sadder'; his wit is curtailed ('governed
by stops'), and he has shaved off his beard, marking his new vulnerability
(III, ii, 15, 56). Claudio, with the other men, takes advantage of him,
reiterating his tale of Beatrice's 'dying'.

The anxieties about sexuality and submission that are the source of the
men's lovesickness then erupt violently in Don John's slander. It is
ironically appropriate that, though Hero has never talked to Claudio at
all and he had 'never tempted her with word too large' (IV, i, 52), he
should immediately accept Don John's report that she 'talk[ed] with a
man out at a window' (IV, i, 308) as proof of her infidelity. Though he
does not 'see her chamber window ent'red' (III, ii, 108), this imagined act
transforms defensive idealization to vicious degradation, as will occur
later with Angelo, Troilus, Hamlet, Othello, Posthumus, and Leontes. His
former cautious, silent workshop inverted, Claudio denounces Hero at
their wedding with extravagantly lascivious, but still conventional,
rhetoric:

> Out on thee, seeming! I will write against it,
> You seem to me as Dian in her orb,
> As chaste as is the bud ere it be blown;
> But you are more intemperate in your blood

. Than Venus, or those pamp'red animals
That rage in savage sensuality.

(IV, i, 55–60)

He perverts the ceremony that had seemed to protect him and seeks from friends confirmation of her corruption, as he had formerly needed proof of her virtues.

When unanchored idealization turns to degradation here, nuptials are shattered more violently and irretrievably than in the other comedies. The possibility of future reconciliation is kept alive, however, by the Friar's scheme for Hero's mock death, by Dogberry and crew's knowledge of the truth about Don John's deceit, and by Beatrice's command to Benedick. The slander of Hero tempers Beatrice's commitment to love. But Claudio's failure of romantic faith in Hero parallels and helps to rectify Benedick's lack of romantic commitment to Beatrice. Both men, along with Hero, must risk a comic death and effect a comic transformation to affirm their love. Although only Dogberry's revelation influences the plot, the three 'deaths' function together to engender the play's comic reconciliations and festive release.

Hero's mock death, transforming the strategies of self-concealment through masking, disguise, or withdrawal practiced by women in romantic comedies, anticipates the development of the motif in later plays. The women in *Love's Labour's Lost* mask themselves, and they go into seclusion at the end; Kate plays shrew and Titania evades Oberon; Julia, Rosalind, Portia and Viola are disguised. The literal masks of Beatrice and Hero at the ball mirror their defensive facades of wit and silence. But, unlike these festive disguises, women's mock deaths do not merely parody or postpone nuptials voluntarily; they are designed by the woman and/or her confidantes to mend nuptials shattered by the men. It is now not idealization of women which must be qualified but their slander and degradation which must be reformed. The mock death is both an involuntary, passive escape from degradation and a voluntary constructive means to alter it.[12]

But in *Much Ado* the festive conclusion is not only made possible by Hero's mock death, Claudio's enforced penance, and Dogberry's apprehension of the 'benefactors' who expose the deceit. Equally important is Benedick's willingness to comply with Beatrice's command to 'Kill Claudio' (IV, i, 88). Benedick's acquiescence signals his transformation and reconciles him with Beatrice. Although the gullings bring Beatrice and Benedick to acknowledge their affections to themselves, they have not risked doing so to each other. The broken nuptials provide the impetus for this commitment. The seriousness of the occasion tempers their wit and strips away their defenses. Weeping for Hero, Beatrice expresses indirectly her vulnerability to Benedick, just as Benedick's assertion of trust in Hero expresses indirectly his love for Beatrice and leads to his direct, ungrudging expression of it: 'I do love nothing in the world so well as you' (IV, i, 267). This reciprocates Beatrice's earlier vow to 'tame her wild heart' for him. But the broken nuptials have encouraged Beatrice to be wary still; her vow is witty, and she asks for more than vows from Benedick, taking seriously his romantic promise, 'Come, bid me do anything for thee.' 'Kill Claudio', she replies (IV, i, 287–8).

Extravagant and coercive as her demand may be, Benedick's willingness to comply is a necessary antidote to the play's pervasive misogyny and a necessary rehabilitation of romance from Claudio's corruption of it.[13] Benedick's challenge to Claudio, by affirming his faith in both Hero's and Beatrice's fidelity, repudiates his former mistrust of women and breaks his bonds with the male friends who shared this attitude. Because romantic vows and postures have proved empty or unreliable – 'But manhood is melted into cursies, valor into compliment, and men are only turned into tongue, and trim ones too' (IV, i, 317–20) – they must now be validated through deeds. The deed Beatrice calls for is of a special sort. Male aggression is to be used not in war but for love, not against women but on their behalf. Beatrice calls on Benedick to become a hero of romance in order to qualify his wit and verify his commitment to her. Similar transformations are demanded by the women of other men in the comedies: the lords in *Love's Labour's Lost* must test their wit and prove their vows during a year of penance; Bassanio must relegate friendship to surety for his marriage; Orsino and Orlando are led to abandon silly poses for serious marriage vows. But while the grave estrangement of Claudio and Hero is displaced by Beatrice's and Benedick's movement into romantic love, the wits' love for each other is also protected by their commitment to the cause of Hero. Beatrice can weep for her friend as she does not weep for Benedick, and Benedick is 'engaged' simultaneously to Beatrice and on behalf of Hero.

The scene of the challenge itself also deftly intertwines two tones – the romantic and the comic – and the two plots. Although it shows the bankruptcy of Claudio's wit, it also absorbs Benedick's challenge back into a witty comic context before actual violence can disrupt this context irrevocably. Benedick, having abandoned his wit, proposes to substitute a sword for it: 'It [wit] is in my scabbard. Shall I draw it?' (V, i, 126). Seriously challenging Claudio, he refuses to join in his friend's effort to use wit to transform swords back into jests, a duel to a feast, his adversary to a dinner: 'he hath bid me to a calf's head and a capon; the which if I do not carve most curiously, say my knife's naught. Shall I not find a woodcock too?' (V, i, 154–7).[14] In fact, swordplay *is* absorbed back into wordplay when the slandering of Hero is revealed, Claudio guiltily does penance, and the challenge is dropped. Benedick's delivery of it releases him and Beatrice into the affectionate banter through which, 'too wise to woo peaceably' (V, ii, 71), they reanimate the conventions of romantic rhetoric as they did those of romantic valor: 'I will live in thy heart, die in thy lap, and be buried in thy eyes; and, moreover, I will go with thee to thy uncle's' (V, ii, 99–101). The dynamics of the Beatrice/ Benedick plot invert and counteract the dynamics of the Claudio/Hero plot. Whereas Hero must 'die' in response to Claudio's misogynistic fantasies of her corruption in order to restore his romantic attachment, Benedick must agree to kill Claudio in compliance with Beatrice's demand in order to establish the replacement of witty misogyny by romantic affection.

At the conclusion, Claudio's and Hero's pat reaffirmation of their wedding vows ignores rather than transforms the conflicts which erupted through the broken nuptials. First Claudio performs a ritualistic but impersonal penance: 'Pardon, goddess of the night,/Those that slew thy virgin knight;/For the which, with songs of woe,/Round about her tomb they go' (V, iii, 12–15). Then he asserts his faith in women by agreeing to accept a substitute bride. But his willingness to 'seize upon' any bride seems to suggest that the possessiveness and conventionality which fuel romance are not exorcised. When she unmasks, Claudio declares, 'Another Hero', and it is Don Pedro who must assert the continuity between the two Heros, one 'defiled' and destroyed, the other pure, a 'maid': 'The former Hero! Hero that is dead!' (V, iv, 62–5). But there is no sense of rebirth. Claudio and Hero give no sign of establishing a new relationship or of incorporating desire. They move mechanically back into their former roles: 'And when I lived I was your other wife/And when you loved you were my other husband' (V, iv, 61).[15] In the problem comedies, Bertram's and Angelo's repentance and acceptance of substitute brides is even less spontaneous; in them the crucial presence of two women at the endings – the one the chaste object of lust (Diana, Isabella), the other the substitute bride and enforced marriage partner (Helen, Mariana) – emphasizes the continuing division between idealization and degradation, between romance and desire, which is glossed over here.[16]

In *Much Ado*, however, Beatrice and Benedick, displacing the Claudio/ Hero plot one final time, create the festive conclusion. Disruptive elements continue to be expressed and exorcized in their bantering movement into marriage. Their refusal to love 'more than reason' or other than 'for pity' or 'in friendly recompense' (V, iv, 74–93) acknowledges wittily the fear each still has of submission and the desire each has that the other be subordinate. They are finally brought to their nuptials only by a wonderfully comic 'miracle', (91) but one not dependent on removal of disguise, recognition of other kinds, or the descent of a god. The discovery of their 'halting' sonnets signals their mutual release into the extravagance of romance and is followed by the kiss which, manifesting their mutual desire, serves as a truce in their merry wars. This kiss 'stop[s]' Beatrice's mouth as she had earlier urged Hero to 'stop' Claudio's at their engagement (V, iv, 97; II, i, 299). But while affirming mutuality in one way, the kiss ends it in another, for it silences Beatrice for the rest of the play. Similarly, other strong, articulate women are subdued at the ends of their comedies – Julia, Kate, Titania, Rosalind, Viola.[17] This kiss, then, may be seen as marking the beginning of the inequality that Beatrice feared in marriage and that is also implicit in the framing of the wedding festivities with male jokes about cuckoldry, in the re-establishment of male authority by means of these jokes, and in Benedick's control of the nuptials.

This inequality is confirmed as Benedick presides over the play's conclusion, using his wit to affirm the compatibility of manhood, friendship and marriage. Through the cuckoldry motif, Benedick has transformed a potentially humiliating submission in marriage into a proof of power. He likewise transforms the women's 'light heels' into a sign of joy, not infidelity (V, iv, 119). His final unifying gesture invites Don Pedro to join him and Claudio in marriage to alleviate his sadness, attain authority, and re-establish ties with his war companions: 'get thee a wife, get thee a wife! There is no staff more reverend than one tipped with horn' (V, iv, 122–5). Beatrice's and Benedick's sparring is transformed by the broken nuptials into romantic attachment, and Hero's mock death and the revelation of her innocence transform Claudio's degradation of her into a ritualistic penance. Throughout the comedies broken nuptials, even when initiated by men, give women the power to resist, control, or alter the movement of courtship. But with the celebration of completed nuptials at the end of the comedies, male control is re-established, and women take their subordinate places in the dance.

While rejoicing in the festive conclusion of *Much Ado* we should perhaps remember Beatrice's acute satire on wooing and wedding – and their aftermath:

> wooing, wedding, and repenting is as a Scotch, jig, a measure, and a cinquepace. The first suit is hot and hasty like a Scotch jig (and full as fantastical); the wedding, mannerly modest, as a measure, full of state and ancientry; and then comes Repentance and with his bad legs falls into the cinquepace faster and faster till he sink into his grave.
>
> (II, i, 69–75)

Beatrice's description, which sees marriage as a precarious beginning, not a happy ending, is anticipated by the many irregular nuptials of earlier comedies and is embodied in the troubling open endings of *All's Well That Ends Well* and *Measure for Measure*. In these plays the balance between wit and romance, between male authority and female power is lost. The culmination 'fantastical' romance and 'hot and hasty' desire in a 'mannerly modest' ceremony does not preclude the repenting which

151

follows in the problem comedies and tragedies. In the romantic comedies 'the catastrophe is a nuptial', as Armado proclaims with relish in his love letter to Jaquenetta (*Love's Labour's Lost*, IV, i, 78), but later nuptials prove to be catastrophic in a sense other than the one Armado consciously intends. His own reversal of customary nuptials by getting Jaquenetta pregnant before the ceremony foreshadows a source of difficulty. And in *Much Ado About Nothing* there is one final nuptial irregularity: the dancing begins even before the weddings are celebrated.

Notes

1. LEO SALINGAR, *Shakespeare and the Traditions of Comedy*, (Cambridge: Cambridge University Press, 1974), pp. 302–5.

2. BARBER, *Festive Comedy*, and 'Thou that begetst him that did thee beget: Transformation in *Per* and *WT*', *Shakespeare Survey* 22 (1969), 61, focus on the release of emotion and compare this with the transformation of emotion required in the romances. I am indebted to R.P. WHEELER, *Shakespeare's Development and the Problem Comedies* (Berkeley: University of California Press, 1981) which places the festive comedies and the late romances in relation to the problem comedies. See especially pp. 12–19.

3. Most critics accept the Claudio/Hero story as the 'main plot', although they literally or figuratively put the term in quotation marks and are quick to point out that Beatrice and Benedick overshadow this 'plot', however 'main' it is. See, for example, GRAHAM STOREY, 'The Success of *MAdo*', in *Twentieth Century Interpretations of MAdo* (Englewood Cliffs: Prentice-Hall, 1969), p. 14; JOHN CRICK, 'Messina', in ibid, p. 33; and ELLIOTT KRIEGER, 'Shakespeare and the Social Order in "*Much Ado About Nothing*"', *Shakespeare Survey* 32 (1979), 50, n. 3. JAMES SMITH, '*Much Ado About Nothing*: Notes from a Book in Preparation', *Scrutiny* 13 (1945–46), 242–57, whose claims seem to be somewhat misrepresented in Krieger's footnote, is one of the few critics who argues, as I will, that the two plots depend on each other and to explore psychological and dramatic interdependence as well as thematic relationships among the different parts of the play: Beatrice/Benedick, Claudio/Hero, Dogberry and the Watch, and Don John. For giddiness, see GRAHAM STORY; for complacency, see JOHN CRICK; for deceptiveness of appearances, see WALTER N. KING, 'Much Ado about *Something*'. *Shakespeare Quarterly* 15 (1964), 143–55; A.P. ROSSITER, *Angel with Horns* (New York: Theatre Arts Books, 1961), pp. 65–81, and many others.

4. KAHN, *Man's Estate*, p. 122.

5. Indeed, Shakespeare's bastards Falconbridge and Edmund, more than Don John, are characterized by their perverse drive and energy and by their need to assert their virility.

6. BARBARA EVERETT, however, analyzes the play as a 'clash' of masculine and feminine worlds in which 'the women's world dominates': '*MAdo*,' *Critical Quarterly* 3 (1961), 320.

7. JANICE HAYS, 'Those "soft and delicate desires": *Much Ado* and the Distrust of

Women', in Lenz et al., *The Woman's Part*, pp. 79–99, discusses in detail Claudio's fears of and defenses against sexual involvement.

8. Some critics insist on the conventional aspects of the courtship and marriage arrangements. See NADINE PAGE, 'The Public Repudiation of Hero', *PMLA* 50 (1935): 739–44, and CHARLES T. PROUTY, *The Sources of Much Ado About Nothing* (New Haven: Yale University Press, 1950), pp. 41–7. Other critics accuse Claudio of being a mere fortune hunter; he is termed 'a brash and ambitious would-be sophisticate' by BERTRAM EVANS, *Shakespeare's Comedies* (London: Oxford University Press, 1960), p. 67. But his concentration on the business arrangements seems to satisfy psychological needs even more than financial ones.

9. In contrast, the source, Bandello's *novella* is explicit about the passionate desires of Claudio's prototype, Timbreo, for Fenicia: 'The gentleman grew warmer every day and the more he gazed on her, the more he felt his desires to burn, and the fire increasing in his heart so much that he felt himself consumed with love for the beautiful maiden, he determined that he must have her at any cost' (Geoffrey Bullough, *Narrative and Dramatic Sources of Shakespeare* (New York: Columbia University Press), 2: 113). As is common in Italian *novelle*, Timbreo woos Fenicia for his wife only after she refuses to be his mistress.

10. Editions commonly gloss 'bachelors' in this speech as 'male or female unmarried persons', claiming that the source of this meaning is the biblical passage, 'For when they shall rise from the dead, they neither marry, nor are given in marriage; but are as angels which are in heaven' (Mark 12: 25). But the *OED* cites this meaning (5) as rare and obsolete and gives only one reference (Ben Jonson: 1632). In all nineteen other Shakespearean uses, *bachelor* refers exclusively to unmarried men, as it must, for example, in 'Such separation as may well be said,/ Becomes a virtuous bachelor and a maid' (*MND*, II, i, 59–60). When Beatrice claims that 'Adam's sons are my brethren' (II, i, 60), hopes to join the bachelors in heaven, and wishes she were a man to 'eat Claudio's heart out in the market place', she is testifying to the attractiveness of the world of male camaraderie, a world she would be excluded from after marriage.

11. CAROLE MCKEWIN, 'Counsels of Gall and Grace: Intimate Conversations between Women in Shakespeare's Plays', Lenz et al., *The Woman's Part*, pp. 117–32, explores the 'unease' of this scene but does not see as its source Beatrice's and Hero's unacknowledged identification with each other and Margaret's unacknowledged deception.

12. I was first led to consider the function of mock deaths and their combination of passive and aggressive elements by Kirby Farrell's paper, 'Authority and Self-Effacement: Shakespeare's Imagination and Family Structure', presented to a special session, 'Marriage and the Family in Shakespeare', at the annual meeting of the Modern Language Association, New York, 1978. See also his revision, 'Self-Effacement and Autonomy in Shakespeare', *Shakespeare Studies* 16 (1983): 75–99, and his book, *Shakespeare's Creation* (Amherst: University of Massachusetts Press, 1975), chapter 6.

13. JOHN TRAUGOTT, 'Creating a Rational Rinaldo: A Study in the Mixture of the Genres of Comedy and Romance in *MAdo*', *Genre*, 15 (1982), 157–81, analyzes in somewhat similar fashion the effect of the demand to kill Claudio: 'Suddenly our expectations are derailed and they [Beatrice and Benedick] have

stolen away the convention of service to the distressed lady, together with its man on horseback, its idealism, its grace, and incongruously incorporated it into the comic charades they concoct between themselves. The wit plot has absorbed the romance plot' (p. 164).

14. In the first scene of the play, Beatrice similarly deflated killing to eating, real battles to 'merry wars' of wit, and Benedick from a 'good soldier' to a 'good soldier to a lady' (I, i, 36–60).

15. The situation is quite different in Bandello's tale, in which Timbreo is effusively penitent and, after having taken his former beloved, Fenicia, as his wife without recognizing her, must prove his love by asserting that his love for Fenicia is greater than that for his new bride before she will reveal herself to him: 'truly I loved her as much as a woman can be loved by a man, and if I love aeons of years I shall still love her, dead though she is' (BULLOUGH, 2: 130).

16. The vexing double substitution in which not only is Margaret to pretend to be Hero, but Borachio is to imitate Claudio (II, i, 43–4), whether deliberate or a slip, foreshadows the problems plays in which the protagonist himself participates in the bedtricks with a substitute bride. At the end of *All's Well*, Bertram, unlike Claudio here, does assert the identity of the 'dead' Helen he married and the living Helen he slept with, affirming that, now pregnant, she is fully his wife, both the 'name' and the 'thing' (V, iii, 308). Othello, too, at his death affirms the continuity between the actual woman he killed and the reidealized woman he loves: 'I kissed thee ere I killed thee. No way but this/ Killing myself to die upon a kiss' (V, ii, 339–40). And in the ritualistic conclusion of *The Winter's Tale*, Leontes imbues the statue with life, integrating his image of a perfected Hermione with the flesh-and-blood woman: 'Hermione was not so wrinkled, nothing/So aged as this seems' (V, iii, 28–9).

17. CLARA CLAIBORNE PARK, 'As We Like It: How a Girl Can be Smart and Still Popular', in Lenz et al., *The Woman's Part*, pp. 100–16, discusses how the assertiveness of the heroines is curtailed.

7   As You Like It (1599–1600)

PETER B. ERICKSON '*Sexual Politics and the Social Structure in As You Like It*'*

An older tradition of criticism saw *As You Like It* as the quintessential Shakespeare romantic comedy, with a charming, witty heroine and a handsome hero escaping the pressures of an oppressive court and finding, after a suitable maturation, true love and marriage – their developments paralleling, in many readings, the conventional bourgeois pattern of personal growth from pre-adolescent homoerotic friendship to heterosexual romance and marriage. The relaxing pastoral setting, the genial courtly and rustic characters, enveloped in an atmosphere of play, song and wit, and the genial blessings of Hymen thus were seen, according to J.R. Brown, as 'informed to an exceptional degree by Shakespeare's ideal of love's order'.[1] Such a reading sees the play as exquisitely balanced – matched pairs of lovers, a jolly and a bitter fool, with Rosalind herself balanced between ideal and real, romance and disillusion. Such a reading fits Frye's division of Shakespearean comedy into three phases – a disturbing opening in the corrupt court, the escape to a 'green world', and a return to the purged, renewed court.

Though the play is still often read within Frye's scheme, contemporary criticism, however, generally sees it as a little more complicated. The country is far from an ideal escapist paradise. Like the woods of *A Midsummer Night's Dream*, the forest of *As You Like It* produces as much contradiction as contentment. The pastoral mode was (and perhaps remains) the fantasy of an urban ruling class, unwilling to give up its power but aware of destroying something seemingly more natural in the process. 'A culture is no better than its woods', as Auden puts it, and the woods of *As You Like It* have not only poems on trees, but the darkness that haunts other comedies.

Older critics spoke of its concern with 'love'; more recent ones have focused on gender. Peter Erickson argues in this much-praised essay that

---

* Reprinted from *Patriarchal Structure in Shakespearean Drama* (1985), pp. 22–37

the seeming triumph of love at the play's end embodies a conservative compromise with traditional patriarchal gender assignments, embodied in Rosalind's act of 'giving' herself to her father and Orlando, thus re-establishing the conventional order. He reads the forest as an idealized enclave of ultimate male dominance in which both men and women may expand their sense of agency, but where female vitality is not allowed to become too independent. As Jean Howard likewise points out, Rosalind's cross-dressing enables her to redefine the role of a woman in patriarchy, but only to a limited extent: her actions show the constructed nature of gender assignment, but the hierarchical two-gender system is never queried.[2]

Notes

1. JOHN RUSSELL BROWN, *Shakespeare's Dramatic Style* (London, Heinemann, 1970) p. 86.

2. JEAN HOWARD 'Crossdressing, the Theater, and Gender Struggle in Early Modern England' *SQ* 39 (1988), 434–6.

Before entering the forest of Arden, Rosalind's companion Celia/Aliena redefines this pastoral space to mean opportunity rather than punishment: 'Now go we in content/To liberty, and not to banishment' (I, iii, 136–7). This 'liberty' implies overcoming the restrictions of the female role. The idea of the male disguise originates as a strategy for avoiding the normal vulnerability to male force: 'Alas, what danger will it be to us,/Maids as we are, to travel forth so far!/Beauty provoketh thieves sooner than gold' (106–8). Rosalind's male costume, as it evolves, expands her identity so that she can play both male and female roles. Yet the costume is problematic. Though it gives her freedom of action and empowers her to take the initiative with Orlando, it simultaneously serves as a protective device, which temptingly offers excessive security, even invulnerability. In order to love, Rosalind must reveal herself directly to Orlando, thereby making herself vulnerable. She must give up the disguise and appear – as she ultimately promises Orlando – 'human as she is' (V, ii, 67). But in giving up the disguise, she also gives up the strength it symbolizes. As the disguise begins to break down before its official removal, Rosalind's transparent femininity takes the form of fainting – a sign of weakness that gives her away: 'You a man?/You lack a man's heart' (IV, iii, 164–5). This loss of control signals that Rosalind can no longer deny her inner feminine self. The capacity for love that we find so admirable in Rosalind is compromised by the necessity that she resume a traditional female role in order to engage in love.

This traditional image has been present all along. Rosalind willingly confides to Celia that she remains a woman despite the male costume: '. . . in my heart/Lie there what hidden woman's fear there will –/We'll have a swashing and a martial outside' (I, iii, 116–18); 'Good my complexion, dost thou think, though I am caparisoned like a man, I have a doublet and hose in my disposition?' (III, ii, 193–5); and 'Do you not know I am a woman?' (247). By virtue of the costume, Rosalind does have access to both male and female attributes, but the impression she conveys of androgynous wholeness is misleading. Neither Rosalind nor the play questions the conventional categories of masculine and feminine. She does not reconcile gender definitions in the sense of integrating or synthesizing them. Her own insistence on the metaphor of exterior (male) and interior (female) keeps the categories distinct and separable. The liberation that Rosalind experiences in the forest has built into it the conservative countermovement by which, as the play returns to the normal world, she will be reduced to the traditional woman who is sub-servient to men.

Rosalind is shown working out in advance the terms of her return. Still protected by her disguise yet allowing herself to come closer to the decisive moment, she instructs Orlando to 'woo me' (IV, i, 67) and subsequently tells him what to say in a wedding rehearsal while she practices yielding. Though she teases Orlando with the wife's power to make him a cuckold and then to conceal her duplicity with her 'wayward wit' (154–77), this is good fun, and it is only that. It is clear to the audience, if not yet to Orlando, that Rosalind's flaunting of her role as disloyal wife is a put-on rather than a genuine threat. She may playfully delay the final moment when she becomes a wife, but we are reassured that, once married, she will in fact be faithful. Her humor has the effect of exorcising and renouncing her potential weapon. The uncertainty concerns not her loyalty but Orlando's, as her sudden change of tone when he announces his departure indicates: 'Alas, dear love, I cannot lack thee two hours!' (170). Her exuberance and control collapse in fears of his betrayal: 'Ay, go your ways, go your ways; I knew what you would prove' (173–4). Her previous wit notwithstanding, for Rosalind the scene is less a demonstration of power than an exercise in vulnerability. She is once again consigned to anxious waiting for her tardy man: 'But why did he swear he would come this morning, and comes not?' (III, iv, 18–19).

Rosalind's own behaviour neutralizes her jokes about cuckoldry, but this point is sharply reinforced by the brief account of the male hunt that immediately follows (Act IV, scene i). The expected negative meaning of horns as the sign of a cuckold is transformed into a positive image of phallic potency that unites men. Changing the style of his literary response to deer killing, Jaques replaces his earlier lament (II, i, 26–66) with a celebration of male hunt and conquest: 'Let's present him to the Duke like a Roman conqueror, and it would do well to set the deer's horns upon his head, for a branch of victory' (IV, ii, 3–5).[1] The rousing song occasioned by this moment suggests the power of an all-male activity to provide a self-sufficient male heritage, thus to defend against male insecurity about humiliation by women.

The final scene, orchestrated by Rosalind, demonstrates her power in a paradoxical way. She is the architect of a resolution that phases out the control she has wielded and prepares the way for the patriarchal status quo. She accedes to the process by which, in the transition from courtship to marriage, power passes from the female to the male: the man is no longer the suitor who serves, obeys and begs but is now the husband who commands. Rosalind's submission is explicit but not ironic, though her tone may be high-spirited. To each of the two men in her life she declares: 'To you, I give myself, for I am yours' (V, iv, 116–17). Her casting herself in the role of male possession is all the more charming because she does not have to be forced to adopt it: her self-taming is voluntary. We may wish to give Rosalind credit for her cleverness in forestalling male rivalry between her father and her fiancé. Unlike Cordelia, she is smart enough to see that in order to be gratified, each man needs to feel that he is the recipient of all her love, not half of it. Yet Rosalind is not really in charge here because the potential hostility between the younger and older man has already been negotiated in the forest in Act II, scene vii, a negotiation that results in the formation of an idealized male alliance. Rosalind submits not only to two individual men but also to the patriarchal society that they embody. Patriarchy is not a slogan smuggled in from the twentieth century and imposed on the play but an exact term for the social structure that close reading reveals within the play.

II

We are apt to assume that the green world is more free than it actually is. In the case of *As You Like It*, the green world cannot be interpreted as a space apart where a youthful rebellion finds a refuge from the older generation. The forest of Arden includes a strong parental presence: Duke Senior's is the first voice we hear there. Moreover, the green world has a clear political structure. Freed from the constraints of courtly decorum, Duke Senior can afford to address his companions as 'brothers' (II, i, 1), but he nonetheless retains a fatherly command. Fraternal spirit is not equivalent to democracy, as is clarified when the duke dispenses favor on a hierarchical basis: 'Shall share the good of our returned fortune,/

According to the measure of their states' (V, iv, 174–5).

Although interpretations of *As You Like It* often stress youthful love, we should not neglect the paternal context in which the love occurs. Both Rosalind and Orlando acknowledge Duke Senior. Rosalind is aware, as she finds herself attracted to Orlando, that 'My father loved Sir Rowland [Orlando's father] as his soul' (I, ii, 225) and hence that her affection is not incompatible with family approval. Orlando, for his part, does not go forward in pursuit of love until after he has become friends with Duke Senior. Rosalind and Orlando approach the forest in strikingly different ways. Rosalind's mission is love. Upon entering the forest, she discovers there the love 'passion' she has brought with her: 'Alas, poor shepherd, searching of thy wound,/I have by hard adventure found mine own' (II, iv, 42–3). Orlando, by contrast, has two projects (though he does not consciously formulate them) to complete in the forest: the first is his quest to re-establish the broken connection with his father's legacy; the second is the quest for Rosalind. The sequence of these projects is an indication of priority. Orlando's outburst – 'But heavenly Rosalind!' (I, ii, 278) – is not picked up again until he opens Act III, scene ii, with his love poem. The interim is reserved for his other, patriarchal business.

In the first scene of the play, Orlando makes it clear, in a melodramatic but nonetheless poignant way, that he derives his sense of identity from his dead father, an identity that is not yet fulfilled. In protesting against his older brother's mistreatment, Orlando asserts the paternal bond: 'The spirit of my father grows strong in me, and I will no longer endure it' (I, i, 67–9). His first step toward recovery of the connection with his lost father is the demolition of Charles the wrestler: 'How dost thou, Charles?'/'He cannot speak, my lord' (I, ii, 208–9). This victory earns Orlando the right to proclaim his father's name as his own:

> *Duke Frederick*   What is thy name, young man?
> *Orlando*   Orlando, my liege, the youngest son of Sir Rowland de
>   Boys. . . .
>   I am more proud to be Sir Rowland's son.
>
> (210–13, 222)

Frederick's negative reaction to Orlando's statement of identity confirms the concept of heritage being evoked here: 'Thou shouldst have better pleased me with this deed/Hadst thou descended from another house' (217–18). The significance of the wrestling match is that Orlando has undergone a traditional male rite of passage, providing an established channel for the violence he has previously expressed by collaring Oliver in the opening scene. Yet aggression is the epitome of a rigid masculinity that Shakespeare characteristically condemns as too narrow a basis for identity. Orlando's aggressiveness is instantly rendered inappropriate by his falling in love. Moreover, his recourse to violence simply mirrors the technique of the tyrannical Duke Frederick. As it turns out, Orlando must give up violence in order to meet the 'good father'.

While Rosalind's confidante Celia provides the opportunity to talk about love, Orlando is accompanied by Adam, who serves a very different function since he is a living link to Orlando's father. The paternal inheritance blocked by Oliver is received indirectly from Adam when he offers the money 'I saved under you father,/Which I did store to be my foster-nurse' (II, iii, 39–40). The motif of nurturance implied by the 'foster-nurse' image is continued as Orlando, through Adam's sudden collapse from lack of food, is led to Duke Senior's pastoral banquet. Treating this new situation as another trial of 'the strength of my youth', Orlando imagines an all-or-nothing 'adventure' (I, ii, 161–2, 166) similar to the wrestling match: 'If this uncouth forest yield any thing savage, I will either be food for it, or bring it for food to thee' (II, vi, 6–7). In Act II, scene vii, he enters with drawn sword. Unexpectedly finding a benevolent father-figure, Orlando effects as gracefully as possible a transition from toughness to tenderness: 'Let gentleness my strong enforcement be,/In the which hope I blush, and hide my sword' (118–19). This display of nonviolence is the precondition for Orlando's recovery of patriarchal lineage. Duke Senior aids this recovery by his recognition of the father's reflection in the son and by his declaration of his own loving connection with Orlando's father. This transaction concludes the scene:

> If that you were the good Sir Rowland's son,
> As you have whispered faithfully you were,
> And as mine eye doth his effigies witness
> Most truly limned and living in your face,
> Be truly welcome hither. I am the Duke
> That loved your father.
>
> (191–6)

The confirmation of Orlando's identity has the effect of a ritual blessing that makes this particular father–son relation the basis for social cohesion in general. There is much virtue in Orlando's 'If':

> *Orlando* If ever you have looked on better days,
> If ever been where bells have knolled to church,
> If ever sate at any good man's feast,
> If ever from your eyelids wiped a tear,
> And know what 'tis to pity, and be pitied....
> *Duke Senior* True is it that we have seen better days,
> And have with holy bell been knolled to church,

And sat at good men's feasts, and wiped our eyes
Of drops that sacred pity hath engend'red.

(II, vii, 113–17, 120–23)

The liturgy of male utopia, ruthlessly undercut in *Love's Labour's Lost*, is
here allowed to stand. Virgilian piety, founded on ideal father–son
relations and evoked visually when, like Aeneas with Anchises, Orlando
carries Adam on his back, can achieve what Navarre's academe with its
spurious abstinence could not. Orlando's heroic language as he goes off to
rescue Adam is as clumsy as any he uses in the poems to Rosalind, but
whereas the play pokes fun at the love poetry, the expression of duty to
Adam is not subject to irony: 'Then but forbear your food a little while,/
Whiles, like a doe, I go to find my fawn,/And give it food' (127–9). We
are invited simply to accept the doe–fawn metaphor that Orlando invokes
for his obligation to reciprocate Adam's 'pure love' (131).

Just as there is an unlimited supply of food in this scene, so there seems
to be more than enough 'pure love' to go around, Jaques excepted. Love
is expressed in terms of food, and men gladly take on nurturant roles.
Duke Senior's abundant provision of food and of 'gentleness' creates an
image of a self-sustaining patriarchial system. The men take over the
traditional female prerogative of maternal nurturance, negatively defined
by Jaques: 'At first the infant,/Mewling and puking in the nurse's arms'
(II, vii, 143–4). Such discomfort has been purged from the men's
nurturance as it is dramatized in this scene, which thus offers a new
perspective on Duke Senior's very first speech in the play. We now see
that it is the male feast, not the biting winter wind, that 'feelingly
persuades me what I am' (II, i, 11). 'Sweet are the uses of adversity'
because, as Orlando discovers, adversity disappears when men's
'gentleness' prevails, 'translating the stubbornness of fortune/Into so
quiet and sweet a style' (12, 19–20). This sweetness explains why 'loving
lords have put themselves into voluntary exile' with the duke and why
'many young gentlemen flock to him every day' (I, i, 99, 113–14).

The idealized male enclave founded on 'sacred pity' in Act II, scene vii,
is not an isolated incident. The power of male pity extends beyond this
scene to include the evil Oliver, who is threatened by a symbol of
maternal nurturance made hostile by depletion: 'A lioness, with udders
all drawn dry' (IV, iii, 115) and 'the sucked and hungry lioness' (127). The
motif of eating here creates a negative image that might disturb the
comfortable pastoral banquet, but the lioness's intrusion is quickly ended.
Responding with a kindness that can be traced back to his meeting with
Duke Senior, Orlando rescues his brother: 'But kindness, nobler ever than
revenge,/And nature, stronger than his just occasion,/Made him give
battle to the lioness' (129–30). Oliver's oral fulfilment follows: 'my
conversion/So sweetly tastes' (137–8). The tears 'that sacred pith hath

engendered' (II, vii, 123) are reiterated by the brothers' reconciliation –
'Tears our recountments had most kindly bathed' (IV, iii, 141) – and their
reunion confirmed by a recapitulation of the banquet scene: 'he led me to
the gentle Duke,/Who gave me fresh array and entertainment,/
Committing me unto my brother's love' (143–5). Again the pattern of
male reconciliation preceding love for women is seen in Oliver's
confession of his desire to marry Celia (V, ii, 1–12) coming after his
admission to the brotherhood.

The male community of Act II, scene vii, is also vindicated by the
restoration of patriarchal normalcy in the play's final scene. In the end, as
Rosalind's powers are fading, the relationship between Duke Senior and
Orlando is reasserted and completed as the duke announces the
inheritance to which marriage entitles Orlando: 'A land itself at large, a
potent dukedom' (V, iv, 169). Like the 'huswife Fortune' who 'doth most
mistake in her gifts to women' (I, ii, 30, 36), Rosalind plays her part by
rehearsing the men in their political roles:

Rosalind	You say, if I bring in your Rosalind,
	You will bestow her on Orlando here?
Duke Senior	That would I, had I kingdoms to give with her.
Rosalind	And you say you will have her, when I bring her.
Orlando	That would I, were I of all kingdoms king.

(V, iv, 6–10)

The reference the two men make to kingdoms is shortly to be fulfilled,
but this bounty is beyond Rosalind's power to give. For it is not her
magic that produces the surprise entrance of Jaques de Boys with the
news of Duke Senior's restoration. In completing the de Boys family
reunion, the middle brother's appearance reverses the emblematic fate of
the three sons destroyed by Charles the wrestler: 'Yonder they lie, the
poor old man, their father, making such pitiful dole over them that all the
beholders take his part with weeping' (I, ii, 121–3). The image of three de
Boys sons re-establishes the proper generational sequence, ensuring
continuity.

III

C.L. Barber has shown that the 'Saturnalian Pattern' that gives structure
to festive comedy is intrinsically conservative since it involves only 'a
temporary license, a "misrule" which implied rule'.[2] But in *As You Like It*
the conservatism of comic form does not affect all characters equally. In
the liberal opening out into the forest of Arden, both men and women are
permitted an expansion of sexual identity that transcends restrictive

gender roles. Just as Rosalind gains access to the traditional masculine attributes of strength and control through her costume, so Orlando gains access to the traditional female attributes of compassion and nurturance. However, the conservative countermovement built into comic strategy applies exclusively to Rosalind. Her possession of the male costume and of the power it symbolizes is only temporary. But Orlando does not have to give up the emotional enlargement he has experienced in the forest. Discussions of androgyny in *As You Like It* usually focus on Rosalind whereas in fact it is the men rather than the women who are the lasting beneficiaries of androgyny. It is Orlando, not Rosalind, who achieves a synthesis of attributes traditionally labeled masculine and feminine when he combines compassion and aggression in rescuing his brother from the lioness.

This selective androgyny demands an ambivalent response: it is a humanizing force for the men, yet it is based on the assumption that men have power over women.[3] Because androgyny is available only to men, we are left with a paradoxical compatibility of androgyny with patriarchy, that is, benevolent patriarchy. In talking about male power in *As You Like It*, we must distinguish between two forms of patriarchy. The first and most obvious is the harsh, mean-spirited version represented by Oliver, who abuses primogeniture, and by Duke Frederick, who after usurping power holds on to it by arbitrary acts of suppression. Driven by greed, envy, suspicion and power for power's sake, neither man can explain his actions. In an ironic demonstration of the consuming nature of evil, Duke Frederick expends his final rage against Oliver, who honestly protests: 'I never loved my brother in my life' (III, i, 14). In contrast to good men, bad men are incapable of forming alliances. Since Frederick's acts of banishment have now depopulated the court, he himself must enter the forest in order to seek the enemies so necessary to his existence (V, iv, 154–8). But of course this patriarchal tyranny is a caricature and therefore harmless. Oliver and Frederick are exaggerated fairy-tale villains whose hardened characters are unable to withstand the wholesome atmosphere of the forest and instantly dissolve (IV, iii, 136–8; V, iv, 159–65). The second, more serious version of patriarchy is the political structure headed by Duke Senior. To describe it, we seek adjectives like 'benevolent', 'humane', and 'civilized'. Yet we cannot leave it at that. A benevolent patriarchy still requires women to be subordinate, and Rosalind's final performance is her enactment of this subordination.

We can now summarize the difference between the conclusions of *Love's Labour's Lost* and *As You Like It*. In order to assess the sense of an ending, we must take into account the perspective of sexual politics and correlate formal harmony or disharmony with patriarchal stability or instability. Unlike Rosalind, the women in *Love's Labour's Lost* do not give up their independence.[4] The sudden announcement of the death of the princess's father partially restrains her wit. But this news is a *pater ex machina* attempt to even the score and to equalize the situation between the men and the women because nothing has emerged organically within the play to challenge the women's predominance. The revelation that the 'decrepit, sick and bedrid' father (I, i, 138) has died is not an effective assertion of his presence but, on the contrary, advertises his weakness. The princess submits to the 'new-sad soul' (V, ii, 731) that mourning requires, but this provides the excuse for going on to reject the suitors as she has all along. Her essential power remains intact, whereas patriarchal authority is presented as weak or nonexistent. The death of the invalid father has a sobering impact because it mirrors the vacuum created by the four lords' powerlessness within the play. There is no relief from the fear that dominant women inspire in a patriarchal sensibility, and this continuing tension contributes to the uneasiness at the play's end.

Like the princess, Rosalind confronts her father in the final scene. But in her case paternal power is vigorously represented by Duke Senior and by the line of patriarchal authority established when Senior makes Orlando his heir. Festive celebration is now possible because a dependable, that is, patriarchal, social order is securely in place. It is Duke Senior's voice that legitimates the festive closure: 'Play, music, and you brides and bridegrooms all./With measure heaped in joy, to th' measures fall' (V, iv, 178–9). Orlando benefits from this social structure because, in contrast to the lords of *Love's Labour's Lost*, he has a solid political resource to offset the liability of a poetic convention that dictates male subservience. *As You Like It* achieves marital closure not by eliminating male ties but rather by strengthening them.[5]

A further phasing out of Rosalind occurs in the Epilogue when it is revealed that she is male: 'If I were a woman I would kiss as many of you as had beards that pleased me' (18–19). This explicit breaking of theatrical illusion forces us to reckon with the fact of an all-male cast. The boy-actor convention makes it possible for males to explore the female other (I use the term *other* here in the sense given by Simone de Beauvoir in *The Second Sex* of woman as the other). Vicariously taking on the female role enables male spectators to make an experimental contact with what otherwise might remain unknown, forbidden territory. Fear of women can be encountered in the relatively safe environment of the theater, acted out, controlled (when it can be controlled as in *As You Like It*), and overcome. A further twist of logic defuses and reduces the threat of female power: Rosalind is no one to be frightened of since, as the Epilogue insists, she is male after all; she is only a boy and clearly subordinate to men in the hierarchy of things.

The convention of males playing female roles gives men the opportunity to imagine sex-role fluidity and flexibility. Built into the conditions of performance is the potential for male acknowledgment of a 'feminine self' and thus for male transcendence of a narrow masculinity. In the particular case of *As You Like It*, the all-male cast provides a theatrical counterpart for the male community at Duke Senior's banquet in Act II, scene vii. This theatrical dimension reinforces the conservative effect of male androgyny within the play. Acknowledgment of the feminine within the male is one thing, the acknowledgment of individual women another: the latter does not automatically follow from the former. In the boy-actor motif, woman is a metaphor for the male discovery of the feminine within himself, of those qualities suppressed by a masculinity strictly defined as aggressiveness. Once the tenor of the metaphor has been attained, the vehicle can be discarded – just as Rosalind is discarded. The sense of the patriarchal ending in *As You Like It* is that male androgyny is affirmed whereas female 'liberty' in the person of Rosalind is curtailed.

There is, finally, a studied ambiguity about heterosexual versus homoerotic feeling in the play, Shakespeare allowing himself to have it both ways. The Epilogue is heterosexual in its bringing together of men and women: 'and I charge you, O men, for the love you bear to women (as I perceive by your simp'ring, none of you hates them), that between you and the women the play may please' (13–16). The 'simp'ring' attributed to men in their response to women is evoked in a good-natured jocular spirit; yet the tone conveys discomfort as well. In revealing the self-sufficient male acting company, the Epilogue also offers the counter-image of male bonds based on the exclusion of women.

Though he is shown hanging love poems on trees only after achieving atonement with Rosalind's father, Orlando never tries, like the lords of *Love's Labour's Lost*, to avoid women. The social structure of *As You Like It*, in which political power is vested in male bonds, can include heterosexual love because marriage becomes a way of incorporating women since Rosalind is complicit in her assimilation by patriarchal institutions. However, in spite of the disarming of Rosalind, resistance to women remains. It is as though asserting the priority of relations between men over relations between men and women is not enough, as though a fall-back position is needed. The Epilogue is, in effect, a second ending that provides further security against women by preserving on stage the image of male ties in their pure form with women absent. Not only are women to be subordinate; they can, if necessary, be imagined as nonexistent. Rosalind's art does not, as is sometimes suggested, coincide with Shakespeare's: Shakespeare uses his art to take away Rosalind's female identity and thereby upstages her claim to magic power.

We can see the privileged status accorded to male bonds by comparing Shakespeare's treatment of same-sex relations for men and for women. Men originally divided are reunited as in the instance of Oliver and Orlando, but women undergo the reverse process. Rosalind and Celia are initially inseparable: 'never two ladies loved as they do' (I, i, 108); 'whose loves/Are dearer than the natural bond of sisters' (I, ii, 265–6); 'And whereso'er we went, like Juno's swans,/Still we went coupled and inseparable' (I, iii, 73–4); and 'thou and I am one./Shall we be sund'red? shall we part, sweet girl?/No, let my father seek another heir' (95–7). Yet the effect of the play is to separate them by transferring their allegiance to husbands. Celia ceases to be a speaking character at the end of Act IV, her silence coinciding with her new role as fiancée. The danger of female bonding is illustrated when Shakespeare diminishes Rosalind's absolute control by mischievously confronting her with the unanticipated embarrassment of Phebe's love for her. Rosalind is of course allowed to devise an escape from the pressure of his undesirable entanglement, but it is made clear in the process that such ardor is taboo and that the authorized defense against it is marriage. 'And so am I for no woman', Rosalind insists (V, ii, 87). A comparable prohibition is not announced against male friendship.[6]

In conclusion, we must ask: what is Shakespeare's relation to the sexual politics of *As You Like It*? Is he taking an ironic and critical stance toward the patriarchal solution of his characters, or is he heavily invested in this solution himself? I think there are limits to Shakespeare's critical awareness in this play. The sudden conversions of Oliver and Duke Frederick have a fairy-tale quality that Shakespeare clearly intends as an aspect of the wish fulfilment to which he calls attention in the play's title. Similarly, Jaques's commentary in the final scene is a deliberate foil to the neatness of the ending that allows Shakespeare as well as Jaques a modicum of distance. However, in fundamental respects Shakespeare appears to be implicated in the fantasy he has created for his characters.

As You Like It enacts two rites of which Shakespeare did not avail himself in *Love's Labour's Lost*. We have too easily accepted the formulation that says that Shakespeare in the mature history plays concentrates on masculine development whereas in the mature festive comedies he gives women their due by allowing them to play the central role. *As You Like It* is primarily a defensive action against female power rather than a celebration of it.[7] Second, Shakespeare portrays an ideal male community based on 'sacred pity'. This idealized vision of relationships between men can be seen as sentimental and unrealistic, but in contrast to his undercutting of academe in *Love's Labour's Lost*, Shakespeare is here thoroughly engaged and endorses the idealization. These two elements – female vitality kept manageable and male power kept loving – provided a resolution that at this particular moment was 'As Shakespeare Liked it'.

Notes

1. NORMAN O. BROWN, 'Metamorphoses II: Actaeon', *American Poetry Review* 1 (1972), 38–40, employs this passage in his own celebration of the horn.

2. BARBER, *Festive Comedy*.

3. ADRIENNE RICH provides a critique of the conservative use of the concept androgyny and a summary of recent writing on the subject in *Of Woman Born: Motherhood as Experience and Institution* (New York: W.W. Norton, 1976), pp. 62–3. Rich's poem 'The Stranger', in *Diving into the Wreck* (New York: W.W. Norton, 1973), p. 19, declares proudly 'I am the androgyne'. But the revaluation of androgyny in her prose work leads Rich to disavow the term in 'Natural Resources', in *The Dream of a Common Language* (New York: W.W. Norton, 1978), p. 66: 'There are words I cannot choose again/*humanising androgyny*.'

4. I do not mean to suggest that this is a positive ending in the sense of being the best possible outcome, but the women's continued assertion of independence is a valid response to the less-than-ideal circumstances with which they must deal. It allows them to retain their integrity – an alternative preferable to capitulation.

5. In the judgement of ANN BARTON, '*AYL* and *TN*: Shakespeare's Sense of an Ending', in Bradbury and Palmer, p. 161, *AYL* 'stands as the fullest and most stable realization of Shakespearean comic form'. Barton speaks of Shakespeare's loss of 'faith' in comic endings after the perfection of *AYL* and of the 'renewed faith' made possible by his 'readjustment of form' in the late romances (pp. 179–80). Both the loss and recovery of faith involve Shakespeare's changing attitudes towards the viability of benign patriarchy. In particular, *WT* restores this faith (after its shattering in the tragedies) by re-establishing patriarchal harmony in a believable form.

6. In this regard *Mer* offers a useful contrast. The conclusion of *LLL* presents a three-way stalemate. Marital bonds, male bonds and female bonds are all sources of vague discomfort: none can be affirmed. *AYL* affirms marriage by strengthening male bonds and eliminating female bonds. *Mer* breaks the stalemate in a different way. Marriage is achieved by disrupting the bond between Antonio and Bassanio, but the alliance between Portia and Nerissa remains in effect, as their comparatively sharp deployment of the cuckold motif attests. The source of uneasiness in *Mer*, however, is Portia's defeat of a Jewish father in the earlier court scene and, in particular, her problematic speech about Christian bounty (IV, i, 184–202), problematic partly because her own behaviour toward Shylock fails to exhibit the mercy she recommends to him.

7. For an example of this contrast between comedies and histories, see R.J. DORIUS, Shakespeare's Dramatic Modes and *Ant* in *Literatur als Kritik des Lebens: Festschrift zum 65, Geburstag von Ludwig Borinski* (Heidelburg: Quelle & Meyer, 1975), pp. 83–96. Dorius's overview is useful but overdrawn in the way I have suggested.

8   Twelfth Night (1599–1600)

TERENCE HAWKES '*Comedy, Orality and Duplicity: Twelfth Night*'*

Shakespeare, many critics have observed, wrote the same story over and over again. Even in his first comedy, *The Comedy of Errors*, he anticipated the issues, motifs, situations, characters and plots of later plays. Written about halfway through his career, *Twelfth Night* seems to not only look back to *The Comedy of Errors* but also to incorporate many ingredients of the other comedies. *Twelfth Night's* lovers, lost siblings, disguises, mistaken identities, clowns and foolery, coincidental revelations, and Falstaffian buffoonery are all familiar ingredients of other romantic comedies. Its concerns with class and gender, self-delusion and paranoia are also found elsewhere in the comedies.

Hawkes's essay shows how Frye's three-stage structure can be read from the play and how Frye's scheme for the comedies still remains influential. In particular, he extends Frye's argument by the use of the influential Russian critic, Bakhtin. Hawkes relates Malvolio to the denial of 'the fruitful duplicity that Carnival and playing enshrine'. Laughed at as a 'Puritan' in the play, Malvolio has long received more unusual attention than an apparently minor character might justify – in 1623, the play was performed under the title of *Malvolio*, and the traditional interpretation has been that Olivia's steward is a just target of Maria's and Feste's humour. That interpretation has usually been reflected in performances that play up or exaggerate the ridiculousness of his yellow stockings and cross-gartering.

Twelfth Night has long resisted, especially in the theatre, those critics who wish to stress the darker side of the comedies, some of which were discussed in the Introduction (see p. 13). To show how the older view continues to be influential, Joseph Westlund has recently argued for what, working from within a psychoanalytic approach, he terms 'this basic human trait' of idealizing the beloved, citing Melanie Klein that such

---

* Reprinted from *Shakespearean Comedy*, Vols. 5 and 6 of *New York Literary Forum*.

idealization 'derives from the innate feeling that an extremely good breast exists, a feeling which leads to the longing for a good subject and for the capacity to love it'.[1] Such a view may be reassuring to those who continue to find the play enchanting, but it does not explain away the violence and irrationality at the play's end. *Twelfth Night* is thus a source of multiple possibilities. It is, in the words of the play's sub-title, what you will.

Note

1. JOSEPH P. WESTLUND, *Shakespeare's Reparative Comedies: A Psychoanalytic View of the Middle Plays* (Chicago: University of Chicago Press 1984), p. 95.

This essay attempts to link two established views of comedy and to relate them to a third. In the process, it aims to generate a consolidated notion that may be usefully applicable to Shakespearean comedy in general and to *A Midsummer Night's Dream* and *Twelfth Night* in particular.

The first view is Northrop Frye's account of the design of Shakespearean comedy as expressed in his essay 'The Argument of Comedy' (*English Institute Essays*, 1948, New York: Columbia University Press, 1949) and the later *A Natural Perspective* (New York: Columbia University Press, 1965). Frye's view is essentially 'structuralist': 'A comedy is not a play which ends happily: it is a play in which a certain structure is present and works through to its own logical end, whether we or the cast or the author feel happy about it or not' (*A Natural Perspective*, p. 46).

If we combine the arguments of the earlier essay with those of the later book, the case emerges that the themes of Shakespeare's comedies may be said to derive not from the mysteries or the moralities or the interludes, but from a fourth dramatic kind, that of folk ritual, represented by the St. George play, the mummers' plays, the feasts of the Ass and of the Boy Bishop, and so on. These dramas of the 'Green world' embody and record the triumph of life over the waste land, of spring over winter, in a two-step rhythmic movement that can be discerned in the body of Shakespearean comedy.

It has three stages: first, that of an anticomic 'old' society that imposes restrictive laws from the 'outside': a world of uninvolved 'spectators'. Second, there is a stage of confusion and loss of identity, socially and sexually (boy-actors playing girls 'disguise' themselves as boys and so on). The third stage occurs when the confusion is resolved, socially and sexually, through the institution of marriage. The result is a 'new' society whose laws are permissive because concrete: felt, lived, and internalized by people who function, not as spectators of, but as participants in the society.

Festival, carnival and Shakespearean comedy

The second view focuses upon that 'fourth dramatic tradition' and resides in the notions of Festival and Carnival developed respectively by C.L. Barber (*Shakespeare's Festive Comedy*, Princeton University Press, 1959) and Mikhail Bakhtin (*Rabelais and His World*, translated Helen Dwolsky, Cambridge, Mass: MIT Press, 1968).[1]

Barber sees the roots of Shakespearean comedy in the community observance of those feast-days and holidays that formed periodic alternatives to, and inversions of, the pattern of everyday medieval and Elizabethan life. He proposes a kind of subculture (allowed by the dominant culture) that, at regular intervals (Candlemas, Shrove Tuesday, Hocktide, May Day, Whitsuntide, Midsummer Eve, Harvest Home, Halloween, Twelfth Night and so on) offered custom-prescribed ways of release from the constraints of 'normality'.

Bakhtin similarly argues for a tradition of folk carnival existing as a structured opposition to 'the feudal culture' (p. 4). This world of Carnival (erupting at regular intervals, it occupied on average a total of three months of the year in medieval Europe) offered a wholly involving 'second world' and a 'second life' within it of a non-official, extra-political nature to the mass of ordinary people. 'Carnival is not a spectacle seen by the people: they live in it . . . it is the people's second life' (pp. 7–8). The basic mode of this life involved a 'special carnivalesque market-place style of expression', a 'special idiom' featuring a special logic of 'turnabout', with a universal displacement from top to bottom, front to rear:

> From the wearing of clothes turned inside out and trousers slipped over the head, to the election of mock Kings and Popes, the same topographical logic is put to work: shifting from top to bottom, casting the high and the old, the finished and completed, into the material bodily lower stratum for death and rebirth.
>
> (Bakhtin 1968, p. 82)

The ideas of Frye, Barber, and Bakhtin meet in the amalgamated notion of a confusing 'green' 'topsy-turvy' Festive or Carnival world whose operation upon the normal world of everyday that it opposes involves a kind of redemptive duplicity: it serves, by a process of benign, mirroring reversal to change that world to a better place. Clearly, a contrary view is also possible that would take the Carnival world as a simple mirror-image *reinforcement* of the everyday world: it acts as a safety valve and so dissipates opposition. In this view, the everyday world might well seek to encourage Carnival, since the three Carnival months serve to sustain the hegemony of the everyday nine.

Orality as the defining mode of comedy

The third view of comedy focuses upon a particular and central aspect of Elizabethan society: its commitment to oral rather than written language as its defining mode. The major art form that derives from and celebrates orality is, of course, that of drama. Within drama, comedy must stand as the genre in which the factor of orality is raised to the highest power. Its mode is fundamentally interactive and interlocutory. A joke, a comic remark or situation, a funny gesture, all these demand a *response*: not necessarily laughter, but an interjection or reaction or interpolation of some kind from the audience. In this sense, comedy can be said to be an art of the audience: the audience's participation finally constitutes the comedy. This is the same principle that Bakhtin recognized as fundamental to Carnival: it isn't a given spectacle which we passively *watch*, but a 'second life' which we *construct*, by actively taking part in it.

This view suggests, therefore, that in addition to, or as part of, their involvement with the 'green' topsy-turvy world of Carnival, Shakespeare's comic plays show a corresponding and defining commitment to oral interlocution as the fundamental mode of a total way of life whose aptest symbol is the circular, 'including' and 'globe'-like structure of the theater itself. In this context, comic plays offer not merely entertainment or distraction, but by the same token, their opposites: positive involvement in and engagement with the fabric of social life. To use Frye's terms, the structure of comedy mirrors that of actual experience in the Elizabethan theater: it serves to unite the 'extremes' of man and nature by means of art, man's 'second' nature. In such a setting, 'drama is doing, through the identity of myth and metaphor, what its ritual predecessors tried to do by the identity of sympathetic magic: unite the human and the natural worlds' (*A Natural Perspective*, p. 46). Such a unity cannot be achieved in the world of ordinary experience in which man is an alienated spectator. It can only take place in the theater, where, paradoxically, the world of the spectator vanishes, and we become participants in the play, which, as art, is identical with nature at its highest level.

Shakespeare's comic plays can thus be seen not merely to assert the topsy-turvy values of Festival and Carnival in the face of a hegemonic 'everyday', but to do so in quite specific terms, asserting the interactive values of orality and community in the face of literate, book-committed Puritan opposition to the theater. And they also assert the central importance of drama's oral mode as a model for, and emblem of, a 'good', participating, creating society, in the face of a 'bad', passive, inert society of consumer-spectators.

Twelfth Night, or, What You Will

In the case of *Twelfth Night*, it is clear that the eruption of 'green world', carnival confusion in the play is on a massive and complex scale. Its well-known commitment to topsy-turviness permits role-confusion, sex-confusion, and confusion over motives to proliferate. Once more the three-stage structure noted by Frye emerges quite clearly. An initial, anti-comic 'external' prohibition is placed upon love and merrymaking by the uninvolved Olivia and Malvolio. A complex confusion of roles and identities follows: Viola becomes Cesario; the Puritan becomes a cross-gartered lover; the clown becomes a priest, and so on. Finally, in the third stage, a new society clearly appears in which the strictures of Puritanism are banished, together with the stilted 'literary' loving of the play's beginning. A more natural, unlearned and implicating mode of good fellowship and affection (its apogée marriage) replaces them.

The most obvious effect of this structure is to focus attention upon Malvolio and to make him a central figure at every stage. As a result, his predominant anticarnival, antiplaying stance serves to foreground the playing/carnival dimension of the play.

This has various effects. Primarily, it pushes the *theatricality* of the play to the fore. Like *A Midsummer Night's Dream*, *Twelfth Night* has a notable dimension of self-reference. It constantly draws attention to its own 'playing' mode, invoking in the process multiple levels of irony, which undermine the standard presuppositions on which the polarities of fiction and truth, appearance and reality rest. Fabian's 'If this were to be played upon a stage now, I could condemn it as an improbable fiction' (III, iv, 131– 2) supplies an appropriate epigraph for the process.

And 'playing', of course, constitutes the means by which the confusions of the second stage are mounted. Viola plays Cesario; Feste plays Sir Topas; Sir Andrew Aguecheek plays a valorous knight. In fact, 'playing' finally functions as the chief means whereby the Puritan Malvolio is mocked, for he is required to become a 'player' himself, to wear carnivalesque regalia (yellow stockings and cross-garters).

The same general concern provides the basis for what Maurice Charney has termed the play's many 'vigorous affirmations of oral discouse'[2] and, eventually, it reinforces and makes telling the implied context of the action: the carnivalesque Feast of the Epiphany, or Twelfth Night. The play's subtitle, *What You Will*, itself hints at the abandonment or topsy-turvy reversal of accepted categories and distinctions, and comedy of the 'turnabout' sort depends wholly, of course, on the interjected responses of an audience whose knowledge of the 'normal' or 'right' order of things provides the essential basis for the actors' reversal of them. The somersaults, oaths, absurd 'dressing-up' and parodies of Carnival require an active response of everyday 'right way up' awareness in order to generate the humor. The job of deliberately invoking this response and of reinforcing and cementing the play's interactive relationship with its audience falls naturally to its Lord of Misrule, Toby Belch, whose name orally reinforces the Bakhtinian principle that Carnival asserts the lower aspects of the body (the belly) above the higher ones (the head).

Overall, it might be said that the 'double' or interactive nature of oral interchange serves in this play as a model that illuminates and is illuminated by the double or interactive nature of drama, especially comic drama, and the 'double vision' this implies. Effectively, orality involves doubleness: an engagement between at least two persons who alternately speak and listen and, in so doing, have two roles. In comic drama, that which is *single* is anticomic, as we have said, a joke requires another's response to 'complete' it (Rosalind explains the same point in *Love's Labour's Lost*, V, ii, 861ff). The player, like the speaker–hearer, like the participant in Carnival, is two people at the same time: a 'real' person and a 'dressed-up' or 'topsy-turvy' version. The values of comic drama seem somehow to inhere in this interactive, carnivalesque, oral–aural duplicity.

Duplicity certainly stands as a central feature of *Twelfth Night*. Nothing is what it seems to be: 'Nothing that is so, is so' (IV, i, 9). In general terms, the play seems to put the case that the perspective on the world afforded in it proves the more appropriate and the more coherent by reason of the 'double' nature of its vision. The theater itself links the world the actor inhabits on the stage with the one we inhabit in the auditorium: his world 'doubles' or mirrors ours. That benign duplicity, finally symbolized in *Twelfth Night* perhaps by the 'doubling' of Viola/Cesario or of the identical twins at the end of the play, who combine, as actors do, 'One face, one voice, one habit and two persons' (V, i, 215), offers a mode wholly appropriate to our human, social nature. It is, in the Duke's words, 'A natural perspective' which both 'is and is not' (V, i, 216). For to an audience, most of whose members probably engaged in acting in carnival or festive occasions at various points of the year, the duplicity of the player's activity and the doubling, interactive mode of life that it implies must have connoted, to a degree far in excess of our modern experience, the truly natural.

On the other hand, Malvolio's commitment to the single version of

Puritanism is seen to deny the fruitful duplicity that Carnival and playing enshrine. Appropriately, his punishment requires him to be 'carnivalized' and to take part in that dressing-up. Only in the structured Carnival confusion between holiday and everyday – or, in the versions of that which the art of an oral society raises to great heights, such as the duplicity of meanings celebrated by the pun, the *double entendre* or the confusion between male and female, stage and auditorium – is the good society constituted. In comedy, the double worlds of Carnival and everyday find themselves at first opposed, then fruitfully intertwined, and finally essentially twinned.

Since interactive 'conversation' between these worlds generates, it seems, all that we know of the natural and the real, it is important to grasp that its model is the human interaction that orality involves: that characteristic human activity of talking and listening which forms the raw material out of which plays are made. The union between stage and auditorium that occurs at the end of a play, when spectators inherit their own 'doubling' roles as participants, can stand as a continuing memorial to that oral process. Malvolio's single-minded Puritan denial of cakes and ale is also a denial of the 'second', oral world of drama; of those improbable fictions that, as *Twelfth Night* tells us and as experience confirms, in fact, constitute a considerable part of reality.

Notes

1. More recently, the wide-reaching implications of the native comic tradition have been stressed by ROBERT WEIMANN, *Shakespeare and the Popular Dramatic Tradition in the Theatre* (Baltimore: Johns Hopkins University Press, 1978), which pointed to the contribution of earlier studies such as S.L. BETHELL, *Shakespeare and the Popular Dramatic Tradition* (London: Staples, 1944).

2. MAURICE CHARNEY, 'Comic Premises of *TN*', *The New York Literary Forum* 1 (1978), 162.

9   All's Well that Ends Well (1602–04)

CAROLYN ASP *'Subjectivity, Desire and Female Friendship in All's Well That Ends Well'**

In a vague phrase, used as early as 1896, *All's Well that Ends Well* is sometimes described as a 'problem play' rather than a comedy. Unlike the widely used term for the four later comedies, 'the romances', the term has not stuck. It has, somewhat confusedly, been applied to *Measure for Measure, Troilus and Cressida, The Merchant of Venice, Hamlet, Julius Caesar, Antony and Cleopatra, Much Ado about Nothing*, as well as to *All's Well that Ends Well*. The phrase is not a helpful one, except to point to a feature of all the comedies – their propensity to raise serious or difficult issues antithetical to light entertainment, and to encourage responses that are rarely purely comic and that often call into question comedy's expected happy ending. In a sense, all of Shakespeare's plays are problem plays.

The ingredients of the play are familiar. A strong, idealistic heroine and a petulant, reluctant lover give it particular affinities with *Much Ado about Nothing*. One can align the play with the other romantic comedies not merely in terms of its familiar structural elements, but because it raises questions of gender assignment. As Asp shows, it can be read as a proto-feminist play, showing the rise of an assertive woman claiming her choice of marriage partner, and attempting to break beyond traditional passivity. Or, alternatively, the ending might be seen – as with *As You Like It* – as a concession to a recuperative patriarchy.

That man should be at a woman's command and yet no hurt done!
(I, iii, 92)

According to prevailing opinion, *All's Well That Ends Well* is a 'problem play' whose major difficulty is located in the very assertion that the title makes in summarizing the action. In the opinions of many critics the play

---

* Reprinted from *Literature and Psychology* **32** (1986), edited by Richard Feldstein.

175

does not 'end well' because the resolution remains on the structural level rather than moving to the psychological level.[1] The frog prince remains a frog until the end and the princess chooses to overlook his slimy skin. If the reader or theatergoer expects the romance of heterosexual coupling that concludes Shakespeare's 'high comedies', disappointment is inevitable.

Singular among the plays in Shakespeare's canon, *All's Well That Ends Well* is written out of the history of the female subject and this history is the history of her desire. The inadequacy of the male as subject is not only NOT repressed; it is emphasized. In this, the play challenges both culture and theory which both subordinate the issue of woman-as-subject-of-desire to the question of male subjectivity and desire. Renaissance notions of female inferiority (and consequent objectification) were largely based on physiological schemes. The cultural stereotypes that mandated female subordination were (and are) often legitimized by the appeal to the irreducible realm of the real, i.e., nature. Both Aristotle and Galen after him declared that the female is characterized by deprived, passive, material traits and is cold and moist (earthy) in her dominant humours. Because the female is less fully developed than the male, her sexual organs have remained internal; she is therefore incomplete in a teleological scheme that aims toward perfection, i.e., the male. Heat, associated with perfection on the physical level, is a male characteristic; it is the lack of heat in the process of generation that causes the genitalia of the female to remain internal and therefore imperfect. The male characteristic of heat thrusts out the genitalia and produces a perfect human specimen.[2] To round off the paradigm, this assumed frailty of body was thought to be accompanied by mental and emotional weaknesses which were the natural justification of the female's exclusion from responsibility and moral fulfilment. Although the explanations used to justify female subordination to patriarchal structures have become increasingly complex in our day, the figure of the female hero in Renaissance drama, a figure who, especially in the comedies, rebels against her 'natural' inferior position (or better yet, pays it no heed), still serves as a model of self-determination, i.e. as the subject of her desire, not the object of another's. Because there was much of the new in the old, much of the old in the new, I wish to use certain paradigms from psychoanalytic theory that are congruent with Renaissance notions of the character and place of the female to discuss the complexities and ambiguities of the central female character in *All's Well That Ends Well*. Viewed from this perspective Helena can be seen as coming to independent womanhood by surmounting attitudes and theories of female deprivation and inferiority.[3] Psychoanalytic theory is a useful tool for such an investigation because it attempts to account for the phenomenon of female inferiority in terms of structural psychic formations and introjected cultural ideals; but it is also limited in that it insufficiently addresses itself to female psychic formation, i.e., to a female version of the Oedipal crisis. Until recently, despite Freud's late interest in the 'pre-Oedipal phase', which stresses the mother–infant relationship,[4] psychoanalytic theory had largely ignored that stage of development. Helena, in her ambiguity, represents a challenging subject for the psychoanalytic critic in that she breaks out of both the cultural (historical) and psychic (trans-historical) strictures applied to women in both her time and our own. She does this by the assertion of desire, the refusal of objectification and by interaction with other women in the play.

According to psychoanalytic theory, particularly Lacanian theory, the inauguration of subjectivity and desire is based upon a male model, the model of the Oedipal crisis. That model stipulates the phallus as the signifier for the needs and drives which the subject must relinquish to gain access to the symbolic order, the order of language, culture, and symbolization. In the Lacanian scheme the phallus is not identifiable with the penis; it is, however, the signifier for the cultural privileges which define male subjectivity and legitimate his desire within the patriarchal order. The female subject remains isolated from this register, ironically, because she has no penis to lose or exchange for the phallus.[5] As Luce Irigaray comments: 'All theories of the "subject" will always have been appropriated by "the masculine". . . . The subjectivity denied to the woman is, without doubt, the condition which guarantees the constitution of any object: object of representation, of discourse, of desire.'[6] The scene of 'castration' has only one subject as the concept of penis envy implies; the little girl sees herself through the eyes of the boy as 'lacking'. The 'truth' of female sexuality, therefore, is 'truth-as-lack'.

The male subject, on the other hand, gives up the penis (direct expression of his own sexuality) to attain the phallus (the privileges of the patriarchal order). The female subject does not succumb to as radical an alienation from sexuality but neither does she enjoy as full a participation in the patriarchal order. Female sexuality, then, is not represented by the phallus (power) but by 'castration' or lack. Since female sexuality cannot be represented (it is lack or absence) it remains 'a dark continent' that, according to male theory, threatens to overpower both the female and the patriarchal order. According to Antonia Fraser, this 'menacing' aspect of female sexuality was well known and greatly feared by seventeenth-century males. In addition to the testimony of countless *dramatis personae*, there is the witness of such men as Thomas Wythorne and poets from Wyatt to Lovelace.[7]

Although there is a nice logic about this paradigm it is contrary to common sense to assume that the female is outside of signification or that her sexuality is any less structured or repressed by culture than is the male's. In entering into meaning and symbolization the female makes a sacrifice analogous to that of the male, i.e., the sacrifice of the mother and the gratifications she supplies.[8] The difference is that the girl's sexuality is negatively rather than positively defined. This definition occurs on a cultural level which assigns public power and prestige to the male. In developmental processes gender myths of female lack and male fullness are internalized and treated as 'true' and identification with stereotyped characteristics takes place. On this cultural, or symbolic level, then, both men and women are conditioned to think of the male as 'all' and the female as 'not-all'. Prior to the Oedipal crisis, however, the subject is bisexual (Freud, *Standard Edition* XX, p. 118) undetermined by gender myths. Although physiological lack may be used to justify the idea of female inferiority, it is not the cause. Penis-envy, such as it is, is symbolic rather than organic, referring to social power rather than to physical potency. Since the female functions as a signifier of lack in culture the male must accommodate himself to the fact of difference by either establishing the woman's unworthiness or by transforming her into a compensatory object. This objectification of woman (as castrated) is designed to annihilate the threat that she represents. Similar relief is found in the disparagement of women by which the male takes pleasure through control and punishment.[9] (Jacques Lacan, *Séminaire* III, ed. Jacques-Alain Miller (Paris: Seuil, 1973–4), p. 198. Other references to the séminaires in the text refer to the French editions published by Seuil and edited by Miller).

The subject's entry into the Symbolic Order (language, culture, power) displaces the mother as the central object of desire with the father; this transaction is of crucial importance in the constitution of the subject. The son identifies with the father as possessor of cultural power; the daughter with the mother as one who lacks such power. The result of such internalization is a profound sense of inadequacy both for the male and the female – the son can never be equivalent to the symbolic father (the position with which he identifies and with which he identifies the actual father); the daughter is denied even an identification with that position (Silverman, p. 191).

This was especially true in matters of sexuality and marriage in Renaissance England where the role of female desire was widely held to be small, even non-existent. According to Lawrence Stone, the qualities most valued in a woman in the sixteenth and seventeenth centuries were weakness, submissiveness, charity and modesty: 'the theological and legal doctrines of the time were especially insistent upon the subordination of women to men in general and to their husbands in particular'.[10] Ian McLean, after an extensive review of the learned documents devoted to the discussion of women in Renaissance theory, comes to the conclusion that the single greatest force preventing fundamental changes in the notion of women in the Renaissance was the institution of marriage; in the eyes of Renaissance thinkers – all male, by the way – marriage is a divine, natural and social institution and any alternative is considered subversive (p. 85). Rethe Warnicke states that ' . . . women were expected to marry, and those who did not were denied the respect of their communities'.[11] Any change in the position of the silent and submissive wife in relationship to her lordly husband would require a new vision of the mental and physical predispositions of the sexes; this was too radical even for such Utopian writers as Thomas More and Rabelais.

Renaissance handbooks on marriage speak of the 'choice of a wife' but never the choice of a husband. It is the man – the suitor – who seeks, who chooses. He does not expect the woman to seek him or to take the initiative in declaring her love first. It was generally agreed by wise heads that both physical desire and romantic love were unsafe bases of an enduring marriage, since both were regarded as violent mental disturbances which could only be of short duration. Women were especially prone to fits of passion; a menacing aspect of female desire was the woman's suspected carnality as the sixteenth-century mysogynist, Thomas Wythorne, states: 'Though they be weaker vessels, yet they will overcome, 2, 3 or 4 [sic] men in satisfying their carnal appetites' (quoted in Fraser, p. 4). Women were considered incapable of making a wise choice in the best interests of marriage. After arguing against 'enforced marriages' in *The Anatomy of Melancholy*, Robert Burton adds: 'A woman should give unto her parents the choice of her husband lest she be reputed to be malapert and wanton, if she take upon her to make her own choice, for she should rather seem to be desired by a man than to desire a man herself.'[12] Somewhat later in the century (1688) Lord Halifax writes in his *Advice to a Daughter*:

> 'It is one of the disadvantages belonging to your sex, that young
> women are seldom permitted to make their own choice; their friends'
> care and experience are thought safer guides to them than their own
> fancies, and their modesty often forbiddeth them to refuse when their
> parents recommend, though their inward consent may not entirely go
> along with it. . . . You must first lay it down for a foundation in general
> that there is inequality in the sexes, and that for the better economy of
> the world, men, who were to be law-givers, had the larger share of
> reason bestowed upon them, by which means your sex is better pre-
> pared for the compliance that is necessary for the better performance of
> those duties which seem to be most properly assigned to it' [i.e., the
> duties of marriage].
>
> (quoted in Stone, p. 278)

This representative patriarchal statement implies that the duties of compliance and subservience which the marriage doctrine enjoins could only be performed by those limited by nature (biological determinism) to a lesser level of intelligence than man. As late as 1706 Mary Astell still laments: 'A woman, indeed, can't properly be said to choose; all that is allowed her is to refuse or accept what is offered' (Stone, p. 275).

Ruth Kelso, who has surveyed an impressive variety of treatises on female behavior in *The Doctrines of the Lady of the Renaissance*, finally speculates that such emphasis would probably not have been placed on the submission and obedience of women and the inborn superiority of men if women in general were not asserting themselves in the pragmatic sphere. According to Kelso, the womanly ideal as found in male writings represents a most unrealistic separation of theory from fact.[13] Joan Kelly adds another dimension to the pragmatic argument by quoting Lucrezia Marinella who speculates that the psychology of educated men (the authors and authorities) who both vituperated and idealized women was based on both the necessity of feeling superior to women and the displacement of sexual feelings.[14] The received opinion on the value and place of women in a male world was based on male psycho-sexual experiences, not on observation and truth to experience (Kelly, p. 82). Learned treatises on the relations of the sexes and marriage were contaminated by the need to maintain male supremacy even if that meant flying in the face of truth. In the face of such bias, how was a true image of woman to be recovered?

It was in the drama in particular that a new portrait of the female began to emerge during the late sixteenth and early seventeenth centuries. No matter what the various guises in which she appears, this woman has one consistent trait: she does not think of herself merely as an appendage of man; she insists on making her own decisions. It is this insistence that is so threatening to the patriarchal prerogative; it sets her apart from the conventional woman and often subjects her to attack or disapproval. One of the most interesting types of female rebels is the one who, like Helena, insists on the right to choose her own husband, to assert her own desire. This was a radical demand. A woman's right to love and marry according to her own desires could not be admitted without upsetting an established order which regarded women as inferior beings who needed to be governed by the sex for whose pleasure and convenience they had been created. Yet with the recognition that woman as well as man was 'a reasonable creature' came the acceptance of the fact that she should use her reason in one of the most vital concerns of her life – the choice of a marriage partner and her relations with him. To find this type of assertive woman very much alive and extremely articulate in Renaissance drama is surely a surprise, given the repressive nature of the tracts and sermons. But it is a surprise that leads to a deeper understanding of what is actually new in what seems old; it also provides an interesting and often amusing instance of that gradual process by which the new attitudes supplant old ones over a period of time and produce profound societal changes.[15]

Helena, in the opening scene, seems to have internalized the 'lack' mapped onto the female body; she acquiesces in her own powerlessness as defined by her context and tearfully accepts Bertram's inaccessibility as a love object. In this scene she plays out her role as passive, even masochistic female. This problematic first appearance can be explained by looking at her behavior from the viewpoint of psychoanalytic theory which postulates that female masochism is connected with gender identity and sexual desire, both social products. When the girl completes the Oedipal crisis, she also, like the boy must renounce the mother, the first love-object, and turn to the father who will not affirm the phallus in her (as he does for the boy), but instead will give it to her. When she turns to the father, she represses the active part of her libido: 'hand in hand [with turning to the father]' says Freud, 'there is to be observed a marked lowering of the active sexual impulses and the rise of the passive ones . . . The transition to the father is accomplished with the help of passive trends insofar as they have escaped from the catastrophe. The path of femininity now lies open to the girl' (Freud, *SE*, XXI, p. 239). It is this path of powerlessness and dependence which Helena initially believes she must adopt in regard to her desire for Bertram.

The ascendence of passivity in the girl is due to her recognition of the futility of realizing her active desire and of the unequal terms of the struggle. A segment of erotic possibility (female desire) is constrained. This realization, reinforced by cultural norms, prompts Helena's excessive and according to the other characters, unspecified emotional response. The creation of 'femininity' in women as they are socialized also leaves in them a resentment of the constraints to which they were subjected, but they have few ways of expressing this residual anger, even rage. Not only is passivity inculcated in the girl; masochism is as well. When she turns to the father because she must, she discovers that 'castration' (lack of power) is the condition of the father's love, that she must be a woman (signifier of lack) to evoke his love. She therefore begins to desire to be castrated, or powerless, trying to turn a disaster into a wish. In finding her place in the sexual system, then, the woman is robbed of libido and guided into masochistic eroticism (Freud, *SE*, XXII, p. 128).

Although Helena at first seems to embody these psychoanalytic paradigms of psychic masochism and powerlessness, she struggles at several points in the play to defy them and moves from tearful and powerless acceptance of her position – and a concomitant construction of herself as object – to an assertive desire of which she is the subject. How does this shift occur? In her bawdy and witty banter with Parolles on the subject of virginity they both speak of sexuality with the metaphors of warfare. This conversation brings wit into contact with aggressivity and narcissism, thus establishing a contact with unconscious desire. Desire can be restricted within the bounds of societal gender myths or it can follow its own trajectory and operate independently of them. Helena quickly shifts into resolve rooted in desire and determines upon cunning, aggressive action: a woman need not always defend her virginity against attack, i.e., remain an object; she may in fact, go on the offensive and 'lose it to her own liking' (I, i, 145). Desire here overcomes both gender and class; under the impress of its mobile power the unpropertied, educated female had much to gain, even though such a desirous woman was regarded as a usurper of the masculine function and prerogative. Filled with resolve she casts off abjection: 'Who ever strove/To show her merit that did miss her love?' (I, i, 218–19).

Helena is not alone in her struggle, however. In a canon in which mother–daughter relationships are so few, this play is unusual in having several. Although Helena is a ward of the Countess, it is obvious that the Countess extends to her the love of a mother for a child: 'you ne'er oppressed me with a mother's groan', she tells Helena, 'yet I express to you a mother's care (I, iii, 140–1). Helena quibbles, rejecting a fraternal relationship with Bertram: not 'daughter' but 'daughter-in-law' is the title she desires. When Helena admits her love to the Countess as well as her scheme to cure the King, the Countess allows Helena to speak of her desire, gives her an empathetic hearing, and bids her success, promising what aid she can. Helena appeals to the Countess' own youthful female experience thus creating a bond of womanly desire that transcends class.[16] It is obvious that the Countess regards Helena as an appropriate wife for Bertram, but leaves the initiative to her (the King, as Bertram's guardian, has the right to dispose of the young man). Once Helena has legally secured the reluctant Bertram and he rejects her, she returns to the Countess who verbally castigates her son but can do nothing to change the situation. The Countess functions as an emotional center who utters the correct – and truly felt – sentiments, but who is ineffectual to help Helena in any way except through verbal support. Albeit a kind and caring woman, a validator of Helena's desire, the Countess limits her effectiveness and accepts her position of dependence within the patriarchal order.

Helena leaves the maternal aegis of the Countess on the strength of her paternal inheritance; 'prescriptions of rare and prov'd effects', male learning passed on to her as her dowry. She must leave the mother-figure to insert herself with a larger, public group and utilize the skills bequeathed her by her father. Armed with the patriarchal legacy of language and learning, she confronts and confounds 'the schools' and attempts the king's cure. By curing the debilitating fistula (a sexually symbolic disease) Helena restores the king's manly vigor upon which the success of her project depends. But prior to the cure, she engages the royal honor: 'Then shalt thou give me with thy kingly hand/What husband in thy power I will command' (II, i, 194–5). It is in her best interest to restore power to the patriarchy which she plans to engage in her behalf.

This request, which depends upon patriarchal power for its implementation, paradoxically subverts the very order of patriarchy itself. Throughout history women, not men, have been sexual objects, gifts. The 'exchange of women' expresses the social relations of a kinship system that specify that men have certain rights in their female kin and that women do not have such rights over themselves or their male relatives. In this system the preferred female sexuality is one that responds to the desires of others rather than one which actively seeks an object and a response (Lacan, *Séminaire* II, p. 306). We ask: 'What would happen if a woman demanded a certain man as her gift rather than the other way around?' This play shows us what happens. The king's debt to Helena is reckoned in Bertram's flesh; he must become the sexual partner to her to whom he is 'owed' as the reward for the restoration of the king's flesh.[17] Bertram resists this structural 'feminization', loudly voicing the resentment that accompanies objectification, a resentment that arises from having been given no choice: 'I beseech your highness./In such a business give me leave to use/The help of mine own eyes' (II, iii, 105–7).

The play contains a series of triangular exchange transactions of which this is the first. By power the king provides a substitute sexual partner for Helena who will function as his 'stand in'. It is obvious that he values and desires Helena more than any other female in the play – what man does not love the woman who restores his virility? But Helena is determined to have Bertram, and the king, by virtue of his position, is outside the circuit of desire, Subject *par excellence*! Up to this point Helena attempts to control events less through her own sexuality and desire than through patriarchal gifts to her. These gifts come to her in language: prescriptions, learning, promises that will enable her to possess legally what she desires. Even though she is emboldened by desire, she is unable to evoke the desire of the other (Bertram), the ultimate goal in Lacanian psychic dynamics. So what she gets is a marriage in name only – an ironic reward – a marriage that Bertram never intends to honor with his flesh. The letter but not the spirit of the law is fulfilled. So her scheme has both succeeded and failed. This seems to be the limit for female desire that relies too heavily on even the best-intentioned of men.

After the check of Bertram's rejection Helena initiates a complex and indirect action for attaining her desire, an action in which she relies both on her own cunning and on bonding with other women. Taking up the apparently impossible conditions of Bertram's rejection as a challenge – 'When thou canst get the ring upon my finger, which shall never come off, and show me a child begotten of thy body that I am father to, then

call me husband, but in such a "then" I write "never" ' (III, ii, 56–9).
Helena paradoxically weaves her net of capture by literally following his
directives, turning his language into a trap. Her campaign initiatives arise
from the very messages he sends denying her. Responding to his refusal
to return to his ancestral lands 'till I have no wife' she disguises herself as
a pilgrim and sets out for Florence where it is possible she knows he is
stationed. Ostensibly she appears submissive to his will, but her
submission is also a strategy; her success from this point until the end is
linked to her ability to assume a 'feminized' (inferior, powerless) position
and yet remain in cognitive control of the situation. This combination of
positions is exceedingly potent and establishes her mastery in the second
half of the play.

In the early part of the play the ideal that Helena thinks she sees in
Bertram is not merely hidden; it is absent, lacking. She eventually must
come to terms with this fact. Bertram is not a sufficient representation of
the 'virile object' that Helena sees only in her fantasy. We might wonder
why she so desires him. In Lacanian terms, Helena is initially trapped in
the level of consciousness called the Imaginary, i.e., the register in which
opposition and identity are the only possible interrelationships between
self and other. This 'other' is usually someone or something which is
thought to complete the subject or reflects back to him/her an ideal image
(Lacan, *Ecrits* 2–4). The Imaginary is the register of the ego, a construct
that involves a purely dual either/or relationship that resembles that of
the Hegelian master/slave paradigm. The predominance of the Imaginary
in relationships results in the conversion of interdependent similarities
and differences between man and woman into pathological identities and
oppositions (as between images of man and woman). To enter into
productive relationships it is necessary to transcend the oppositional
relationships and reduce mastery to insignificance by means of this
transcendence. During the course of the action Helena traverses this path
of development, passing from the register of the Imaginary to that of the
Symbolic Order (Lacan, *Séminaire* I, p. 215). Early in the play she is almost
overwhelmed by opposition in her relationship with Bertram; she can see
only unbridgeable separations. Then she swings to the opposite,
narcissistically identifying his desire with her own, never doubting her
ability to win him. His severe rejection forces her to align herself with the
limits of the possible. Finally she comes to a third position within the
Symbolic Order, the register of similarities and differences, of the social
and the cultural. She must accept the fact that his desire, whatever it may
be, may be different from her own. Her original desire for Bertram seems
to be displaced by her own maternity and by her return to the mother so
that she is inserted into the larger cultural sphere of social and familial
engagement. Paradoxically she does this by remaining true to her desire
(is this type of maturation initiated, then, by desire within the register of

the Imaginary?); as desiring subject she not only gets what she thinks she wants but more. And it is in this 'more', this excess, that Helena's real triumph is located. This excess has to do with her increasing realization of the pragmatic and psychological support that female bonding provides for her in her erotic adventures.

In contrast to the Countess who is a very real but passive support, the Florentine women, a mother and daughter with whom Helena plots, are active on her behalf. Fallen from fortune, they must make their way in the world and struggle to defend their hard-earned gains. The precious jewel of her treasury is Diana's chastity, a 'commodity' that commands a high price. As a consequence, these women have nothing but distrust and contempt for male language, especially the male language of seduction; instead, they rely on female lore: 'My mother told me just how he would woo,/As if she sat in's heart' (IV, ii, 69–70) says Diana, fore-armed against Bertram's vows. When these women show a willingness to believe her story, Helena grasps the opportunity to fulfil the letter of Bertram's law, an opportunity that Bertram's 'sick desires' for Diana give her. In a scene of many exchanges she buys Diana's place with gold while Bertram thinks he is purchasing Diana's 'ring' (genitals) with the patriarchal ring of Rosillon.[18] What occurs is a triangular transaction between women in the possession of a man. In this circuit of desire Diana remains aloof, Helena gets what she wants and Bertram gets what he does not know he does not want. Without cognitive power, Bertram assumes the role of a circulatable commodity; again he is 'feminized'.

In transactions of heterosexual desire, there can be hidden strategies of bonding which seem to occur here; the bond between Helena and Diana is cemented by means of sexual substitution. Earlier in the play (I, iii) there is an odd conversation between Lavatch and the Countess in which Lavatch describes the use he will make of Isbel to create 'friends' for himself. Voluntary cuckoldry creates a bond among men with the 'other' (the partner of opposite sex) as the object to be exchanged among them. When the Countess remonstrates: 'Such friends are thine enemies, knave', Lavatch points out to her this new type of bonding: 'He that comforts my wife is the cherisher of my flesh and blood; he that cherishes my flesh and blood loves my flesh and blood; he that loves my flesh and blood is my friend; ergo, he that kisses my wife is my friend' (I, iii, 43–7). Lavatch describes a literal series of heterosexual displacements in which implicit homoerotic desire is represented as heterosexual adultery. Isbel will mediate a communion among males. Is Lavatch a fool or a knave or neither? He describes himself as involved in triangular sexual transactions in which he maintains control through knowledge and manipulation. As either thief or distributor he regards women as circulatable commodities, objects of desire. His song invoking Helen of Troy underlines this paradigm of the shared woman, the common ground of male desire.

Helena's sexual experience with Bertram, in which she substitutes her body for that of the desired Diana's, leaves her with the conviction of the impersonality of the act. 'Strange men' – in several senses of that word – make sweet use of what they hate, i.e., the female body with its threatening lack. 'Lust doth play/With what it loathes' (IV, iv, 24–5) in the darkness which hides both the particularity (subjectivity) of the woman and the place of castration. Lacan explains this imbalance by commenting that what man approaches in the sexual act is the cause of his desire (lack). The male identifies the woman with what he has repressed in himself and makes love to complete himself in her. Thus the woman's specificity is subordinate to the man's quest for this own fulfilment (Ragland-Sullivan, p. 292). Helena seems both shocked and disillusioned by this experience of sexual objectification in which she is not seen and in which she may not speak. Yet from this place of apparent lack (her genitals) and seeming powerlessness she traps the cozened Bertram's wild desires and lures them into consummating the legal bond. Publicly commenting on her experience later in the play, Helena admits that Bertram's sexual performance was 'wondrous kind' (V, iii, 305), gentle and natural.

After Helena has fulfilled Bertram's stipulations, the ensuing action is excessive, almost gratuitous. I believe that it is only at this point that Helena moves beyond the Imaginary (projected idealizations) with respect to Bertram and begins to see him as he is. All traces of psychological masochism vanish from her character and she begins to express a residual anger toward him, a desire to punish him for having rejected her desire and objectified her. It becomes clear that she has his public humiliation in mind since she now has achieved a cognitive leverage over him which gives her power. She has sent back word to France that she is 'dead', i.e., she represents 'castration' or loss as the ultimate lack or absence. Paradoxically it is from this position of 'castration' or loss that she is able to achieve her greatest power as an active subject.[19] What is thought to be absent can be ignored; what is regarded as lost can be thought of as without power. Yet the very veil of disappearance allows the subject room to act with impunity. Once again she enlists the aid of the Florentine women to carry out her project.

Having arrived in France Helena sends a letter ahead to the King via messenger. Because of the unforeseen concatenation of events, it becomes clear that this letter had been prepared in advance by Helena although it is signed with Diana's name. It lays claim to Bertram as a fair exchange for the latter's honour. What becomes increasingly apparent is that Helena is preparing a public confrontation between Diana and Bertram based on a non-event, i.e., an absence that will entrap him in a web of signs (rings) and language (lies) from which he will be unable to escape. The effectiveness of Diana's script turns upon an exchange of rings prior to the bed trick. Here the plot becomes increasingly dense since neither the audience nor most of the characters knows the history of the rings. The disclosure that the ring Diana gave to Bertram had been given to Helena by the King is a shocking surprise. What is even more disquieting is the fact that Helena had given it to Diana explicitly to exchange for Bertram's patriarchal ring, a transfer that indicates Helena's intent to entrap, since encoded in this ring is a secret message to the King: she is in need of his help. The sight of Bertram wearing this ring coupled with Helena's fictional account of her own death leads the King to suspect Bertram of foul deeds. On the defensive, Bertram entangles himself more and more tightly in the snare; brazenly lying, he repudiates Diana and denies any knowledge of Helena. As the *pièce de résistance* Diana produces Bertram's ring, alleging that with it he purchased her honor. Although like Parolles, Bertram may play with language, he cannot deny the object, irrefutable proof of his complicity. Publicly revealed as a liar, a coward and a faithless husband, Bertram has no choice but to stand shamed and endure humiliation. At this point Helena enters triumphant as the *dea ex machina* to clarify and forgive.

By reading events of the second half of the play backwards, so to speak, we can see Helena's complex plan to turn Bertram's desires and fears against him and then make his weakness, perfidy and ignorance public through the accusations of others, herself remaining aloof.[20] It is evident that there is little romance in Helena's attitude toward Bertram at the end of the play; when she greets him she merely makes known her fulfilment of his conditions. When he further questions her, her final words to him are distant and almost foreboding: 'If it appear not plain and prove untrue/Deadly divorce step between me and you' (V, iii, 314–5). This marriage is an unknown item, a risk whose outcome is to be determined beyond the limits of the play. In contrast her greeting to the Countess is warm and affectionate: 'O my dear mother, do I see thee living?' (V, iii, 316). These, her last words in the play, seem to indicate that she has readjusted the focus of her desire.

Along with the power shift that occurs in the second half of the play there seems also to be a psychological reversal. I would go so far as to say that lurking behind Helena's apparent psychological masochism of her initial attitude towards Bertram lies its opposite, i.e., anger or rage at having been denied subjectivity by him and a willingness to inflict pain, a psychological form of sadism.[21] In some ways her reversal is quite shocking but it certainly is not an unusual female paradigm. As mentioned earlier in this essay, the constraint of female desire in a patriarchal system leaves a residual resentment and anger in the woman which most women, unlike Helena, do not have the opportunity to act on. Granted, her action is indirect, even cunning, but for all that, it is eminently effective. As Helena moves from object position into subject status, from passive to active (the latter associated with the masculine 'position') she concomitantly exchanges psychological masochism for a certain degree of willingness to inflict pain or humiliation in the assertion of mastery. Shakespeare manages to put Helena in the subject (sadistic) position without depriving her of our sympathy by shielding her behind the accusations and anger of others whom she has convinced to act in her place. Her agency has been displaced, certainly veiled. We cannot deny that Bertram deserves the punishment she arranges; our puzzlement is reserved for the 'reconciliation' on which the play ends. If there is a reconciliation, then how does it come about and whose attitudes must change?

Helena's shift occurs in two phases in an encounter with the Real, i.e., the given field of existence, nature in self and in the world. The first phase is Bertram's rejection and abandonment of her which forces her to see him as he is; the second is her sexual encounter with him which is lustful and procreative rather than romantic. These encounters with the Real shake her out of the narcissism and the false perceptions associated with the Imaginary register and precipitate her into positioning herself within the Symbolic Order as a viable alternative to the delusory projections of the early part of the play. There is loss but there is also gain. Her position in culture and the collective is ratified by her obvious 'wife-li-ness' and maternity. She is the fleshly sign of the link between the generations and as such holds a secure place in the Symbolic Order (Welsh, p. 21). Helena has successfully rejected the powerlessness of her original position in the Imaginary, emerging from it at another level, carrying the signs of her transaction. It is she, not Bertram, who has both the ring and the child and she will exchange both for his acceptance of her as his wife and mother of his child. Helena's desire now locates itself within the social order – the child in her womb is the heir – but that order is not exclusively patriarchal. In the process of pursuing her desire for Bertram, Helena has come to experience the loyalty, support and kindness of women who not only never doubted her but who never failed her. What began as a pursuit of a man developed into a transaction among women. With skill, intelligence and cunning they use Bertram's very desires to bind him to what his position and phallic potency demand of him. Through the trajectory of desire he becomes the victim of the trick. But the paradox does not operate only in Bertram's case. Let us entertain the possibility that in the pursuit of a husband Helena has actually found a mother, has discovered the power of feminine bonding. Although she carries the sign of her heterosexual eroticism and Bertram's potency, her desire seems to have transcended the narrow limits of such eroticism and moved into the larger sphere of female affectivity. Her sexual experiences and her own maternity seem to create a new awareness of and desire for the maternal body.

Is Helena's turning to women at the end of the play unusual in her immediate social context? Or does it signal some kind of change in sensibility that was actually occurring at the time? Although there has not yet been much investigation of primary documents relating to the bonding of women in the Renaissance, there are many collateral sources which refer to this phenomenon, including works of poetry, fiction and drama which depict strong, loyal, and loving relationships between and among women. In addition, it seems likely that in a society so constrained by rigid gender-role differentiations there would be both the emotional segregation of women from the male world and a corresponding development of bonding within the female circle. It is certainly true that biological realities centered around incessant pregnancies and child-birth traumas bound women together in intimacy. Supportive female networks paralleled the social restrictions on intimacy between men and women. Courtesy books, advice books, sermons, and other male-originated texts all stress gender-role differentiations as well as the social segregation characteristic of the culture.[22]

Although generally speaking the mother–daughter relationship is at the heart of the female world, in Renaissance literature we see bonds of kinship and service forming the basis of intense friendships. The literature frequently depicts a 'conspiracy of women' that organizes itself around female desire. When the male is indifferent or hostile to such desire, the female characters find support in female kin, friends, or servants. Celia conspires with Rosalind; Emilia defends Desdemona to the death; Paulina refuses to abandon Hermione; Cleopatra surrounds herself with her women in the hour of her final triumph. This woman's world has a dignity and integrity that spring from mutual affection and the shared experiences of being a woman in a man's world. The drama of late sixteenth- and early seventeenth-century England, then, provides many examples of not only strong women but of strong friendships between women. According to Juliet Dusinberre, the struggles of many of the heroines in Shakespeare's plays are struggles against the male idea of womanhood; they are efforts to be considered human in a world that sees them only as female, i.e., as powerless, 'castrated', devoid of initiating desire. In these conflicts women are intimate not just as individuals but as women; they develop a loyalty to their sex which can express itself in confederacy, even cunning.[23] For example, in the play under consideration, the Countess is more sympathetic toward Helena than she is to her own son. She assures Helena: '. . . be sure of this/What I can help thee to, thou shalt not miss' (I, iii, 248–9).

Helena succeeds in her scheme because she heeds and follows her desire even though the caveats of internalized gender values and the constraints of society make her task seem impossible. Frequently she occupies the so-called male position, the position of knowledge and

189

power, through the very paradox of her 'castration'; in this position she sets up the exchanges upon which society depends for its continuation. By the play's end she has come to value and depend on the world of women whose power Bertram, with some humility, is forced to acknowledge. Her success argues for a re-evaluation of the patriarchal denigration of female desire and a reconsideration of that desire's power and validity in the social order. Through Helena's single-minded action a redefinition of gender prerogatives has occurred and as a consequence the patriarchal order is modified, if ever so slightly.[24] Fired by her desire, Helena refuses to submit to gender myths that link the female with loss unless that loss can be turned to gain. The play ends as well as it can – all only 'seems well' the king states at the conclusion – given the fact that sexual relations will never be harmonious, that psychic unity is tenuous at best.[25]

Notes

1. P.S. BERGGREN, 'The Woman's Part: Female Sexuality as Power in Shakespeare's Plays', in Lenz, Greene and Neely, pp. 22–3; G.K. HUNTER, 'Introduction' to *AWell* (London: Methuen, 1959), pp. xxix–xxxi. Hunter also comments (pp. liv-lv) that 'in [the problem plays] the strand of psychological realism makes the absence of personal reconciliation seem wanton and careless'. That the ending of the play is not a true resolution but merely a superficial denial of the hero's rebellion is stated by RICHARD WHEELER, 'Marriage and Manhood in *AWell*', *Bucknell Review* 21 (1973), 103–24. R. WARREN, 'Why Does it End Well? Helena, Bertram, and the Sonnets', *Shakespeare Survey* 22 (1969), 79–92, faults Shakespeare for failing to provide a 'powerful and reassuring speech' for Helena at the finale, a definite dramatic weakness in his opinion.

2. IAN MCLEAN, *The Renaissance Notion of Women* (Cambridge: Cambridge University Press, 1980), p. 33.

3. WARREN sees Helena as 'unbearably poignant' and tends to idealize her masochistic tendencies; my argument follows Hunter's insight that 'to fit Helena into the play or to adapt the play to Helena is obviously the central problem of interpretation' (p. xlviii). I agree with Hunter that 'her role is a complex one, but there is an absence of adequate external correlatives to justify this complexity; we are drawn to regard her as an isolated, complex individual' (p. xlix). In his enlightening study of the play, Wheeler, *Shakespeare's Development*, p. 63, keeps to a middle ground when he asserts both her humble, adoring love for Bertram and her 'viperous, cunning and determined pursuit' of him. Psychoanalytic theory can provide paradigms to account for her complex attitudes and behaviours.

4. SIGMUND FREUD, *The Standard Edition of the Complete Psychological Works* (London: The Hogarth Press, 1964), Vol. XXII pp. 112–35. NANCY CHODOROW, *The Reproduction of Mothering* (Berkeley: University of California Press, 1978), has developed this theory in great detail.

5. JACQUES LACAN, *Ecrits: A Selection*, trans. Alan Sheridan (New York: Norton, 1977), p. 66.

6. IRIGARAY, *Speculum*, p. 165.

7. ANTONIA FRASER, *The Weaker Vessel* (New York: Knopf, 1984), p. 4.

8. ELIE RAGLAND-SULLIVAN, *Jacques Lacan and the Philosophy of Psychoanalysis* (Chicago: University of Illinois Press, 1985), pp. 297-8.

9. KAJA SILVERMAN, *The Subject of Semiotics* (London: Oxford University Press, 1983), p. 198.

10. LAWRENCE STONE, *The Family, Sex, and Marriage in England: 1500–1800* (New York: Harper and Row, 1977), p. 199.

11. RETHA WARNICKE, *Women of the English Renaissance and Reformation* (Westport: Greenwood Press, 1983), p. 178.

12. ROBERT BURTON, *The Anatomy of Melancholy* (New York: Vintage, 1932), 'Third partition', p. 238.

13. RUTH KELSO, *The Doctrine of the Lady in the Renaissance* (Urbana: University of Illinois Press, 1978), p. 208.

14. JOAN KELLY, *Women, History and Theory* (Chicago: University of Chicago Press, 1984), p. 81.

15. JOAN GAGEN, *The New Woman* (New York: Twayne, 1954), p. 119.

16. CAROL McKEWIN, 'Counsels of Gall and Grace: Intimate Conversations between Women in Shakespeare's plays' in Lenz, Greene and Neely, pp. 117–32.

17. EVE SEDGEWICK, 'Sexualism and the Citizen of the World', *Critical Inquiry* 10 (1984), 233. See also WHEELER, *Shakespeare's Development*, pp. 49–51, on the deflection of male sexual interest from women to men.

18. ALEXANDER WELSH, 'The Loss of Men and the Getting of Children: *A Well* and *Meas*', *Modern Language Review* 73 (1978), 17–28, argues against Wheeler and later Alexander Kirsch, *Shakespeare and the Experience of Love* (Cambridge: Cambridge University Press, 1981), in their emphasis on the 'threat of castration inherent in the Oedipal situation', i.e. Bertram's identification of Helena with her mother. He asserts that 'inheritance and succession are far more important concerns than Oedipal jealousies (p. 21). Although my focus is not on Bertram, I agree with Welsh that the Oedipal argument is quite weak and unconvincing. Aside from the 'punning' scene between the Countess and Helena, there is no reference to such a motive in the play. In that scene Helena specifically and somewhat playfully, refers to brother/sister incest.

19. Here I disagree with HUNTER, p. xxxii, on the power of coincidence and submission to supernatural forces as the dynamic forces of the second half of the play. Helena actively uses and arranges the circumstances that lead to her success.

20. R.B. PARKER, 'War and Sex in *A Well*', *Shakespeare Survey* 37 (1984), 111–12.

21. Wheeler, *Shakespeare's Development*, pp. 72–3, states that 'the exposure of Bertram releases a righteous feeling of moral outrage and with it a kind of vindictive pleasure that corresponds to the sadistic attack on the internalized object lost in reality described by Freud'.

22. CARROL CAMDEN, *The Elizabethan Woman* (New York: Elsevier Press, 1952), quotes from many such treatises which lead us to believe that women spent a great deal of time together. Henry Parrot, *The Gossips Greeting*, inveighs against

talkative and outgoing women. Burton also refers to gossiping among women as 'their merrie meetings and frequent visitations, mutual invitations in good times . . . which are so in use'. A Dutch traveller named VAN METEREN found this mode of entertainment a notable one among Elizabethan women. He writes: 'all the rest of their time they employ in walking and riding, in playing cards or otherwise, in visiting their friends and keeping company, conversing with their equals and their neighbours and making merry' (p. 162). Educated women also spent their time carrying on an extended correspondence with their female friends.

23. JULIET DUSINBERRE, *Shakespeare and the Nature of Women* (London: Macmillan, 1975), p. 282.

24. Even at the end of the play the king proposes to repeat the process he inaugurated with Helena by finding Diana, the professed virgin, a husband. Lafew's daughter is offered to Bertram and then summarily withdrawn without any consultation with her. The tableau of women at the end of the play is intriguing; it ranges from Diana, who has vowed not to marry, to 'fair Maudlin' who is given and taken back. The widow Countess stands with the newly restored wife–mother, Helena. What seems to be emphasized is the lack of or the problematic nature of heterosexual relationships

25. JACQUES LACAN, *Séminaire XX*, ed. Jacques-Alain Miller (Paris: Seuil, 1973–4), p. 14.

10 Measure for Measure (1604)

JONATHAN DOLLIMORE *'Transgression and Surveillance in Measure for Measure'**

Another comedy often described as a 'problem play', *Measure for Measure* has undergone some startling transformations in the past sixty or so years. Until the 1960s, the dominant view of the play was that it was a Christian allegory, with the Duke representing God, Isabella the human soul, Lucio (and sometimes Angelo) the devil, and built on themes of repentance, salvation and divine grace. The play then was read as a triumphant assertion of the overcoming of temptation and moral relativism by Christian virtues, or as the triumph of 'love', including Christian love, over the 'law', the triumph (in explicitly theological readings) of the New Dispensation over the Old. Such readings, however, needed to explain away the realistic, even seamy setting of the play, ignore the moral ambiguity of some of the Duke's actions, and see the ending – with its use of the familiar comic ending of the principal characters forgiven, reconciled and (especially) married – as an appropriately beneficent one. Sexual excess – both the 'licence' of Claudio and Lucio, and the self-denial of Isabella – are, according to such a reading, overcome by the moderation of the Duke.

More recently, both directors and critics have seen the play very differently, as a study in ethical relativism and sexual politics, and therefore particularly attuned to the moral indeterminacy of our time. The BBC television production worked unusually well, as it enticed us to peer to voyeuristically into the little room of the screen, seeing and overhearing what we should not – Angelo's manipulation of the masochistically sensual Isabella, his present fixation on what his own puritanism had previously repressed. The production was startlingly contemporary despite the trappings of costume drama: we were brought face to face with what Freud opened for our century – the normality that lies in perversion, the perversions that underlie the normal.

---

* Reprinted from *Political Shakespeare*, edited by Jonathan Dollimore and Alan Sinfield (1986).

Likewise, in recent criticism, as Dollimore's essay notes, an alternative reading has become especially popular – one that emphasizes the manipulative, sinister side of the Duke's power, and the '*positively* anarchic, ludic, carnivalesque ... subversion from below of an oppressive official ideology of order'. By such a reading, Pompey's anarchic disregard of the law is the protest of ordinary life against authoritarianism, Lucio's relaxed sensuality is a positive, the Duke's manipulation an expression of his power, and Isabella's and Angelo's prudery require correction by the necessary material complications of real life as opposed to religious or legal dogma. However startlingly different, as Dollimore points out, such a reading remains 'within the same problematic, only reversing the polarities of the binary opposition which structures it (order/chaos)'. Dollimore's essay is an attempt to go beyond such polarities, both in his reading of the play and as part of the agenda of Cultural Materialism (see Introduction on Cultural Materialism, pp. 20–2).

Nonetheless, it is by means of the polarities criticized by Dollimore that debates on the play have raged in the past twenty or so years. All the crucial questions seem capable of equally plausible, yet contradictory, answers. The Duke's behaviour and morality, Isabella's religious strictness and defence of her chastity against Angelo and, in effect, her brother (though not her capitulation to the Duke, which certainly needs explaining), the moral status of Lucio, Pompey, Claudio and Juliet; the struggles, moral and sensual, of Angelo; the relation of power, law and morality. The ending remains particularly difficult for readers and directors alike. Is it a happy comic ending, in which case the darkness and contradictions it has revealed are only defeated by a trick and remain to haunt us? Is such an ending Shakespeare's desperate or cynical gesture towards other romantic comedies, an inevitable yet shallow conclusion to a situation that has opened up more than he can handle? Or do we read it ironically, as the grim assertion of sexist politics where the strongest and most cunning male authority figure gets the prize – in this case the body of Isabella, fought over by Angelo, the Duke, and the Church? In which case, what happens to the benevolence of the Duke? Whichever way we read it, *Measure for Measure* is certainly – but like all the other comedies, one might add – a problem play.

It might be that the fascination of the play – evidenced by the many recent provocative essays on it, as well as some spectacularly successful productions – is based (as so often) on Shakespeare's trying to extend his and his audiences' expectations of comedy. As in the late romances, he mixes ingredients that, in theory, should not work – and yet he produces a script of such power that his readers make it do so. Or is it rather that, at this stage in his career, he was attempting to do too much? *Measure for Measure* might usefully be read as Shakespeare's last attempt at comedy, one that, as it proceeds, exceeds the possibilities of the genre. It looks forward to the late romances, especially *The Winter's Tale*'s radical juxtaposition of violence and harmony, tragedy and redemption, 'joy' and 'terror'. Thus, without achieving the goal, *Measure for Measure* anticipates another kind of play, one that takes us beyond comedy – and perhaps beyond tragedy as well.

In the Vienna of *Measure for Measure* unrestrained sexuality is ostensibly subverting social order; anarchy threatens to engulf the state unless sexuality is subjected to renewed and severe regulation. Such at least is the claim of those in power. Surprisingly critics have generally taken them at their word, even while dissociating themselves from the punitive zeal of Angelo. There are those who have found in the play only a near tragic conflict between anarchy and order, averted in the end, it is true, but unconvincingly so. Others, of a liberal persuasion and with a definite preference for humane rather than authoritarian restraint, have found at least in the play's 'vision' if not precisely its ending an ethical sense near enough to their own. But both kinds of critic have apparently accepted that sexual transgression in *Measure for Measure* – and in the world – represents a real force of social disorder intrinsic to human nature and that the play at least is about how this force is – must be – restrained.

J.W. Lever, in an analysis of the play noted for its reasonableness,[1] draws a comparison with Shakespeare's romantic comedies where disorders in both society and individual, especially those caused by the 'excesses of sentiment and desire' are resolved: 'not only the problems of lovers, but psychic tensions and social usurpations or abuses, found their resolution through the exercise of reason, often in the form of an adjudication by the representatives of authority'. In *Measure for Measure* the same process occurs but more extremely: 'Not only are the tensions and discords wrought up to an extreme pitch, threatening the dissolution of all human values, but a corresponding and extraordinary emphasis is laid upon the role of true authority, whose intervention alone supplies the equipoise needed to counter the forces of negation.' Lever draws a further contrast with *Troilus and Cressida* where 'no supreme authority exists; age and wisdom can only warn, without stemming the inevitable tide of war and lechery'. On this view then unruly desire is extremely subversive and has to be countered by 'true' and 'supreme authority', 'age and wisdom', all of which qualities are possessed by the Duke in *Measure for Measure* and used by him to redeem the state (pp. lx and lxxi). Only these virtues, this man, can retrieve the state from anarchy.[2]

But consider now a very different view of the problem. With the considerable attention recently devoted to Bakhtin and his truly important analysis of the subversive carnivalesque, the time is right for a radical reading of *Measure for Measure*, one which insists on the oppressiveness of the Viennese state and which interprets low-life transgression as *positively* anarchic, ludic, carnivalesque – a subversion from below of a repressive official ideology of order. What follows aims (if it is not too late) to forestall such a reading as scarcely less inappropriate than that which privileged 'true' authority over anarchic desire. Indeed, such a reading, if executed within the parameters of some recent appropriations of Bakhtin, would simply remain within the same problematic, only reversing the polarities of the binary opposition which structures it (order/chaos). I offer a different reading of the play, one which, perhaps paradoxically, seeks to identify its absent characters and the history which it contains yet does not represent.

Transgression

Whatever subversive identity the sexual offenders in this play possess is a construction put upon them by the authority which wants to control them; moreover control is exercised through that construction. Diverse and only loosely associated sexual offenders are brought into renewed surveillance by the state; identified in law as a category of offender (the lecherous, the iniquitous) they are thereby demonised as a threat to law. Like many apparent threats to authority this one in fact legitimates it: control of the threat becomes the rationale of authoritarian reaction in a time of apparent crisis. Prostitution and lechery are identified as the causes of crisis yet we learn increasingly of a corruption more political than sexual (see especially V, i, 316ff). Arguably then the play discloses corruption to be an effect less of desire than authority itself. It also shows how corruption is downwardly identified – that is, focused and placed with reference to low-life 'licence'; in effect, and especially in the figure of Angelo, corruption is displaced from authority to desire and by implication from the rulers to the ruled. The Duke tells Pompey:

Fie, sirrah, a bawd, a wicked bawd;
The evil that thou causest to be done,
That is thy means to live. Do thou but think
What 'tis to cram a maw or clothe a back
From such a filthy vice. Say to thyself,
From their abominable and beastly touches
I drink, I eat, array myself, and live.

Canst thou believe thy living is a life,
So stinkingly depending?

(III, ii, 18–26)

This is in response to Pompey's observation that such exploitation not
only exists at other levels of society but is actually protected 'by order of
law' (l.8). This is just what the Duke's diatribe ignores – cannot
acknowledge – fixating instead on the 'filthy vice' and its agents in a way
which occludes the fact that it is Angelo, not Pompey, who, unchecked,
and in virtue of his social position, will cause most 'evil . . . to be done'.
But, because Angelo's transgression is represented as growing from his
desire rather than this authority, his is a crime which can be construed as
a lapse into the corruption of a lower humanity, a descent of the ruler
into the sins of the ruled. Provocatively, his crime is obscurely theirs.

If we can indeed discern in the demonising of sexuality a relegitimation
of authority we should not then conclude that this is due simply to an
ideological conspiracy; or rather it may indeed be conspiratorial but it is
also ideological in another, more complex sense: through a process of
displacement an imaginary – and punitive – resolution of real social
tension and conflict is attempted.

The authoritarian demonising of deviant behaviour was common in the
period, and displacement and condensation – to and around low life –
were crucial to this process (see also Paul Brown's analysis on these lines
in *Political Shakespeare*). But what made displacement and condensation
possible was a prior construction of deviancy itself. So, for example,
diatribes against promiscuity, female self-assertion, cross-dressing and
homosexuality construed these behaviours as symptomatic of an
impending dissolution of social hierarchy and so, in effect, of civilisation.[3]
This was partly because transgression was conceived in public and even
cosmic terms; it would not then have made sense to see it in, say,
psychological or subjective terms – a maladjustment of the individual
who, with professional assistance, could be 'normalised'. On the one hand
then homosexuality was not considered to be the 'defect' of a particular
personality type since 'the temptation to debauchery, from which
homosexuality was not clearly distinguished, was accepted as part of the
common lot, be it never so abhorred. For the Puritan writer John Rainolds
homosexuality was a sin to which "men's natural corruption and
viciousness is prone".' And this was because homosexuality 'was not a
sexuality in its own right, but existed as a potential for confusion and
disorder in one undivided sexuality' (Alan Bray, *Homosexuality in
Renaissance England*, pp. 16–17, 25). On the other hand it was
distinguished sufficiently to be associated with other cardinal sins like
religious and political heresy and witchcraft. This association of sexual
deviance with religious and political deviance – made of course in

relation to Marlowe by the informer Richard Baines[4] and rather more recently by the British tabloid press in relation to Peter Tatchell[5] – facilitates the move from specific to general subversion: the individual transgressive act sent reverberations throughout the whole and maybe even brought down God's vengeance on the whole.

Stuart Clark has shown how the disorder which witches and other deviants symbolised, even as it was represented as a threat to order, was also a presupposition of it. Contrariety, he argues, was 'a universal principle of intelligibility as well as a statement about how the world was actually constituted' and 'the characterisation of disorder by inversion, even in relatively minor texts or on ephemeral occasions, may therefore be taken to exemplify an entire metaphysic' ('Inversion, Misrule and Witchraft', pp. 110–12). On this view then the attack on deviancy was not just a diversionary strategy of authority in times of crisis but an elementary and permanent principle of rule. Nevertheless, we might expect that it is in times of crisis that this principle is specially operative. The work of Lawrence Stone would seem to confirm this. He argues that in the early seventeenth century the family household becomes, at least in contemporary propaganda, 'responsible for, and the symbol of, the whole social system, which was thought to be based on the God-given principle of hierarchy, deference and obedience'. Such propaganda was stimulated in part by the experienced instability of rapid change, change which was interpreted by some as impending collapse. According to Stone then, 'the authoritarian family and the authoritarian nation-state were the solutions to an intolerable sense of anxiety, and a deep yearning for order' and the corollary was a ruthless persecution of dissidents and deviants. Sexuality became subject to intensified surveillance working in terms of both an enforced and an internalised discipline.[6] *Measure for Measure*, I want to argue, is about both kinds of discipline, the enforced and the internalised. Their coexistence made for a complex social moment as well as a complex play.

J.A. Sharpe's recent and scrupulous study of crime in seventeenth-century England confirms this discrepancy between the official depiction of moral collapse among the lower orders and their actual behaviour. Sharpe also confirms that the suppression of sexuality was only 'one aspect of a wider desire to achieve a disciplined society. Fornication, like idleness, pilfering, swearing and drunkenness, was one of the distinguishing activities of the disorderly'. Further, the Elizabethan and early Stuart period marked an historical highpoint in an authoritarian preoccupation with the disorderly and their efficient prosecution.[7] Nevertheless, many of those concerned with this prosecution really did believe standards were declining and the social fabric disintegrating. Puritan extremists like Stubbes saw prostitution as so abhorrent they advocated the death penalty for offenders (Lever, p. xlvi). But if, as Stone and others argue, their fervour is the result of insecurity in the face of change, then, even if that fervour was 'sincere', the immorality which incited it was not at all its real cause. This is one sense in which the discourse of blame involved displacement; but there was another: while the authorities who actually suppressed the brothels often exploited the language of moral revulsion it was not the sexual vice that worried them so much as the meeting together of those who used the brothels. George Whetstone was only warning the authorities of what they already feared when he told them to beware of 'haunts . . . in Allies, gardens and other obscure corners out of the common walks of the Magistrate' whose guests are 'masterless men, needy shifters, thieves, cutpurses, unthrifty servants, both serving men and prentices'.[8] Suppression was an attempt to regulate not the vice, nor apparently, even the spread of venereal disease, but the criminal underworld.[9] Similarly, in *Measure for Measure*, the more we attend to the supposed subversiveness of sexual licence, and the authoritarian response to it, the more we are led away from the vice itself towards social tensions which intersect with it – led also to retract several distinct but related processes of displacement.

The play addresses several social problems which had their counterparts in Jacobean London. Mistress Overdone declares: 'Thus, what with the war, what with the sweat, what with the gallows, and what with poverty, I am custom shrunk' (I, ii, 75–7). Lever points out that this passage links several issues in the winter of 1603–04: 'the continuance of the war with Spain; the plague in London; the treason trials and executions at Winchester in connection with the plots of Raleigh and others; the slackness of trade in the deserted capital' (p. xxxii). Significantly, all but the first of these, the war, are domestic problems. But even the war was in prospect of becoming such: if peace negotiations then under way (and also alluded to in the play – at I, ii, 1–17) proved successful it would lead to a return home of 'the multitude of pretended gallants, banckrouts, and unruly youths who weare at this time settled in pyracie' (Lever, p. xxxii). In this political climate even peace could exacerbate domestic ills.

This play's plague references are especially revealing. Both here and at I, ii, 85–9, where Pompey refers to a proclamation that 'All houses in the suburbs of Vienna must be plucked down' there is a probable allusion to the proclamation of 1603 which provided for the demolition of property in the London suburbs in order to control the plague. But the same proclamation also refers to the 'excessive numbers of idle, indigent, dissolute and dangerous persons, and the pestering of many of them in small and strait room'.[10] Here, as with the suppression of prostitution, plague control legitimates other kinds of political control. (Enemies of the theatre often used the plague threat as a reason to have them closed.) As this proclamation indicates, there was a constant fear among those in charge of Elizabethan and Jacobean England that disaffection might escalate into organised resistance. This anxiety surfaces repeatedly in official discourse: any circumstance, institution or occasion which might unite the vagabonds and masterless men – for example famine, the theatres, congregations of the unemployed – was the object of almost paranoid surveillance. Yet, if anything, *Measure for Measure* emphasises the lack of any coherent opposition among the subordinate and the marginalised. Thus Pompey, 'Servant to Mistress Overdone' (list of characters), once imprisoned and with the promise of remission, becomes, with no sense of betrayal, servant to the state in no less a capacity than that of hangman.

Yet those in power are sincerely convinced there is a threat to order. At the very outset of the play Escalus, described in the list of characters as an 'ancient' Lord, is praised excessively by the Duke only to be subordinated to Angelo, the new man. The traditional political 'art and practice' (I, i, 12) of Escalus is not able to cope with the crisis. Later, the Duke, speaking to the Friar, acknowledges that this crisis stems from a failure on the part of the rulers yet at the same time displaces responsibility on to the ruled: like disobedient children they have taken advantage of their 'fond fathers' (I, iii, 23). Hence the need for a counter-subversive attack on the 'liberty' of the low-life. Yet even as we witness that attack we see also that the possibilities for actual subversion seem to come from quite another quarter. Thus when Angelo resorts to the claim that the state is being subverted (in order to discredit charges of corruption against himself) the way he renders that claim plausible is most revealing:

> These poor informal women are no more
> But instruments of some more mightier member
> That sets them on. Let me have way, my lord,
> To find this practice out.
>
> (V, i, 235–7)

Earlier the Duke, pretending ignorance of Angelo's guilt, publicly denounces Isabella's charge against Angelo in similar terms:

> thou knowest not what thou speak'st
> Or else thou art suborn'd against his honour
> In hateful practice . . .
> . . . Someone hath set you on.
>
> (V, i, 108–10; 115)

The predisposition of Escalus to credit all this gives us an insight into how the scapegoat mentality works: just as the low-life have hitherto been demonised as the destructive element at the heart (or rather bottom) of the state, now it is the apparently alien Friar (he who is 'Not of this country', III, ii, 211) who is to blame. The kind old Escalus charges the Friar (the Duke in disguise) with 'Slander to th'state!' and cannot wait to torture him into confession (V, i, 320, 309–10). That he is in fact accusing the Duke ironically underpins the point at issue: disorder generated by misrule and unjust law (III, ii, 6–8) is ideologically displaced on to the ruled – 'ideologically' because Angelo's lying displacement is insignificant compared with the way that Escalus really believes it is the subordinate and the outsider who are to blame. Yet even as he believes this he is prepared to torture his way to 'the more mightier member' behind the plot; again there is the implication, and certainly the fear, that the origin of the problem is not intrinsic to the low-life but a hostile fraction of the ruling order.

Oddly the slander for which Escalus wants to have this outsider tortured, and behind which he perceives an insurrectionary plot, is only the same assessment of the situation which he, Angelo and the Duke made together at the outset. What does this suggest: is his violent reaction to slander paranoid, or rather a strategy of *realpolitik*? Perhaps the latter – after all, it is not only, as Isabella reminds Angelo (II, ii, 135–7) that rulers have the power to efface their own corruption, but that they need to do this to remain in power. And within the terms of *realpolitik* the threat of exposure is justification enough for authoritarian reaction. But the problem with the concept of *realpolitik* is that it tends to discount the non-rational though still effective dimensions of power which make it difficult to determine whether crisis is due to paranoia generating an imaginary threat or whether a real threat is intensifying paranoia. And, of course, even if the threat is imaginary this can still act as the 'real' cause of ensuing conflict. Conversely, terms like paranoia applied to a ruling class or fraction, while useful in suggesting the extent to which that class's discourse produces its own truth and apprehends that truth through blame, can also mislead with regard to the class's power to rationalise its own position and displace responsibility for disorder. Put another way, *realpolitik* and paranoia, in so far as they are present, should be seen to coexist more at a social rather than an individual level. An interesting case in point is George Whetstone's *A Mirror for Magistrates* (1584), a possible source for Shakespeare's play. This work related the story of how the Roman emperor, Alexander Severus, re-establishes order in the state by setting up a system of sophisticated surveillance and social regulation which includes himself going disguised among his subjects and observing their transgressions at first hand. These are denounced with moral fervour and the implication of course is that they are condemned just because they are sinful. But as Whetstone's retelling of the story develops we can see a pragmatic underside to his blameful discourse. In fact, as so often in this period, political strategy and moral imperative openly coexist. The focus of Whetstone's reforming zeal are the 'Dicing-houses, taverns and common stews' – 'sanctuaries of iniquity'. But what gives him most cause for concern is not the behaviour of the low but that of the landed gentry who are attracted to them: 'Dice, Drunkenness and Harlots, had consumed the wealth of a great number of ancient Gentlemen, whose Purses were in the possession of vile persons, and their Lands at mortgage with the Merchants. . . . The Gentlemen had made this exchange with vile persons: they were attired with the Gentlemen's bravery, and the Gentlemen disgraced with their beastly manners' (Izard, *George Whetstone*, p. 135).

Here, apparently, hierarchy is subverted from above and those most culpable the gentlemen themselves. Yet in Whetstone's account the low are to blame; they are held responsible for the laxity of the high, much as a man might (then as now) blame a woman for tempting him sexually whereas in fact he has coerced her. The gentlemen are 'mildly' reproached and restored to that which they have transacted away while the low are disciplined. Whetstone believed that the survival of England depended on its landed gentry; in rescuing them from the low-life he is rescuing the state from chaos and restoring it to its 'ancient and most laudable orders' (Izard, *George Whetstone*, p. 136). A reactionary programme is accomplished at the expense of the low, while those who benefit are those responsible for precipitating 'decline' in the first place. The same process of displacement occurs throughout discourses of power in this period. One further example: one of the many royal proclamations attempting to bring vagabonds under martial law asserts that 'there can grow no account of disturbance of our peace and quiet but from such refuse and vagabond people' (*Tudor Royal Proclamations*, III, 233) – and this despite the fact that the proclamation immediately preceeding this one (just six days before) announced the abortive Essex rebellion. The failure of the rebellion is interpreted by the second proclamation as proof of the loyalty of all other subjects with the exception of that 'great multitude of base and loose people' who 'lie privily in corners and bad houses, listening after news and stirs, and spreading rumours and tales, being of likelihood ready to lay hold of any occasion to enter into any tumult or disorder' (p. 232). For the authoritarian perspective as articulated here, the unregulated are by definition the ungoverned and always thereby potentially subversive of government. At the same time it is a perspective which confirms what has been inferred from *Measure for Measure*: in so far as the socially deprived were a threat to government this was only when they were mobilised by powerful elements much higher up the social scale. Moreover the low who were likely to be so mobilised were only a small part of the 'base and loose people' hounded by authority. In fact we need to distinguish, as Christopher Hill does, between this mob element, little influenced by religious or political ideology but up for hire, and the 'rogues, vagabonds and beggars' who, although they 'caused considerable panic in ruling circles were incapable of concerted revolt' (*The World Turned Upside Down*, pp. 40–1). Of course there were real social problems and 'naturally' the deprived were at the centre of them. Moreover, if we recall that there *were* riots, that fornication *did* produce charity-dependent bastards, that drunkenness *did* lead to fecklessness, it becomes apparent that, in their own terms there also real grounds for anxiety on the part of those who administered deprivation. At the same time we can read in that anxiety – in its very surplus, its imaginative intensity, its punitive ingenuity – an ideological displacement (and hence misrecognition) of much deeper fears of the uncontrollable, of being out of control, themselves corresponding to more fundamental social problems.[11]

Surveillance

In II, i, we glimpse briefly the state's difficulties in ensuring the levels of policing which the rulers think is required. Escalus discreetly inquires of Elbow whether there are any more officers in his locality more competent than he. Elbow replies that even those others who have been chosen happily delegate their responsibility to him.

A similar anxiety about the ungovernability of his subjects leads the Duke to put those of them he encounters under a much more sophisticated and effective mode of surveillance; though remaining coercive, it seeks additionally to get subjects to reposition themselves. First though, a word about the Duke's use of disguise. The genre of the disguised ruler generally presented him in a favourable light. But in Jacobean England we might expect there to have been an ambivalent attitude towards it. In Jonson's *Sejanus*, contemporary with *Measure for Measure*, it is a strategy of tyrannical repression; Jonson himself was subjected to it while in jail, apparently with the intention of getting him to incriminate himself.[12] Next there is the question of the Duke's choice of *religious* disguise. As I've argued elsewhere, there was considerable debate at this time over the 'Machiavellian' proposition that religion was a form of ideological control which worked in terms of internalised submission.[13] Even as he opposes it, Richard Hooker cogently summarises this view; it represents religion as 'a mere politic devise' and whereas state law has 'power over our outward actions only' religion works upon men's 'inward cogitations . . . the privy intents and motions of their heart'. Armed with this knowledge 'politic devisers' are 'able to create God in man by art'.[14]

The Duke, disguised as a friar, tries to reinstate this kind of subjection.

Barnardine is the least amendable; 'He wants advice', remarks the Duke grimly (IV, ii, 144) and is infuriated when the offer is refused. Barnardine is especially recalcitrant in that he admits guilt yet is unrepentant and even disinclined to escape; he thus offers no response on which the Duke might work to return him to a position of dutiful submission. But the Duke does not give up and resolves to 'Persuade this rude wretch willingly to die' (IV, iii, 80; cf. II, i, 35). A similar idea seems to be behind his determination to send Pompey to prison – not just to rot but for 'Correction and instruction' (III, ii, 31). Earlier the Duke had been rather more successful with Claudio. His long 'Be absolute for death' speech (III, i, 5ff) does initially return Claudio to a state of spiritual renunciation, but Claudio has not long been in conversation with Isabella before he desires to live again. Isabella, herself positioned in a state of intended renunciation, struggles to restore Claudio to his. She fails but the Duke intervenes again and Claudio capitulates.

The Duke makes of Mariana a model of dutiful subjection. Predictably, he is most successful with those who are least powerful and so most socially dependent. He tells Angelo to love Mariana, adding: 'I have confess'd her, and I know her virtue' (V, i, 524). He has indeed, and earlier Mariana confirms his success in this confessional positioning of her as an acquiescent, even abject subject (IV, 1, 8–20); for her he is one 'whose advice/Hath often still'd my brawling discontent' (IV, i, 8–9). His exploitation of her – 'The maid will I frame, and make fit for his attempt' (III, i, 256–7) – is of course just what she as confessed subject must not know, and the Duke confirms that she does not by eliciting from her a testimony:

> Duke   Do you persuade yourself that I respect you?
> *Mariana*   Good friar, I know you do, and so have found it
>
> (IV, i, 53–4)

Thus is her exploitation recast and indeed experienced by Mariana, as voluntary allegiance to disinterested virtue.

The Duke's strategy with Isabella is somewhat different. Some critics of the play, liking their women chaste, have praised Isabella for her integrity; others have reproached her for being too absolute for virtue.[15] Another assessment, ostensibly more sympathetic than either of these because psychological rather than overtly moralistic, is summarised by Lever. He finds Isabella ignorant, hysterical and suffering from 'psychic confusion', and he apparently approves the fact that 'through four ... acts' she undergoes 'a process of moral education designed to reshape her character' (pp. lxxx, lxxvii, lxxix, xci). Here, under the guise of normative categories of psychosexual development, whose objective is 'maturity', moralistic and patriarchal values are reinstated the more insidiously for being ostensibly 'caring' rather than openly coercive. But in the play the coercive thrust of such values suggests that perhaps Isabella has recourse to renunciation as a way of escaping them. When we first encounter her in the nunnery it is her impending separation from men that is stressed by the nun, Francisca. The same priority is registered by Isabella herself when she affirms the prayers from 'preserved souls,/From fasting maids, whose minds are dedicate/To nothing temporal' (II, ii, 154–6). She seeks in fact to be preserved specifically from men:

> Women? – Help, heaven! Men their creation mar
> In profiting by them. Nay, call us ten times frail;
> For we are soft as our complexions are,
> And credulous to false prints.
>
> (II, iv, 126–9)

If we remember that in the play the stamp metaphor signifies the formative and coercive power of authority, we see that Isabella speaks a vulnerability freed in part from its own ideological misrecognition; she conceives her weakness half in terms of women's supposed intrinsic 'frailness', half in terms of exploitative male coercion. Further, we see in Isabella's subjection a conflict within the patriarchal order which subjects: the renunciation which the Church sanctions, secular authority refuses. The latter wins and it is Isabella's fate to be coerced back into her socially and sexually subordinate position – at first illicitly by Angelo, then legitimately by the Duke who 'takes' her in marriage.

His subjects' public recognition of his own integrity is important in the Duke's attempt to reposition them in obedience. Yet the play can be read to disclose integrity as a strategy of authority rather than the disinterested virtue of the leader. The Duke speaks frequently of the integrity of rulers but the very circumstances in which he does so disclose a pragmatic and ideological intent; public integrity legitimates authority, and authority takes sufficient priority to lie about integrity when the ends of propaganda and government require it (IV, ii, 77–83). And the Duke knows that these same ends require that integrity should be publicly displayed in the form of reputation. Intriguingly then, perhaps the most subversive thing in the play is the most casual, namely Lucio's slurring of the Duke's reputation. Unawares and carelessly, Lucio strikes at the heart of the ideological legitimation of power. Along with Barnardine's equally careless refusal of subjection, this is what angers the Duke the most. Still disguised, he insists to Lucio that he, the Duke, *'be but testimonied in his own bringings-forth*, and he shall appear to the envious a scholar, a statesman, and a soldier' (III, ii, 140–2, italics added). After Lucio has departed he laments his inability to ensure his subject's dutiful respect: 'What king so strong/Can tie the gall up in the slanderous tongue?' (II,

181–2; cf. IV, i, 60–5). If the severity of the law at this time is anything to go by, such slander was a cause of obsessive concern to Elizabethan and Jacobean rulers,[16] just as it is here with the Duke and, as we have already seen, with Escalus.

The ideological representation of integrity can perhaps be judged best at the play's close – itself ideological but not, it seems to me, forced or flawed in the way critics have often claimed. By means of the Duke's personal intervention and integrity, authoritarian reaction is put into abeyance but not discredited: the corrupt deputy is unmasked but no law is repealed and the mercy exercised remains the prerogative of the same ruler who initiated reaction. The Duke also embodies a public reconciliation of law and morality. An omniscience, inseparable from seeming integrity, permits him to close the gulf between the two, one which was opening wide enough to demystify the one (law) and enfeeble the other (morality). Again, this is not a cancelling of authoritarianism so much as a fantasy resolution of the very fears from which authoritarianism partly grows – a fear of escalating disorder among the ruled which in turn intensifies a fear of impotence in the rulers. If so it is a reactionary fantasy, neither radical nor liberating (as fantasy may indeed be) but rather conservative and constraining; the very disclosure of social realities which make progress seem imperative is recuperated in comedic closure, a redemptive wish-fulfilment of the status quo.

In conclusion then the transgressors in *Measure for Measure* signify neither the unregeneracy of the flesh, nor the ludic subversive carnivalesque. Rather, as the spectre of unregulated desire, they are exploited to legitimate an exercise in authoritarian repression. And of course it is a spectre: desire, culturally manifested, is never unregulated, perhaps least of all in Jacobean London. Apart from their own brutally exploitative sub-cultural codes, the stews were controlled from above. This took several forms, including one of the most subtly coercive of all: economic investment. Some time between 1599 and 1602 the Queen's Lord Chamberlain, Lord Hunsdon, appears to have leased property for the establishing of an especially notorious brothel in Paris Gardens, while Thomas Nashe declared in 1598 that 'whoredom (the next doore to the Magistrates)' was set up and maintained through bribery, and Gāmini Salgādo informs us that 'Most theatre owners . . . were brothel owners too.'[17]

At the same time in this period, in its laws, statutes, proclamations and moralistic tracts, the marginalised and the deviant are, as it were, endlessly recast in a complex ideological process whereby authority is ever anxiously relegitimating itself. *Measure for Measure*, unlike the proclamation or the statute, gives the marginalised a voice, one which may confront authority directly but which more often speaks of and partially reveals the strategies of power which summon it into visibility.

Even the mildly transgressive Claudio who, were it not for the law, was all set to become law-abiding, becomes briefly that 'warped slip of wilderness' (III, i, 141). But if Claudio's desire to live is momentarily transgressive it becomes so only at the potential expense of his sister. The same is true of Pompey and Lucio who, once put under surveillance or interrogation by authority voice a critique of authority itself (III, ii, 6–8; 89–175), yet remain willing to exploit others in their position by serving that same authority when the opportunity arises. Ironically though, it is Angelo's transgressive desire which is potentially the most subversive; he more than anyone else threatens to discredit authority. At the same time his transgression is also, potentially, the most brutally exploitative. This is an example of something which those who celebrate transgression often overlook: even as it offers a challenge to authority, transgression ever runs the risk of re-enacting elsewhere the very exploitation which it is resisting immediately.

What Foucault has said of sexuality in the nineteenth and twentieth centuries seems appropriate also to sexuality as a sub-category of sin in earlier periods: it *appears* to be that which power is afraid of but in actuality is that which power works through. Sin, especially when internalised as guilt, has produced the subjects of authority as surely as any ideology. At the same time it may be that not everyone, indeed not even the majority, has fallen for this. The 'sin' of promiscuity, for example, has always been defended from a naturalistic perspective as no sin at all – as indeed we find in *Measure for Measure*. But those like Lucio who cheerfully celebrate instinctual desire simultaneously reify as natural the (in fact) highly *social* relations of exploitation through which instinct finds its expression, social relations which, we might say, determine the nature of instinct far more than nature itself:

Lucio   How doth my dear morsel, thy mistress? Procures she still, ha?
Pompey   Troth sir, she hath eaten up all her beef, and she is herself in the tub.
Lucio   Why, 'tis good: it is the right of it: it must be so. Ever your fresh whore, and your powdered bawd; an unshunned consequence; it must be so.

(III, ii, 52–8)

And Pompey, whom he refuses to bail, Lucio perceives as 'bawd born' (III, ii, 66). Mistress Overdone, her plight as described here notwithstanding, was one of the lucky ones; after all, the life of most prostitutes outside the exclusive brothels was abject. Overdone is at least a procuress, a brothel keeper. For most of the rest poverty drove them to the brothel and, after a relatively short stay in which they had to run the hazards of disease, violence and contempt, most were driven back to it.

In pursuing the authority–subversion question, this essay has tried to exemplify two complementary modes of materialist criticism. Both are concerned to recover the text's history. The one looks directly for history in the text including the historical conditions of its production which, even if not addressed directly by the text can nevertheless still be said to be within it, informing it. Yet there is a limit to which the text can be said to incorporate those aspects of its historical moment of which it never speaks. At that limit, rather than constructing this history as the text's unconscious, we might instead address it directly. Then at any rate we have to recognise the obvious: the prostitutes, the most exploited group in the society which the play represents, are absent from it. Virtually everything that happens presupposes them yet they have no voice, no presence. And those who speak for them do so as exploitatively as those who want to eliminate them. Looking for evidence of resistance we find rather further evidence of exploitation. There comes a time of course when the demonising of deviant sexuality meets with cultural and political resistance. From the very terms of its oppression deviancy generates a challenging counter-discourse and eventually a far-reaching critique of exploitation. That is another and later story.

Notes

1. J.W. Lever, ed., *Meas* (London: Methuen, 1965).

2. For another kind of critic sexuality in *Meas* continues to be seen as something deeply disruptive though now it is the individual psyche rather than the social order which is under threat. Thus for Marilyn French this is a play which 'confronts directly Shakespeare's own most elemental fears' – hence its 'sexual obsessiveness, mixed guilt, abhorrence'. She writes further of the 'hideous and repellent quality sex has throughout the play. It is, it remains, evil, filthy, disgusting, diseased': *Shakespeare's Division of Experience* (London: Jonathan Cape, 1982), pp. 195–7.

3. Alan Bray, *Homosexuality in Renaissance England* (London: Gay Men's Press, 1982); Stuart Clark, 'Inversion, Misrule, and the Meaning of Witchcraft', *Past and Present* 80 (1980), 98–127; Christopher Hill, *The World Turned Upside Down: Radical Ideas During the English Revolution* (Harmondsworth: Penguin, 1975).

4. For the Baines document, see C.F. Tucker Brooke, *The Life of Marlowe and the Tragedy of Dido Queen of Carthage* (London: Methuen, 1936), pp. 98–100.

5. Peter Tatchell, *The Battle for Bermondsey* (Preface by Tony Benn), (London: Heretic Books, 1983).

6. Stone, *Family*, pp. 653, 217, 654, 623–4. F.G. Emmison has estimated that in the county of Essex around 15,000 people were summoned on sexual charges in the forty-five years up to 1603: *Elizabethan Morals and the Church Courts* (Chelmsford: Essex County Council, 1973), p. 1. Commenting on these figures

STONE, *Family*, p. 519, remarks that 'in an adult lifespan of 30 years, an Elizabethan inhabitant of Essex . . . had more than a one-in-four chance of being accused of fornication, adultery, buggery, incest, bestiality, or bigamy'.

7. J.A. SHARPE, *Crime in Seventeenth-Century England: a County Study* (Cambridge: Cambridge University Press, 1983), pp. 57, 70, 215–16.

8. *A Mirror for Magistrates*, quoted from the helpful study by THOMAS C. IZARD, *George Whetstone: Mid-Elizabethan Gentleman of Letters* (New York, AMS Press, 1942, reprinted 1966), p. 140.

9. See the proclamation of 1546 ordering London brothels to be closed, in *Tudor Royal Proclamations*, 3 vols, ed. P.L. Hughes and J.I. Larkin (New Haven: Yale University Press, 1964–69), Vol. I, pp. 365–6; also WALLACE SHUGG, 'Prostitution in Shakespeare's London', *Shakespeare Studies* 10 (1977), 291–303, especially 306.

10. *Stuart Royal Proclamations*, ed. J.F. Larkin and P.L. Hughes (Oxford: Clarendon Press, 1973), p. 47.

11. See especially LEONARD TENNENHOUSE, 'Representing Power: *Meas* in its Time', in *The Forms of Power in the English Renaissance*, ed. Stephen Greenblatt (Norman: Pilgrim Books, 1982); David Sundelson, 'Misogyny and Rule in *Meas*', *Women's Studies* 9 (1981), 83–91.

12. BEN JONSON, *Works*, ed. C.H. HERFORD and P. Simpson, 11 vols (Oxford: Clarendon, 1922–52), Vol. I, pp. 19, 139.

13. JONATHAN DOLLIMORE, *Radical Tragedy: Religion, Ideology and Power in the Drama of Shakespeare and His Contemporaries* (Brighton: Harvester Press, 1984), pp. 9–17.

14. RICHARD HOOKER, *Of the Laws of Ecclesiastical Polity* (introduction by Christopher Morris), 2 vols (London: Dent, 1969), Vol. II, p. 19.

15. In the nineteenth century, for example, A.W. SCHLEGEL praised 'the heavenly purity of her mind . . . not even stained with one unholy thought' and Edward Doughtie her 'pure zeal' and 'virgin sanctity'. By contrast Coleridge found her 'unamiable' and Hazlitt reproved her 'rigid chastity'. These other passages from earlier critics are conveniently collected in C.K. STEAD, ed. *Shakespeare: Meas, a Casebook* (London: Macmillan, 1971); see especially pp. 43–5, 59–62, 45–7, 47–9.

16. See especially JOEL SAMAHA, 'Gleanings from Local Criminal Court Records: Sedition among the Inarticulate in Elizabethan Essex', *Journal of Social History* 8 (1975), 61–79.

17. E.J. BURFORD, *Queen of the Bawd* (London: Neville Spearman, 1974); THOMAS NASHE, *The Unfortunate Traveller and Other Works*, ed. J.B. Steane (Harmondsworth: Penguin, 1972); GĀMINI SALGĀDO, *The Elizabethan Underworld* (London: Dent, 1977), p. 58.

Glossary

The following is a list of terms not otherwise discussed or contextualized in the introduction, headnotes and essays. For more detailed discussion of these and other formative concepts in current criticism, see e.g. RAMAN SELDEN, *A Reader's Guide to Contemporary Literary Criticism* (Brighton: Harvester Press, 1985, 2nd edn, 1989), KATHLEEN McCORMICK and GARY WALLER, *Reading Texts* (Lexington: D.C. Heath, 1987), or *Critical Terms for Literary Study*, ed. Thomas McLaughlin and Frank Lentricchia (Chicago: University of Chicago Press, 1990).

ARCHETYPAL CRITICISM Drawing on early twentieth-century studies of myth and dreams by, among others, Carl Jung and Joseph Campbell, archetypal criticism relates textual images and themes in texts to what are believed to be deep-rooted, 'universal' patterns of belief and experience. Typical archetypal patterns are those relating to natural cycles, birth and death, motherhood, etc.

DOMINANT, EMERGENT All societies contain contradictory and conflicting values, practices and beliefs that are articulated in the language and other codes current in that society. Those that are more powerful in any particular conjunction of history and exert more influence are called 'dominant'. 'Emergent' refers to those new practices that any society produces, which are initially on the margins of that society, even though they may at some time move into more dominant positions.

IDEOLOGY The conscious and unconscious beliefs, habits and social practices of a society, which mark that society's understanding of the 'real'. Such understandings invariably seem true, correct (even universally so) to members of that society, or at least to its dominant members. In this sense ideology is not, as often in popular parlance, a synonym for a partisan point of view, or even a term nearly synonymous with 'politics', as opposed to pragmatism or common sense. It is the system of representations of 'reality' by which men and women, usually willingly, are subject to their societies. In the context of reading 'literature', we can usefully distinguish between 'literary' and more 'general' ideology.

PARADIGM A term predominantly used in the history of science to designate a model of reality or field of enquiry, which is constructed or develops over time to explain, as exhaustively as possible, the phenomena that appear to be significant. A paradigm shift occurs when the model of reality changes.

READING FORMATION A term defined by Tony Bennett ('Texts in History: the Determinations of Readers and their Texts', *JMMLA* (Journal of the Midwest Modern Language Association), 18 (1985), 1–16) to indicate a repertoire, or 'set', of 'discursive and intertextual determinations that organize and animate the practice of reading', constituting readers as 'reading subjects of particular types and texts as objects-to-be-read in particular ways'. Texts thus have no existence 'independently of such reading formations'. A reading formation is thus derived from and a sub-set of a society's literary and more general ideology.

REPERTOIRE The particular sub-set of beliefs, assumptions, practices that an individual subject (or text) has absorbed from the general ideological formation in which he or she (or it) occupies a place.

RESIDUAL Those practices that a particular society inherits from its past and which remain active, even dominant, in the cultural process. Examples in contemporary society would include beliefs in racial or gendered subjection, or organized religion. Raymond Williams, who uses the term most helpfully, gives the monarchy as an example for Britain (*Marxism and Literature* (Oxford: Oxford University Press, 1977), p. 123). By contrast, in contemporary America, the monarchy would be said to be an *archaic* institution.

SUBJECT A term that, as widely used in contemporary criticism, particularly marks it off from earlier work. We often think of ourselves as 'individuals', with unique rights, and an 'essential' nature that is 'ours'. The concept of 'subject' as opposed to 'individual' stresses that we are all produced by and within our society's distinctive ideological formations. However much we try to achieve a measure of agency, we are not independent of ideology: the 'individual' or 'person' is not a fixed and indissoluble point but a process.

Notes on Contributors

Carolyn Asp is Associate Professor of English at Marquette University. She has published in a number of journals, including *Shakespeare Quarterly*, *Shakespeare Studies*, *Literature and Psychology*, and *Studies in English Literature*. She is working on a book that addresses itself to psychoanalytic–feminist readings of Shakespeare's plays.

Jonathan Dollimore is Senior Lecturer in the School of English and American Studies at the University of Sussex. He is the author of *Radical Tragedy* (1985), coeditor (with Alan Sinfield) of *Political Shakespeare* (1986), and many articles in the fields of theory, politics, and Renaissance and modern literature and culture. He is currently working on a book on transgression.

Peter Erickson, of the Sterling and Francine Clark Art Institute, Williamstown, Massachusetts, is the author of *Patriarchal Structures in Shakespeare's Drama* (1985) and coeditor of *Shakespeare's 'Rough Magic': Renaissance Essays in Honor of C.L. Barber* (1985). He is currently completing two further books. The first, *Rewriting Shakespeare, Rewriting Ourselves*, concerns Shakespeare's changing status in a revised literary canon; the second is a study of the comedies for Routledge's series on Feminist Readings of Shakespeare. In addition to his work on Shakespeare, he has published essays on contemporary women writers, including Maya Angelou, June Jordan, Toni Morrison, Gloria Naylor, Adrienne Rich and Alice Walker.

Helen Golding is a graduate of Anglia College (formerly Cambridgeshire College of Arts and Technology), where she read English and European Studies. Her essay on *A Midsummer Night's Dream* was first published in *Ideas and Production*, and grew out of her Honours thesis.

Terence Hawkes is currently Professor of English at the University of Wales, Cardiff. He has lectured in a number of countries for the British Council. His books include: *Shakespeare and the Reason* (1964), *Metaphor* (1972; rev. edn 1977), *Shakespeare's Talking Animals: Language and Drama in Society* (1973), *Structuralism and Semiotics* (1977; rev. edn 1983), and *That Shakespearean Rag* (1986). He is also general editor of the New Accents series of books, and editor of the journal *Textual Practice*.

Norman N. Holland holds an Eminent Scholar's Chair at the University of Florida, where he founded the Institute for Psychological Study of the Arts, and he has held Guggenheim and ACLS Fellowships. Holland has published nearly 150 articles in popular and professional magazines all over the world, but he is best known for his ten books. After two purely literary studies (of Restoration comedy and Shakespeare) his next five books focused psychoanalytic psychology on literary problems: *Psychoanalysis and Shakespeare* (1966), *The Dynamics of Literary Response* (1968), *Poems in Persons* (1973), *5 Readers Reading* (1975), and *Laughing* (1982). *The I* (1985) is purely psychological, drawing not only on psychoanalysis, but experimental psychology, linguistics, anthropology and philosophy of science to provide a model of the human being across the humanities and social sciences. His most recent book, *The Brain of Robert Frost* (1988), applies cognitive science and recent studies of the brain to literary criticism. A recent textbook, *Holland's Guide to Psychoanalytic Psychology and Literature and Psychology* (1990) sums it all up.

COPPÉLIA KAHN is Professor of English at Brown University. She is the author of *Man's Estate: Masculine Identity in Shakespeare* (1981), and has coedited three anthologies, including *Making a Difference: Feminist Literary Criticism* (1986). She is currently writing on the sexual politics of Shakespeare's Roman plays.

W. THOMAS MACCARY is Adjunct Professor of Classics at Brooklyn College, and the author of *Friends and Lovers: The Phenomenology of Desire in Shakespearean Comedy* (1985).

LOUIS ADRIAN MONTROSE is Professor of Literature at the University of California, San Diego. He is the author of a study of *Love's Labour's Lost* (1977), and many influential essays on Elizabethan and Jacobean literature, in such journals as *English Literary Renaissance, ELH, Representations, Shakespeare Quarterly* and *Helios*.

CAROL THOMAS NEELY is Professor of English and Women's Studies at the University of Illinois at Urbana-Champaign, and a past president of the Shakespeare Association of America. She is the author of *Broken Nuptials in Shakespeare* (1985) and the coeditor of *The Woman's Part: Feminist Criticism of Shakespeare* (1980). She has published essays on Shakespeare, Renaissance sonnet sequences and feminist literary theory, and is currently working on a study of madness, gender and subjectivity in early modern England.

KAREN NEWMAN, Associate Professor of Comparative Literature and English at Brown University, has published articles on a variety of topics including psychoanalysis, Shakespeare, Jonson and Renaissance comedy. She is the author of *Shakespeare's Rhetoric of Comic Character* (1985) and has just completed a new book on female subjectivity and Renaissance drama in early modern England.

GARY WALLER is Professor of Literary and Cultural Studies in the Department of English at Carnegie Mellon University, where he was for six years Head of Department. He is the author of some fifteen books, mainly on Renaissance literature and culture, including *The Strong Necessity of Time* (1976), *Mary Sidney, Countess of Pembroke* (1979), *Sir Philip Sidney and Renaissance Culture* (1984), *English Poetry in the Sixteenth Century* (1986), *Reading Texts* (1987) and editions of the poetry of the Countess of Pembroke and Lady Mary Wroth. Forthcoming books include a study of Spenser's imperialism for Macmillan, a volume of essays on Mary Wroth which he is coediting for Tennessee, and a study of gender construction in the seventeenth century, *The Sidney Family Romance*. His essays and articles range across Renaissance literature, contemporary fiction and poetry, theory and curricular studies. He has published one volume of poetry and has just completed a second collection. In 1987 he was a Guggenheim Fellow.

FRANK WHIGHAM is Associate Professor of English at the University of Texas, Austin. He is the author of *Ambition and Privilege* (1984), and has published widely on Renaissance poetry and drama in such journals as *Shakespeare Studies* and *Renaissance Drama*.

Further Reading

General studies of Shakespeare's comedies

BARBER, C.L. 1959 *Shakespeare's Festive Comedy*. Princeton: Princeton University Press. A foundational study for much important recent work. Relates comedy to Elizabethan rituals and holidays.

BELSEY, CATHERINE 1985 'Disrupting Sexual Difference: Meaning and Gender in the Comedies'. In John Drakakis, ed. *Alternative Shakespeares*. Methuen, pp. 166–90.

FRYE, NORTHROP 1965 *A Natural Perspective: the Development of Shakespearean Comedy and Romance*. New York: Columbia University Press.

MacCARY, W. THOMAS 1985 *Friends and Lovers: The Phenomenology of Desire in Shakespearean Comedy*. New York: Columbia University Press.

WHEELER, RICHARD P. 1981 *Shakespeare's Comedies and the Problem Comedies: Turn and Counter-Turn*. Berkeley: University of California Press.

Theatrical, film and television criticism

BULMAN, J.C. and COURSEN, H.R. (eds) 1988 *Shakespeare on Television*. Hanover: University Press of New England. A seminal collection including detailed accounts and reviews of productions and a videography.

GOLDMAN, MICHAEL 1972 *Shakespeare and the Energies of Drama*. Princeton: Princeton University Press.

GOLDMAN, MICHAEL 1985 *Acting and Action in Shakespeare*. Princeton: Princeton University Press.

McGUIRE, PHILIP C. 1985 *Speechless Dialect: Shakespeare's Open Silences*. Berkeley: University of California Press.

WALLER, GARY 1988 'Decentering the Bard: the Dissemination of the Shakespearean Text'. In *Shakespeare and Deconstruction* ed. G. Douglas Atkins and David Bergeron. New York: Peter Lang, pp. 21–46.

WORTHEN, W.B. 1989 'Deeper Meanings and Theatrical Technique', *SQ*, 40: 441–55

Feminist criticism

ERICKSON, PETER 1985 *Patriarchal Structures in Shakespeare's Drama*. Berkeley: University of California Press.

215

HOWARD, JEAN 1988 'Crossdressing, the Theater, and Gender Struggle in Early Modern England', *SQ* 39 : 418–41

LENZ, CAROLYN, RUTH SWIFT, GREENE GAYLE and NEELY, CAROL THOMAS, (eds) 1980 *The Woman's Part: Feminist Criticism of Shakespeare*. Urbana: University of Illinois Press.

MCEACHERN, CLAIRE 1988 'Fathering Herself: A Source Study of Shakespeare's Feminism', *SQ* 39: 269–91

NEELY, CAROL THOMAS 1985 *Broken Nuptials in Shakespeare's Plays*. New Haven: Yale University Press.

NEELY, CAROL THOMAS 1988 'Constructing the Subject: Feminist Practice and the New Renaissance Discourses', *English Literary Renaissance* 18: 5–18.

NOVY, MARIANNE 1984 *Love's Argument: Gender Relations in Shakespeare*. Chapel Hill: University of North Carolina Press.

Psychoanalytic criticism

ADELMAN, JANET 1985 'Male Bonding in Shakespeare's Comedies'. In Peter Erickson and Coppélia Kahn (eds) *Shakespeare's Rough Magic: Renaissance Essays in Honor of C.L. Barber*. Newark: University of Delaware Press, pp. 73–103.

BARBER, C.L. and RICHARD P. WHEELER 1986 *The Whole Journey: Shakespeare's Power of Development*. Berkeley: University of California Press.

FREEDMAN, BARBARA 1990 *Staging the Gaze: Psychoanalysis, Post-modernism, and Shakespearean Comedy*. Ithaca: Cornell University Press.

HOLLAND, NORMAN N. 1966 *Psychoanalysis and Shakespeare*. New York, McGraw-Hill.

HOLLAND, NORMAN N., HOMAN, SIDNEY and PARIS, BERNARD J. (eds) 1990 *Shakespeare's Personality*. Berkeley: University of California Press.

KAHN, COPPÉLIA 1981 *Man's Estate: Masculine Identity in Shakespeare*, Berkeley: University of California Press.

SCHWARTZ, MURRAY M. and KAHN, COPPÉLIA (eds) 1980 *Representing Shakespeare: New Psychoanalytic Essays*. Baltimore: Johns Hopkins University Press.

WESTLUND, JOSEPH P. 1984 *Shakespeare's Reparative Comedies: A Psychoanalytic View of the Middle Plays*. Chicago: University of Chicago Press.

Cultural Materialist and New Historicist criticism

BRISTOL, MICHAEL D. 1985 *Carnival and Theatre: Plebeian Culture and the Structure of Authority in Early Modern England*. London: Methuen.

DOLLIMORE, JONATHAN and SINFIELD, ALAN (eds) 1985 *Political Shakespeare*. Manchester: Manchester Ur 'ersity Press. Contains seminal essays in Cultural Materialism.

DRAKAKIS, JOHN (ed.) 1985 *Alternative Shakespeares*. London: Methuen. Contains provocative essays on gender in the comedies by Catherine Belsey, on ideology by James Kavanagh, and deconstructing the comedies by Malcolm Evans.

EAGLETON, TERRY 1986 *William Shakespeare*. Oxford: Basil Blackwell. A post-structuralist *jeu d'ésprit*, sometimes random, often cryptic, but very suggestive on *MSND, TN, Mer, Meas*.

GREENBLATT, STEPHEN 1988 *Shakespearean Negotiations: the Circulation of Social Energy in Renaissance England*. Berkeley: University of California Press. A major study by the leading American New Historicist in the field of Renaissance studies. Comments suggestively on *AYL, Meas* and *TN*.

HOLDERNESS, GRAHAM (ed.) 1988 *The Shakespeare Myth*. Manchester: Manchester University Press. Excellent on Shakespeare's place in contemporary culture and theatre.

HOWARD, JEAN and O'CONNOR, MARION (eds) 1987 *Shakespeare Reproduced*. London: Methuen. Includes useful overviews of recent political and New Historicist criticism.

MONTROSE, LOUIS A. 1983 'Shaping Fantasies: Figurations of Gender and Power in Elizabethan Culture', *Representations* 1: 61–94.

MULLANY, STEPHEN P. 1988 *The Place of the Stage: License, Play, and Power in Renaissance England*. Chicago: University of Chicago Press.

RYAN, KIERNAN 1989 *Shakespeare*. Brighton: Harvester Press. Combines materialist and historicist perspectives. Contains a detailed re-reading of *Mer* and provocative remarks on comedy and romance.

WEIMANN, ROBERT 1978 *Shakespeare and the Popular Dramatic Tradition in the Theater*. Baltimore: Johns Hopkins University Press.

Individual plays

All's Well that Ends Well

ADELMAN, JANET 1989 'Bed Tricks: On Marriage as the End of Comedy in *A Well* and *Meas*', In Holland, Homan and Paris, pp. 151–74.

FRYE, NORTHROP 1983 *The Myth of Deliverance*. University of Toronto Press: Toronto. Also contains discussion of *Meas*.

HODGDON, BARBARA 1987 'The Making of Virgins and Mothers: Sexual Signs, Substitute Scenes and Doubled Presences in *A Well*', *Philological Quarterly* 66: 47–71.

SNYDER, SUSAN 1988 '*A Well* and Shakespeare's Helens: Text and Subtexts, Subject and Object', *English Literary Renaissance* 18: 66–67.

As You Like It

CARLSON, SUSAN 1987 'Women in *AYL*: Community, Change, and Choice' *Essays in Literature*', 14.ii: 151–69.

ISER, WOLFGANG 1983 'The Dramatization of Double Meaning in Shakespeare's *AYL*', *Theatre Journal* 35: 307–32.

MONTROSE LOUIS A. 1981 ' "The Place of a Brother" in *AYL*: Social Process and Comic Form', *SQ* 32: 28–54.

TURNER, JOHN '*AYL*: The Outlaw Court'. In Graham Holderness, Nick Potter, and John Turner, *Shakespeare out of Court*, pp. 86–104. New York: St Martin's Press 1990.

The Comedy of Errors

CREWE, JONATHAN V. 1982 'God or the Good Physician: the Rational Physician in *Err*', *Genre* 15: 203–23.

FREEDMAN, BARBARA 1980 'Error in Comedy: a Psychoanalytic Theory of Farce'. In Maurice Charney, (ed.) *Shakespearean Comedy*. New York: New York Literary Forum.

Love's Labour's Lost

ASP, CAROLINE '*LLL*: Language and the Deferral of Desire', *Literature and Psychology*, 35 (1989), 1–21. A Lacanian reading of the lords' banishment of women.

EVANS, MURRAY 1975 'Mercury versus Apollo: A Reading of *LLL*', *SQ* 26: 113–27. A deconstructive/semiotic reading.

TURNER, JOHN '*LLL*: The Court at Play'. In Graham Holderness, Nick Potter and John Turner, *Shakespeare out of Court*, pp. 19–48. New York: St Martin's Press, 1990.

Measure for Measure

DAWSON, ANTHONY B. 1988 '*Meas*, New Historicism, and Theatrical Power', *SQ* 39: 328–41.

McLUSKIE, KATHLEEN 'The Patriarchal Bard: Feminist Criticism and Shakespeare: *KL* and *Meas*'. In Dollimore and Sinfield, *Political Shakespeare*, pp. 88–108.

ROSE, JACQUELINE 'Sexuality in the Reading of Shakespeare: *Ham* and *Meas*'. In Drakakis, *Alternative Shakespeares*, 95–118.

SKURA, MEREDITH 1979 'New Interpretations for Interpretation in *Meas*', *Boundary 2*, 8.ii: 39–59.

TENNENHOUSE, LEONARD 1982 'Representing Power: *Meas* in its Time'. In Stephen Greenblatt (ed.) *The Power of Forms in the English Renaissance*. Norman: Pilgrim Books, pp. 139–56. Argues that the play represents the recuperation of unruly social elements.

WEILL, HERBERT S., JR., 1986 ' "Your Sense Pursues Not Mine": Changing Images of Two Pairs of Antagonists'. In *Images of Shakespeare*, pp. 163–73. Berlin: Verlag.

The Merchant of Venice

BULMAN, J.C. 1990 *Mer*. Manchester University Press. Concentrates on political readings and performative dimension.

TENNENHOUSE, LEONARD 1980 'The Counterfeit Order of *Mer*'. In Schwartz and Kahn, *Representing Shakespeare*, pp. 57–66.

JIJI, V. 1975 'Portia Revisited: The Influence of Unconscious Factors Upon Theme and Characterization in *Mer*'. *Literature and Psychology* 26: 5–15.

NEWMAN, KAREN 1987 'Portia's Ring: Unruly Women and Structures of Exchange in *Mer*', *SQ* 38: 18–33.

COHEN, WALTER 1983 '*Mer* and the Possibilities of Historical Criticism', *English Literary History* 49: 765–89. Excellent on social and class tensions.

MOISAN, THOMAS 1987 ' "Which is the Merchant here? and which the Jew?": Subversion and Recuperation in *Mer*'. In Howard and O'Connor, *Shakespeare Reproduced*, pp. 188–206.

The Merry Wives of Windsor

COTTON, NANCY 1987 'Castrating (W)itches: Impotence and Magic in *MWW*'. *SQ* 38: 321–326.

ERICKSON, PETER 1987 'The Order of the Garter, the Cult of Elizabeth, and Class–Gender Tension in *MWW*'. In Howard and O'Connor, pp. 116–40.

A Midsummer Night's Dream

KOTT, JAN 1981 'The Bottom Translation', *Assays* 1: 117–49.

MONTROSE, LOUIS A. 1986 '*MSND* and the Shaping Fantasies of Elizabethan Culture: Gender, Power, Form'. In Margaret Ferguson, Maureen Quilligan and Nancy J. Vickers, (eds) *Rewriting the Renaissance: the Discourses of Sexual Difference in Early Modern Europe*. Chicago: University of Chicago Press.

PATTERSON, ANNABEL 1988 'Bottoms Up: Festive Theory in *MSND*'. *Renaissance Papers*, pp. 25–39.

Much Ado about Nothing

DAWSON, ANTHONY 1982 'Much Ado about Signifying', *Studies in English Literature* 22: 211–21.

COOK, CAROLYN 1986 ' "The Sign and Semblance of her Honor": Reading Gender Difference in *MAdo*', *PMLA*, 101: 186–202.

HAYS, JANICE 1980 'These "soft and delicate desires": *MAdo* and the Distrust of Women'. In Lenz, Greene and Neely, pp. 79–100.

HOWARD, JEAN 1987 'Renaissance Antitheatricality and the Politics of Gender and Rank in *MAdo*'. In Howard and O'Connor, *Shakespeare Reproduced*, pp. 163–87.

The Taming of the Shrew

ANDRESEN-THOM, M. 1982 'Shrew-Taming and other Rituals of Aggression: Baiting and Bonding on the Stage and in the Wild', *Women's Studies* 9: 121–43.

BEAN, JOHN C. 1980 'Comic Structure and the Humanizing of Kate in *Shr*'. In Lenz, Greene and Neely, *The Woman's Part*, pp. 65–78.

FINEMAN, JOEL 1985 'The Turn of the Shrew'. In Patricia Parker and Geoffrey Hartman (ed.) *Shakespeare and the Question of Theory*. New Haven: Yale University Press.

KAHN, COPPÉLIA 1975 '*Shr*: Shakespeare's Mirror of Marriage', *Modern Language Studies* 5: 88–102.

McLUSKIE, KATHLEEN 1982 'Feminist Deconstruction: Shakespeare's *Shr*', *Red Letters* 12: 15–22.

Two Gentlemen of Verona

GOLDBERG, JONATHAN 1986 *Voice Terminal Echo: Postmodernism and English Renaissance Texts*. London: Methuen.

McLUSKIE, KATHLEEN 1989 *Renaissance Dramatists*. Atlantic Highlands: Humanities Press International, pp. 104–7. Discusses the blurring of gender roles.

Twelfth Night

FREEDMAN, BARBARA 1987 'Separation and Fusion in *TN*'. In Maurice Charney, and John Reppon (eds) *Psychoanalytic Approaches to Literature and Film*. Rutherford: Fairleigh Dickinson University Press, pp. 96–119.

FREUND, ELIZABETH 1986 '*TN* and the Tyranny of Interpretation', *English Literary History* 53: 471–89.

POTTER, NICK '*TN*: The Court in Transition'. In Graham Holderness, Nick Potter, and John Turner, *Shakespeare out of Court*, pp. 10–21. New York: St Martin's Press, 1990.

Index